# THE PHANTOM PIRATE

## Tales of the Irish Mafia and the Boston Harbor Islands

by

## DAVID KALES

authorHOUSE

*1663 LIBERTY DRIVE, SUITE 200*
*BLOOMINGTON, INDIANA 47403*
*(800) 839-8640*
*www.authorhouse.com*

*The places mentioned in this book are real. The characters are fictitious. However, they are based on some of the things that actual people have said and done. To make my story credible, I have blended fact with fiction. If the reader finds some resemblance of the book's characters to persons now living or dead, then, perhaps, it is a good story. But it is still a story after all--DK.*

*First published by AuthorHouse 07/27/04*

*ISBN: 1-4184-5997-6 (sc)*
*ISBN: 1-4184-5998-4 (dj)*

*Library of Congress Control Number: 2004094309*

*Printed in the United States of America*
*Bloomington, Indiana*

*This book is printed on acid-free paper.*

*Maps by Kenneally Creative, Arlington, MA. www.kenneallycreative.com*

*For my family--Emily, Matthew, Michelle, and Eli*

# ACKNOWLEDGEMENTS

Special thanks to my editor, Avi Salzman, who helped shape the narrative of this story, as well as took on the editing with diligence and enthusiasm.

There were many sources that gave me the background and understanding to write this book. Most notable among them were: Edward Rose Snow's *The Islands of Boston Harbor*; Dick Lehr and Gerard O'Neil's *Black Mass--The Irish Mob, the FBI, and a Devil's Deal*; Thomas O'Connor's *South Boston: My Home Town*; and the archives and reporting of *The Boston Globe* and *The Boston Herald*.

Special appreciation as well to the many people who shared their memories and personal stories, through which I learned how deeply connected these characters in the book were to the lives of so many Boston families and neighborhoods.

Thanks, also, to Eileen Kenneally, whose maps of The Boston Harbor Islands illustrate an essential theme of the book--that of place.

Most importantly, a very special thanks to my wife, Emily, whose love and support made this book a reality.

# Table of Contents

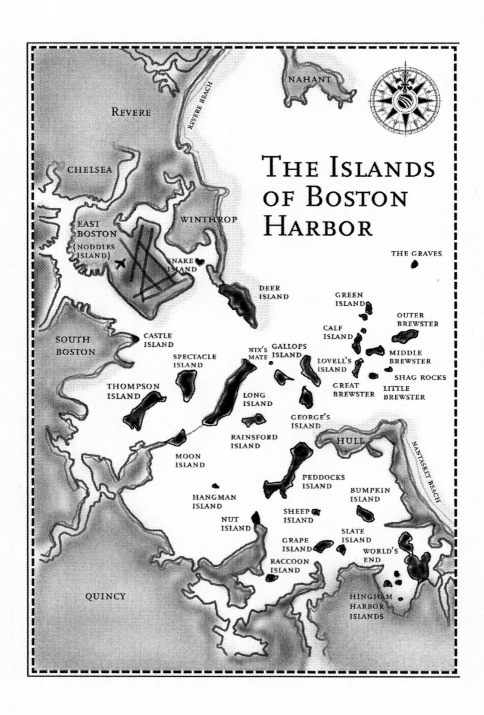

# THE ISLANDS OF BOSTON HARBOR

NAHANT

REVERE

REVERE BEACH

CHELSEA

EAST BOSTON (NODDLES ISLAND)

WINTHROP

SNAKE ISLAND

THE GRAVES

DEER ISLAND

GREEN ISLAND

SOUTH BOSTON

CASTLE ISLAND

SPECTACLE ISLAND

NIX'S MATE

GALLOPS ISLAND

CALF ISLAND

OUTER BREWSTER

LOVELL'S ISLAND

MIDDLE BREWSTER

THOMPSON ISLAND

LONG ISLAND

GREAT BREWSTER

SHAG ROCKS

LITTLE BREWSTER

GEORGE'S ISLAND

RAINSFORD ISLAND

HULL

NANTASKET BEACH

MOON ISLAND

PEDDOCKS ISLAND

HANGMAN ISLAND

BUMPKIN ISLAND

NUT ISLAND

SHEEP ISLAND

GRAPE ISLAND

SLATE ISLAND

WORLD'S END

RACCOON ISLAND

QUINCY

HINGHAM HARBOR ISLANDS

# PROLOGUE

There are many kinds of islands. Romantic islands. Real islands. Fantasy islands. Holy islands. Haunted islands. Utopian islands. Volcano Islands. Prison islands. Pirate islands. There is hardly an island that has not yet been imagined. Down through the centuries, these little fragments of land surrounded by water have inspired so many great stories.

*Arran*, the Irish island paradise in Celtic legend. Shipwreck and survival in Defoe's *Robinson Crusoe*. Pirates in Stevenson's *Treasure Island*. The legendary island of Atlantis said to have sunk beneath the sea in Plato's *Timaeus*. Good laws versus bad laws on the island of Utopia in Rabelais' *Gargantua and Pantagruel*. The alienated individual on the island of Lilliput in Swift's *Gulliver's Travels*. The self-sufficient woman, Calypso, on the island of Ogygia in Homer's *The Odyssey*. Evil, beasts, witches, and spirits of Caliban Island in Shakespeare's *Tempest*. The transition from civilized to barbaric in Golding's *Lord of the Flies* — to name just a few of the stories that have intoxicated our collective consciousness over the centuries. Indeed, as one romantic wrote: "Man's fascination with islands inspires one of the world's most passionate and enduring geographic love stories."

---

Few people, outside of Boston, have ever heard of them, although seven million people live within a fifty-mile radius of them.

ix

Even most Bostonians are only dimly aware of the islands of Boston Harbor.

There are some thirty-four islands in Boston Harbor. These islands were formed eons ago when the crust of the earth shifted, setting off earthquakes, and unleashing titanic floods. As the earth shook and rocked, a block of its crust broke off and sank, forming a lowland plain — Boston Basin. Millions of years passed and then the glaciers moved down from the north, grinding down ridges of land and leaving smooth, narrow hills of glacial till called drumlins. The two most famous examples of these formations are Beacon Hill and Bunker Hill. As the glaciers melted, the sea rose in the basin and surrounded many of the drumlins. Some of these drumlins, such as Peddocks and Spectacle, became the islands of Boston Harbor. Other islands in the harbor are rocky outcroppings, such as the Outer Brewster and Hangman's Island, formed as the ice sheet tore away pre-glacial soils and ground down the hills to be bedrock. Still others — Governor's, Bird, and Apple islands — are no more, obliterated many years ago to make way for the expanded runway system of Logan International Airport.

The islands are scattered throughout Boston Harbor, a harbor divided into five distinct areas — the Inner Harbor, Outer Harbor, Dorchester Bay, Quincy Bay, and Hingham Harbor. A harbor comprised of some fifty square miles of unpredictable weather, of sudden squalls that turn calm waters into six foot swells, of howling gales, nor'easters and hurricanes that pound ships against rocky ledges and capsize boats. A harbor where fogs sneak in, blanketing ships and shoals alike, leaving inexperienced navigators totally unaware of pending danger. Only the most skilled skippers are capable of navigating the Narrows, Black Rock Passage, and Hypocrite Channel, their names as forbidding as the hidden underwater crags beneath these waters.

———————

This is a story about the islands of Boston Harbor, whose history is filled with legends about pirates and plunder, smuggling and buried treasure, forts and dungeons — and treachery and murder. It is also the story about a modern-day pirate, the most ruthless gangster and feared crime boss to ever come off the streets of Boston.

Some readers would no doubt recognize this man and many of the people in his world; so the names of the characters in this story have been changed to protect the dead and those who could become the dead. These characters — gang members, co-conspirators, fellow mobsters, lawmen, harbor denizens, victims, and seanchies (Irish storytellers) — each spin their tale about him in the pages of this book.

For twenty-five years, a man named James Freney ruled the Boston underworld, controlling illegal gambling, loan-sharking, and drug dealing in Boston, up and down the East Coast from Maine to Rhode Island. He was the Don of Boston's Irish Mafia. They say that he even sat at the table with the Five Families of New York when La Cosa Nostra was big. The FBI credits him with murdering twenty-two people, but who knows how many more bodies he's dumped into Boston Harbor?

Freney went on the lam in 1995 when he found out that he was going to be indicted for racketeering and murder, and the FBI, along with every other law enforcement agency across the country, is still looking for him. The FBI has put Freney on its Ten Most Wanted List, right behind Osama Bin Laden, and posted a $1 million reward for his capture.

Although his story has been reported for years by newspapers and television in Boston and across the nation, providing many facts about his life, little is certain about the myth and mystery that shroud him. We are not even sure whether he is still alive. But dead or alive, his ghost haunts the present, and is doomed to haunt the future. Time, in the end, is the best storyteller.

The setting — the Boston Harbor Islands — is real. The intersection where characters and setting meet is imaginary. But it could have happened this way.

# CHAPTER I     IRELAND

To understand the story of the Boston Harbor Islands and the intrigue that later occurred there, one must first take a trip across the Atlantic to another island, Ireland, where the spirit of this story was born. It was here that an outlaw named James Freney lived and died and here that his legend began.

The outlaw is among the most popular figures in Irish folklore. The Irish outlaw represents more than a criminal. As one Irish writer put it, "he is the hero through whom ordinary Irishmen and women can vicariously enjoy brief victories, and imagine their collective dignity in the midst of political defeat." He is like Jesse James in America and Robin Hood in England, embodying "a sense of justice based on kinship and community rather than on the impersonal, bureaucratic laws of the state."

"We may be poor," boasted the Irish outlaw, "but we are intelligent and brave. We may not command armies, but we have our own captains and princes who do not need superior forces to successfully resist. We may be governed by hostile foreigners, but we know right from wrong and recognize higher authorities."

In the eighteenth century, a type of rogue, descendents of earlier outlaws, appeared in Ireland. They were called highwaymen, daring bandits who robbed and racketeered for personal gain, but whose activities were seen as robbing the rich to give to the poor and defying the hated landlords and the oppressive English authority.

Woven through the stories of these outlaw heroes, though, is another, more sinister theme — the theme of betrayal. This theme is embodied by the informer, whose opportunism, treachery and temptation for money ultimately lead to the outlaw hero's defeat.

Down through the centuries, there are many notorious highwaymen celebrated in Irish folklore; men such as Redmond O'Hanlon, William Brennan, Donal O'Keefe — and James Freney.

## THE SEANCHIE'S STORY

They call Frank Doherty the seanchie, or Irish storyteller of South Boston. Whenever he can find an audience, Doherty will spin some tale of local history or ancestral lineage in that inimitable Irish blend of fact and blarney. "He beats Banaghan," as the Irish saying goes of one who tells wonderful stories.

It was a summer evening. The sun was setting in the west, spreading a golden light across the harbor. Sitting on a park bench on Castle Island, I listened to Doherty tell his tale.

"My story begins long ago — in 1719. That was the year James Freney was born in Inistioge, a beautiful village nestled in the Valley of the Nore in County Kilkenny. His fatha' was a servant in the home of Joseph Robbins, a very respectable gentleman, who took a likin' to young James, encouragin' the lad to become a butler in his home.

"But ah, James, 'is heart was not inna bein' a servant. He preferred spendin' 'is time at cock-fightin', hurlin', and gamblin'.'

"Freney married a local girl named Ann in 1743. But that didn't change his dissipatin' habits, as he spent his wife's dowry on gamblin', and fell deep into debt.

"At wit's end, he rounded up all the idle and worthless fellows in the neighborhood and formed a gang of robbers. He took absolute control over his gang, demandin' obedience and loyalty from 'em. The gang called 'im 'Captain Dead-eye,' 'cause you see he lost the sight of one eye from smallpox that he contracted in 1746. But that didn't diminish his shootin' skills.

"Aye, they be the devil's horsemen, Freney and his gang they was. At night, they would ride to some rich man's home and stake out the house. Freney would then order 'is gang to go in with sledges, breakin' down the doors, smashin' the windows, and haulin' out all the valuables. Durin' the day, they stopped travelers and robbed 'em on the highway. Indeed, they were a brazen lot, 'cause they would blackmail the driver, demandin' a ransom for the goods they just had stolen.

"There was one occasion when five wagons proceedin' from Waterford to Thomastown, loaded with valuable shop goods, were stopped. Freney demanded a ransom of 150 pounds and sent one of the drivers to fetch it. While waitin' for the return, one of the scouts ran back with information that a body of merchants from Waterford, accompanied by a strong militia force was near at hand to capture 'im.

"Freney looked out and saw the posse comin' down the road. He ran and after some pursuit, concealed 'imself in a cleft of a rock, covered with spiny shrubs and bramble. Here he laid his loaded musket across his body and two cocked pistols at his sides. After waitin' for some time, expectin' his pursuers, he fell fast asleep.

"One of the party in search of 'im heard 'im snorin', and looked into the cleft. Seein' Freney fast asleep, he dashed back to announce 'is discovery to the others. Freney was immediately surrounded by the posse, who began firin' into the spot were 'e lay. The sounds of musket balls awakened Freney and 'e sees the ground 'round 'im riddled and torn by the balls passin' over 'is body.

"'e lay still until some of the party, supposin' 'e must be dead, were 'bout to pull 'im out by the legs, when 'e suddenly jumped up, rushed out of the bramble with 'is pistols cocked, bellowin'—'So you thinkin' ya can capture James Freney do yer?'

"The terror of 'is name and the suddenness of 'is appearance, frightened the party, scatterin' 'em all, merchants and military alike, in different directions, like a bunch of scared rabbits. Availin' 'imself of the momentary panic, Freney escaped under cover of a neighborin' hedge. From there, he jumped on a horse and rode off unda a showa of musket balls to the River Nore, not far distant, dashed into it, swimmin' 'cross and found safety at the other side. 'Is pursuers stopped on the bank of the river and fired at 'im without effect as 'e disappeared into the fields on the other side.

"By such darin' deeds and hairs-breadth escapes did Freney, for five years, sow terror 'cross the land. It came to be that no one thought of resistin' 'im on the highway or defendin' their house when attacked — or ever refusin' 'im the ransom he demanded for the goods he had stolen.

"But at length his gang, one by one, melted away. They turned informers against one another, got caught, and were hanged in succession, till but one remained with 'im. I know it sounds stranger than fiction, but it's true, I swear to ya'. The name of 'is remainin' accomplice was James Bulger.

"The law finally caught up with 'em in 1747. Freney and Bulger were in a cabin, surrounded by lawmen. While makin' their escape, Bulger was wounded by a musket ball in the leg, yet Freney took 'im on his back and they both escaped.

"But Freney seein' no prospect of findin' safety for 'imself decided to purchase 'is freedom by betrayin' 'is last friend. He told the lawmen of where Bulger was hidin' and he was captured. For 'is treachery, Freney was granted a pardon by Councilor Robbins, 'is old employer's brother, and Lord Carrick. Freney also received a small reward for turnin' in Bulger and a job as a custom's official at New Ross Port — a post that 'e held until 'e died quietly in 'is bed in 1788.

"Freney is buried in an unmarked grave in Inistioge. Some of 'is hoard is reputed to be buried on Brandon Hill, near Graiguenamanagh. It has never been discovered — yet."

---

"There was a young boy from County Kilkenny. No one remembas 'is name. They say 'e was an orphan. Like so many of the poor youths at that time, 'e received 'is general instruction, that is 'is readin' and writin', at a 'hedge' school. They called 'em hedge schools 'cause the benches were loosely laid either in a cabin or under a hedge by the wayside. The only books of instruction were crude, six penny books, the most popular bein' *The Irish Rogues and Rapparees* and an autobiography of *The Life and Adventures of James Freney.*

"Whateva 'is original name was, the boy changed it to 'is hero — James Freney. In the late 1850s, in the wake of the 'Great Famine,' 'e sailed on a 'fever' ship bound for Boston."

4

"After the passengers in the ship carryin' young James Freney were quarantined at Spectacle Island for a few days, fearin' there was a smallpox case onboard, the ship finally arrived in East Boston. There young Freney worked on the docks of East Boston 'til wooden shipbuildin' collapsed after the Civil War and he moved to South Boston in search of work.

"Sometime later, young Freney married and raised a family. 'Is first born bein' a boy, 'e was named James Freney. Like 'is father, James Freney, Jr. worked on the docks, married, and raised a family. 'Is first born also bein' a boy, 'e stuck with tradition and named his son James Freney.

"James Freney, the grandson of the Irish patriarch, was known to be a dour man, even a bitta' man. Took to the bottle to dull 'is bitta' pain. They say 'e wasn't always that way, but somethin' happened to 'im durin' the Depression that changed 'is personality.

"Before the incident, Freney was known to be a passionate man, a fightin' man. Always speakin' out for the little guy and railin' against the injustice and the discrimination against 'is fella workers on the docks. As a union organizer 'e was always leadin' the workers' demonstrations against the shippin' companies, fightin' for betta workin' conditions and betta wages.

"The shippin' companies weren't about to give into no redneck mick-run unions, so they locked out the unions and brought in the scabs. The workas marched down to the docks, threw up the pickets, and started demonstrations against the lockout. The companies called on the city to send in the police to break up the demonstrations.

"The police commissioner, no lova of those 'Irish hooligans' from South Boston, ordered 'is men to bash a few 'eads in breakin' up the demonstrators. Wieldin' their billy clubs, the police waded into the union ranks, and Freney, bein' at the front was among the first to feel their blows. After the demonstrators were dispersed, Freney lay bleedin' and unconscious on the ground — left layin' there with an arm that was broken and crippled for life, a heart full of hate, and a legacy of vengeance toward 'is oppressors."

"But that vengeance was not unleashed upon the people of Boston for anotha' full generation, when James Freney's son elbowed his way into this world. The authorities mighta taken blood from the union organiza' James Freney, but that blood was returned with interest by his son, the most ruthless gangsta' South Boston eva' saw. And what was the name of this gangsta'? You guessed it. James Freney.

"For decades he ruled the Boston underworld, extortin' from bookies and drug pushas and terrorizin' the neighborhood. Every buck in Southie, you hadda' give a dime of it to Freney, and if you didn't, well, they're still findin' bodies washin' up on the shore. Ya see, Freney didn't just own the bookies and the drug pushas. He had the cops right unda his thumb. They were the sons of those same cops that beat up his ol' man. He told 'em that as long as they didn't touch his business, he would hand over the other gangstas in the town. By the time Freney was finished with them, all the no-good crooks and petty thieves in this city were wonderin' what hit 'em. And then, well, one day James Freney just disappeared."

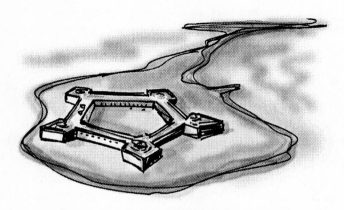

## CHAPTER II CASTLE ISLAND

No one knows how Castle Island got its name. They called it Castle Island even before there were buildings on it. The Puritans thought the island was the best site to defend the harbor so they built a pine wood and stone fort there in 1634 and called it Castle William, after the King of England. Some say the Castle was haunted, even cursed. Governor Winthrop recorded in 1643 "mysterious and unexplained lights" hovering over the fort. In 1665, lightening struck the captain of the garrison as he stood on the ramparts. In 1673, a fire set apparently by the "Awful Hand of God" demolished the wooden fort, requiring the building of a new stone citadel. During a gun salute marking the inauguration of the new fort, a cannon exploded, killing two of the Castle's gunners.

The British occupied the island during the Revolutionary War. From the fort, their cannons bombarded Washington's troops positioned on Dorchester Heights. But Washington had the British surrounded in Boston. Realizing their situation hopeless, on a stormy March night in 1776, Royal engineers blew up the fort, spiked its great guns, and set sail out of Boston for good. Official Boston celebrates March 17th as Evacuation Day — the day the British left town. But far more important for the residents of South Boston, the Irish section of Boston, as well as for every other Irish man in the country, March 17th is celebrated as Saint Patrick's Day.

After the Revolutionary War, the U.S. Army built a new fort in 1799 and President John Adams renamed it Fort Independence.

The gray granite stone fort, shaped like a pentagon, looking like a medieval fortress, with massive walls five feet thick and thirty feet high, with five, diamond-shaped bastions at the corners — is the same fort you see on the hill there today.

Castle Island isn't an island anymore. It hasn't been since it was connected by a bridge in the 1890s and then in 1916 by land fill to South Boston—"Southie" the natives call it. For the Irish, the connection existed long before the bridge. Even though they were immigrants, the Irish in America have never lost their love for Ireland — nor their hatred of England. They've always dreamed of an independent Ireland. Back in 1858, some Irish revolutionaries organized a secret society called the Fenian Brotherhood. The name Fenian was derived from Fionna Eirinn, an ancient military organization which existed in Ireland, taking its name from Finn, the celebrated hero of Irish legend. The society's object was the overthrow of English authority in Ireland.

In America, the Fenian's first objective was to supply money and arms to the Irish branch. But the United States was a vast, spacious country; the Fenians could be more open in their efforts to recruit members and raise money. So after the Civil War, with many Irish-American veterans bolstering their ranks, the American Fenians took the initiative and declared the independence of the Irish Republic. Its leaders decided the best way to win independence was to establish a foothold in Canada, which was a part of the British Empire, sow terror among the inhabitants, and set up a provisional organization as the first government of the Irish Republic. An invasion was planned with Irish-American soldiers filling the ranks of a special army called Fenians' Raiders.

Battery E 5th Artillery, an Irish-American unit stationed on Castle Island, was among the 900 raiders from Kentucky, Tennessee, Indiana, and New York who heeded the call to arms. With 'green flags waving and with Irish cheers,' they marched into Canada. Twice, the raiders pressed into Canadian territory, and twice, the Canadian militia beat them back. The invasion was a failure. Irish independence was to remain a distant dream. Even today, as you walk past a weedy, vacant lot, a few blocks from the waterfront in

Southie, you can see a faded mural that proclaims "Ireland Unfree Will Never be at Peace."

Since the Revolutionary War, Castle Island has played a role in the defense of Boston in most of the major wars America has fought — the War of 1812, the Civil War, the Spanish-American War, World Wars I and II — but through them all, the fort never fired at any enemy in anger. Down through the centuries, though, strange, unexplainable occurrences have continued to happen there, as if a spell still were cast over the island.

The steamboat *Ella*, carrying a group of youngsters to the island on Farragut Day in June 1896 capsized at the dock and four boys were drowned. A mine mysteriously exploded on the island's seawall during the Spanish-American War, killing three men. During World War II, mines were spotted floating close to the island. The mines were swept away by the Navy, but they never said where the mines came from. Was it a German submarine? Captured German documents revealed that in June 1942, the submarine U-87 entered the harbor. Did the sub plant the mines there?

Some people say ghosts continue to haunt the castle. The last record of one, according to a local historian, is more than 60 years old. He told me this story.

"One night, in the early days of World War II, after Pearl Harbor, sentries atop the ramparts heard strange wailings and noises of clanking chains. Then, all of a sudden, someone screamed. In what seemed to be the headlights from a truck, a ghostly white apparition glided across the parade ground. Shots rang out. All of the sentries on the ramparts claimed they were not drunk or seeing things. But daylight found a parade ground sentry in total shock, unable to move or speak, his rifle and helmet lying on the ground."

After World War II, the army pulled out of Castle Island and for a time the fort wasn't used for anything. The Metropolitan District Commission took over the crumbling Fort Independence, and gradually restored it. Today, the fort is open to the public for scheduled tours. You can climb to the ramparts which loom eighty feet above the water and look out at the sail and power boats, commuter and excursion boats, ferries, trawlers, tug boats, container ships, Coast Guard cutters, LNG tankers and, maybe, if they're in port, the QE II or an aircraft carrier. Overhead you can see the big jets taking off and landing at Logan. From the ramparts, you can descend the stone stairways to the parade-ground and explore the storehouses, bakeries, ordnance-rooms, and cavernous, gloomy, cold stone casements where soldiers slept near the cannons.

The grounds around the fort are open to the public. There is a paved path that winds around the fort and goes out to the causeway encircling Pleasure Bay. The causeway leads to a little rotunda called the "Sugar Bowl," then continues to Day Boulevard and back to the fort. It's a favorite course for walkers, joggers, and bikers.

On a balmy summer night, the area is filled with people standing in line to buy hot dogs and ice cream at Sullivan's, old-timers sitting on the benches in quiet reverie or talking about the good old days, families pushing baby carriages along the boardwalk, roller-bladers, and skate-boarders weaving in and out of groups of strolling walkers. If you look up to the sky, you'll see the stars twinkling over the harbor mingling with the lights of the city.

---

What people don't know is that Castle Island was a secret meeting place, you might say the private castle of James Freney.

Freney had a number of hangouts. There was Triple O's, a tavern on the first floor of a dingy, four-story red brick building on West Broadway in South Boston. Above the door was a sign *Triple O's Lounge* with *Coors Light* and *Rolling Rock* advertised on each side. The dimly lit bar was noisy and rowdy, and brawls were breaking out all the time. One newsman dubbed the tavern "the bucket of blood," as many a night the police would respond to a call complaining about a "disturbance of the peace," barge into the tavern, bash a few heads with their billy clubs, and hustle the bloody combatants into the paddy wagon.

Freney's office was on the second floor, where his mail was delivered, where drug money got laundered, and where bookies went to pay back their loans. If they didn't pay back in time they got a few bones broken, and if they still didn't pay up the second time, they got whacked, stuffed in a trash bag and dumped into the South End.

The Farragut Liquor Mart on Old Colony Avenue was another meeting place. Freney took it over by pointing a gun at the owner, and saying, "I'm buying your store." Renaming the store Atlantic Wine & Spirits, Freney turned it into a front for fencing stolen merchandise, and running his loan-sharking protection rackets and his drug dealing network. Dope pushers like Stan "My Man" Moore and Craig "Bobcat" Reed, nicknamed because of his fast hands and feet, hung out at the store, as well as characters like Marty "The Match" Miller, who burnt down buildings and then collected the insurance money on them.

Outside of South Boston, Freney's hangout was the Lancaster Street garage. The garage was located near the old Boston Garden, now the Fleet Center, and was within walking distance from the North End, the heartland of Boston's Italian Mafia. A steady stream of mobsters visited the garage, including Mafia big boys like Guido Massaroni, brother to Dante Massaroni, underboss of Boston's Mafia, and Sammy Salerno, second to Dante Massaroni.

Freney, though, never felt comfortable doing business in these places. The fights that constantly broke out at Triple O's attracted the police's attention. The police knew Atlantic Wine & Spirits was a front, and from time to time staked out the store, hoping to catch Freney and his gang engaged in some criminal activity. From a flophouse across the street, the state police set up a twenty-four hour surveillance of the Lancaster Street garage, and then tried bugging the garage. But nothing worked. Freney knew they were watching and listening. He showed nothing, he said nothing, and instead moved his meeting places elsewhere — to the parking lot along Wollaston Beach in Quincy, to the Café Pompeii in the North End, to Anthony Hawthorne Restaurant in Swampscott, to Boston City Hall. He was even seen leaning against the statue of John Harvard in Cambridge's Harvard Yard talking to a gang member. With law enforcement constantly on his tail, Freney took to conducting business out of telephone booths around town, never using the same pay phone twice in a row.

Castle Island was one place where Freney felt safe to conduct his business. Maybe it was because Castle Island was a part of South Boston, his home territory, and he felt his back was covered. Or maybe because Castle Island overlooked the main channel in and out of the harbor, his escape route in case he got trapped. But I think Freney liked to conduct his business at the Castle because under the cover of its massive walls he could meet his most entrusted lieutenants privately and deal with people one on one. Freney was a suspicious character. For him, as the old Irish saying goes: "It is not a secret if it is known by three people." Deep down, though, he really trusted no one, and lived by another motto: "Two men can keep a secret as long as one of them is dead."

There were only a handful of men entrusted with James Freney's secrets who lived to tell about them. And even they didn't know everything.

### CONTI

Robert "The Sniper" Conti was Freney's partner in crime. Conti got his nickname "The Sniper" as a marksman in the Korean War. He enlisted in the Army at the age of seventeen and served two tours in Korea as a paratrooper. He was highly decorated, rescuing a wounded soldier during a bloody battle with Chinese Communists in the Kumwha Valley. When he was honorably discharged from the army in 1955, he brought his gun back home with him.

Home was Roxbury, a section of Boston where Conti made his name as a loan shark. Conti was a little guy, five foot eight and slender, but he was tough, quick to use his gun when any hood had second thoughts about paying off a debt. He was a survivor of Boston's gangland wars of the 1960s. He met Freney when they were both hit men and bill collectors for the Winter Hill gang in Somerville. They hung out together — Freney the Irishman from South Boston, Conti the Italian from Roxbury. Conti had personal ties to the Italian Mafia. His brother Charlie "The Wolf" Conti was a strong man for the Mafia. His boyhood chum, Luigi "Limousine Lou" Farnese, rose to become a Mafia boss. Top Mafia boss Carmen Borgia in Providence and Sammy Salerno both liked Conti and wanted him to join La Cosa Nostra. Salerno was also Conti's chief banker for his loan-sharking business. Salerno would loan money to Conti at an interest of 1% a week, and, Conti, in turn, would loan the money out on the street at a rate of 5% a week, working out to be

260% interest on an annual basis, if the borrower lived that long to pay off his debt.

## CONTI'S ACCOUNT

I rememba' one day. It was in the dead of winter. Me and Jim, we unfold our lawn chairs on the slope of Castle Island to catch some rays. I pick up my binoculars to scan the harbor, lookin' for any DEA patrol boat that may be spyin' on us.

"How's things goin' with our Italian friends on Prince Street?" Jim asks me.

"Do ya remember Larry Fatricia, the little Italian wop who screwed us outa' $50,000 he owed us for fixin' the horses?" I answers, puttin' down my binoculars and pullin' my chair closer to Jim's so we can have a conversation. "Let me tell ya what Salerno did.

"His boys escort Larry over to Prince Street and Salerno says to him: 'Look ya little shit, if ya screw someone close to us, I'm goin' to give you a shake now. Do ya know Freney's and Conti's gang is us?' 'These are nice people,' he tells Fatricia, who's shittin' in his pants. 'These are the kind of people that straighten a thing out....Anything I ever asked them. They're with us. We're together. And we cannot tolerate them gettin' screwed, Okay?'

"Good," Jim nods. "That shows our Italian friends still trust us. Now let's get down to business."

"We got a few bar and liquor store owners who are refusin' to replace their vendin' machines with ours. I think it's time to put a little muscle on these guys," I says.

"Ya, it's time to send a message," says Jim with that sneer of his.

"How should we handle the master horse-race fixer, 'Fat' Harry Fontana?" I goes on. "Ya know he's netted us $8 million fixin' horses for us. But I don't like what's happenin'. Those jockeys that cooperated with the police got him busted and now he's facin' four to six years in the federal pen for race fixin'. I hear Fat Harry don't like prison. He promises to rat on all of us if the FBI drops his prison charges and gets him into the Witness Protection Program."

"Let me handle this, Bobby," says Jim. "I've been talkin' to our friends over at the FBI. Tip tells me that they can keep our names out of the investigation."

Me and Jim, we get up from our chairs, we do a little stretchin' and pushups. Me and him, we're always workin' out. Pumpin' iron. Keepin' in shape. I pick up my binoculars again, scannin' the harbor and the path below the fort.

"Look at those two broads, Jim. What tits and asses on them! Come on, let's go say hello to them."

"Ya keep your pants on, Bobby. Let's stick to business. How's Suspenders doin' with our investments?"

"He's got some new properties he wants us to buy. Some condos in South Boston, the South End, Back Bay, and Medford. And a couple of restaurants. There's one in the South End and one in Quincy Market — that's the hot area down near the waterfront."

"Where's those Back Bay condos?" Jim asks.

"They're on Marlborough Street and Commonwealth Ave. They come with swimmin' pools, saunas, and rooftop decks. They're real upscale, real class. Suspenders says they'll be worth two million in a few years.

"Hey, Jim! How's the missis doin'?" I asks him, wantin' to talk about somethin' else.

"Mary?" he growls in that voice he gets when somethin' irritates him. "She's doin' okay, except she's still on the sauce. I tell her she's got to get more control over her life. Be a family. Have her kids at the supper table when I get home."

"And you, Romeo, how you doin' with Marcia these days?" he asks, turnin' the conversation around again. "Does she know you're screwin' Barbara what's-her- face?"

"Barbara Bennet?" I says. "Who gives a shit? I got a new chick, Jim. What a honey! But don't tell anybody. She's Marcia's daughter."

"Ya know, Bobby. Someday, somebody is goin' get hurt with all your fuckin' around."

**NEELEY**

Garrett Neeley was Freney's trusted lieutenant. He was a leg-breaker, an enforcer, Freney's pit bull and grave digger. Freney hired Neeley as a bouncer at Triple O's right after he got out of South Boston High School in the 1970s. The son of a boxing trainer, Neeley was a tough guy with flashing fists. One of his functions was to break up the brawls at Triple O's.

Neeley became like a son to Freney, and in short time his bodyguard. Neeley was the supreme loyalist — always telling people he would rather serve hard time than ever bad mouth his boss. Some say he would even sell his own grandmother down the river before ever letting Freney come in harm's way. Neeley was hot-tempered and would tick off a lot of people, like the time he bragged about the Italian Mafioso "bein' a bunch of old guys who were no match for the 'shooters' of Freney's Irish gang."

## NEELEY'S ACCOUNT

Me and Jimmy, we'd spend a lot of time strollin' round Castle Island, 'specially in the summer when the breeze from the harba' cooled ya off. Jimmy would be wearin' sunglasses and his Red Sox cap. Me, I had an Afro in those days. I liked the ol' white tight-fittin' T-shirts to show off my muscles. None of those baggy, extra-long ones ya see today. I'd be wearin' bell-bottoms. Rememba dem? And my gold chain with tiny gold boxin' gloves round my neck. I'd always be wearin' dem. Brings me luck and shows everyone who I am.

"I hear our safecracker friend Dicky Hudson doesn't want to share some of the $1.5 million he made in the Medford bank heist. I don't like the word gettin' out that the 'Dick' is screwin' us. It's not good for our reputation," Jimmy says to me. "If ya let one guy get away with screwin' us, others will try screwin' us, too. It sets a bad example."

"What do ya want me to do, Jimmy?" I ask.

"Take him off the street, beat the shit out of him, and then drop him back on the street — alive, so others get the message. In time Sir Dick is goin' to have to go 'bye-bye.'"

"I got the picture, Jimmy. The job's as good as done," I tell him.

"And Garrett, I want you with me when we talk to Skippy Shaw about sellin' his liquor store to us. He may need a little convincin'. Do ya know what I mean?"

"Rememba the time we're at Logan?," he says, puttin' his arm on my shoulder like he's my father. "I was checkin' two duffle bags through on a Delta flight to Montreal. The duffle bags were stuffed with stacks of hundred dollar bills, five hundred grand was in 'em. This female security broad was monitoring the X-ray machine as my bags moved through. She starts to take a closer look. I grab the bag and shout, 'That's my fuckin' money', bolt to the terminal door, and shout again: 'Garrett...Garrett catch this.' I pitch the two bags to ya just like a quarterback hittin' his tight end. Ya catch 'em, jump over the guard rail and out of the terminal. With everyone lookin' at ya, I just walked away into the night."

## DOYLE

Paul Doyle was the gang's money launderer. He steered money from drug dealing, extortion, and loan sharking into legitimate businesses like Triple O's tavern and Atlantic Wine & Spirits. The mob called him "Suspenders" because he needed suspenders to hitch his pants up over his huge belly. Doyle's face was scarred from acne, his hair was graying, he sported a couple of double chins and he weighed well over 300 pounds. To the world outside, he presented himself as a legitimate businessman, a family man and solid citizen in the community. Doyle never finished high school, but he was good with numbers. He knew how to keep the books for Triple O's and Atlantic Wine & Spirits. With Doyle as the front man, the mob set up Shamrock Realty Trust to buy into properties all over South Boston, rooming houses, appliance and variety stores as well as condos and O'Toole's Bar and Grill in the Back Bay. Besides the real estate business, Doyle's job was to "collect the rent" — that's the payment a drug dealer, loan shark, or bookie had to make to Freney and his gang if they wanted to operate in South Boston.

## DOYLE'S ACCOUNT

I remember meetings with Jim at Castle Island. It always felt like they were taking place on an April spring day. You know the weather around Boston at that time of year — overcast, damp, chilly. The temperature is in the low 50s, but the east wind off the harbor makes it feel like it's in the 30s. I'd sit down on a park bench near the fort and we'd talk about what's going on.

"How's our realtor friend Raymond Stubbs doin'?," Jim asks.

"He's welshing out on us," Jim," I answer. "He says he doesn't have the fifty grand he owes us."

"I guess it's time for us to pay Stubbs a visit," Jim says in that icy tone of his. "Get Garrett to soften him up with a few bruises and then make him an offer he can't refuse. Because if he does, Garrett will blow his fuckin' head off. Tell 'im to come up with ten thousand, then every week you'll stop by his office and pick up another two thousand."

"I'll get right on it, Jim."

## O'DONNELL

William O'Donnell was a little boy of eight when he first met Freney. As the story goes, O'Donnell was getting beat up on a playground in Southie by an older, bigger kid. Freney, who was eleven years older than O'Donnell, comes out of nowhere, pounds the bully to the ground, and chases him away. Later, Freney took O'Donnell and his friends to a soda shop for ice cream. O'Donnell never forgot what Freney did for him that day.

But it was Freney's younger brother, Dan Freney, who really shaped the course of O'Donnell's life. Dan, born five years after Jim, would become an iron-fisted state assemblyman for seventeen years. He put little Billy under his wing and told him to hit the books, not the streets. "Books are like magic carpets," Dan would tell him. "They can take you anywhere you want to go." Dan steered O'Donnell to college at Boston College, his own alma mater.

After college, O'Donnell joined the FBI. He was first posted to Baltimore where he worked on bank robberies and fugitives cases, then briefly to San Francisco, and then to New York in 1971 where he worked East Harlem and the Bronx, tracking the Lucchesse family, one of the Mafia families that controlled the docks and rackets in New York City. O'Donnell's big break came when he arrested Luigi Farnesse on Third Avenue near Gimbel's. At that time, Farnesse was a Mafia hood wanted in Boston. After serving fifteen years in the pen from that arrest, Farnesse later rose in the ranks to become an underboss in the Boston Mafia with the nickname "Limousine Lou" because he liked to drive around in big chauffer-driven cars.

Agents score points in the FBI when they nab a Mafioso. It puts them on a fast track. Farnesse's arrest was O'Donnell's ticket to the bureau in his hometown.

Back in the 1970s, the FBI was waging a crusade across the country against the Italian Mafia on orders from Attorney General Robert F. Kennedy and J. Edgar Hoover. In Boston, the bureau thought the best strategy to break up La Cosa Nostra was to pit the Irish gangs against the Mafia, make an unholy alliance with the Irish against the Italians, divide and conquer the underworld. How do you do it? Recruit informants to tip off the FBI to Mafia moves. Find out how the Mafia operates. As a "son of Southie," one who was very familiar with the territory, O'Donnell was picked to become Freney's handler, to recruit James Freney as a TE (Top Echelon) informant.

From all appearances, Freney would make a good informer, or so the bureau thought. Through Conti, Freney was friendly with the Mafia. The Mafia trusted Freney as much as they trusted anybody. His gang and the Mafia had become partners, dividing greater Boston up into governing zones. The Mafia held forth in the North End, East Boston, Revere, Chelsea and the North Shore, while Freney's gang was in South Boston, the South End, Charlestown, Dorchester, Somerville, and the South Shore. Given his reputation as a notorious criminal, James Freney would be the last person anyone would suspect of becoming a rat for the FBI.

## O'DONNELL'S ACCOUNT

It was an evening in October of 1975. I parked my car in the parking area near Fort Independence on Castle Island. Out of the shadows comes Jim Freney and slides into the front seat.

"How did you get here, by parachute?" I asked, surprised at being taken off guard. We exchanged greetings and made small talk about what's happening in Southie.

And then I continued: "Jim, your buddies in the Mafia want to give you up to the cops. Why not give up your buddies in the Mafia to us? I've got a proposition. Why don't you use us to do what they're trying to do to you? Take them down.

"Here's the deal: Use the FBI to eliminate your Mafia rivals. We won't be looking to take you down if you were cooperating with us.

"Come aboard, we'll protect you. You can count on the FBI keeping the other law enforcement agencies off your back."

Freney pondered the proposition. Several moments ticked by and then he responded: "You can't survive without friends in law enforcement. All right. Deal me in."

After our initial meeting, we would meet hundreds of times over the next twenty years. Many of our meetings took place at Castle Island. We met in all seasons. If the weather was cold or rainy, we sat in my car in the parking area near Fort Independence. If the weather was clear or balmy, we met outside the fort, on Day Boulevard, or at the Sugar Bowl, the little pavilion on the causeway encircling Pleasant Bay. We usually met around midnight when the park was deserted. The only sounds you could hear were the seagulls out in the harbor, a distant fog horn, and the surf beating gently against the seawall.

At these meetings, Freney passed on tips to me, giving me more and more credibility with my superiors as a TE handler.

"Billy, ya know the big Mafia guy who faked a heart attack to avoid the federal grand jury subpoena?...His name is Domenic Brasco," Freney tells me.

"I found out what ya wanted to know about that bank heist at Workers Trust in Medford over last Memorial Day weekend. Yah, there were Mafia guys involved, a couple of soldiers. Salerno was in on it, too. This should help ya keep the heat on them."

"'Do ya know who gunned down Joey Barboza Brambilla in San Francisco for turnin' state's evidence? It was a wiseguy — Jimmy Barrows.'

"'Jim, the U.S. and state attorneys are making cases against the big bookies," I say to him. "They're threatening ten years in the can if these guys don't become government witnesses. It would help me if you would tell me who the big bookies in Boston are."

"'Skinny' Vinnie Giordano is the Mafia's biggest bookie,' Freney says. "But lay off Ziggi Schwartz and his Jew buddies — Eddie Kravitz, Irv Stolz, and Abe Gold. These bookies pay me."

"Billy, I got a hot tip that'll blow your mind," Freney boasts in his Irish whisper. (an Irishman's way of pretending he's telling a secret without lowering his voice.) "I found out that the Mafia is holdin' a big induction ceremony. It's planned for October 29 at Gino Moretti's home in Medford. All the big boys will be there — Moretti, J.R. Ricci, Albert Bruno and thirteen other guys. I hear that Carmen "Junior" is coming in from Providence to run the show. They're inductin' four new soldiers."

I passed this tip along to the bureau. On the night of October 29, 1980, we secretly videotaped a Mafia induction ceremony. The tape showed Carmen Borgia, Jr., son of the deceased New England godfather, Carmen Borgia, welcoming all:

"We're all here to bring some new members into our Family.... and more than that, to start making a new beginning."

One by one each of the new soldiers pricked his finger and swore a blood oath to enter into the Mafia to protect his Family and Friends, swearing never to divulge this secret — to obey with love and *omerta*, the code of silence.

Then all together they recited: " I want to enter alive this organization and leave it dead."

Then Borgia continued:

"If I told you, your brother was wrong, he's a rat, he's gonna do one of us harm, you'd have to kill him, would you do that for me?"

"Yes."

"Your mother's dying in bed, and you have to leave her because we called you. It's an emergency. You have to leave. Would you do that?"

"Yes."

It was the first time a Mafia ceremony was recorded on tape. It was a big step in taking down the Boston Mafia. It made me a top agent in the Boston bureau of the FBI. And it made James Freney my "Untouchable."

## GRECO

Not every one of Freney's visitors to the Castle received the same reception as O'Donnell or the inner circle. Johnny Greco was Freney's number one trigger-man. Greco was said to have gunned down over twenty men in cold blood. The bodies of many of his victims have never been found. Some of his known victims were hoods or stool pigeons like Billy Puddu and Norm Jackson. Others were like Richie Cattaneo, a Revere night club owner and mob associate who became a government informant, and Philip Newton, a business tycoon, who was shot while sitting in his car at a Dallas, Texas country club because he had found out that Freney's gang had skimmed $1 million from his North American Jai Alai company in Florida.

## GRECO'S ACCOUNT

I'm waitin' and waitin' on the ramparts, my nitchees freezin' off. The fog was like soup, I couldn't even see my hand in front of my face. Then I see two lights, they looked like headlights, comin' closer and closer. There's a moanin' and groanin' sound — *'J-o-h-n-ny, J-o-h-n-ny, J-o-h-n-ny Gre--co'.* A rattlin' of chains, and a sound like a step and a foot bein' dragged — *thump — scrape — thump — scrape —* like ya see in one of 'em old Frankenstein flicks. Suddenly, somethin' taps me on the shoulder. I turn 'round and there's this face lit by a flashlight, like kids do at Halloween to scare you. All I could see was this face like Dracula. This figure wearin' a black hat. Ya know, with the brim kinda' slouching down over his forehead. He's wearin' a black cape, and his eyes are like marbles. I felt like I was lookin' into the cold, empty eyes of the devil.

"How ya' doin, Johnny."

"Geezees! it's you, Jim. You had me shittin' in my pants."

"Relax, Johnny, and tell me what's up."

"It's Ralph Taggert, our fat CPA friend. The FBI wants to question him about the Dallas murder. I don't know if he can take the heat. He'd talk to save his skin. Taggert was with me when I whacked Newton. He knows you and Bobby gave the orders."

"Whack him," says Freney.

"Geezees! Are you sure, Jim? I hate to do this. He was a friend of mine. Lent me money when I was on the lam livin' in Florida. He's got a lot of connections in the bankin' community which we can always use."

"Whack him," says Freney.

## MCGIVERS

Charlie "Mack" McGivers, an ex-marine and New England champion kick boxer, was a leg-breaker and cocaine dealer in Freney's gang. He had a high school diploma and a bachelor's degree in legal education from the University of Massachusetts. He fancied himself a favorite of Freney's and pictured himself as the chronicler of Freney's gang, the one who someday would write a book — and sell the movie rights — about the organization in which he would describe himself as an 'urban predator', and Freney as 'the ultimate urban predator.'

## MCGIVERS ACCOUNT

It was an overcast hot summer day. The humidity felt suffocatin', no coolin' breezes. Freney told me to meet him on the ramparts. I see him joggin' up the ramp to the ramparts. He's wearin' a black joggin' outfit and black sneakers. He comes up to me. We exchange a couple of 'How ya doin's,' all the while he's lookin' at me with that blank stare of his. I see death in those eyes, nothin' but death. No compassion. Nothin'.

Then he starts givin' me a lesson. Freney likes givin' lessons. This time it's on the art of beatin'. "Ya break his ribs, jump on his ankles, break his ankles, hit all the spots, his non-lethal spots," he says. 'That sends a clear message onto the streets.'

"No one challenges James Freney."

"Come on, let me show ya somethin'," says Freney, leadin' me down the stone ramp to the parade grounds and then into a room. I think it was the officers' quarters and a gun casement in the old days.

"Look at that wall," says Freney, pointing toward a brick wall cemented over. "I'm gonna tell ya the story behind that wall."

"It seems that back on Christmas Day in 1817, two officers fought a duel 'cause one accused the other of cheatin' at cards the night before. A young lieutenant, Robert Massie, was killed in the duel by a lieutenant named Gustavus Drane, who nobody liked. Massie's friends were really pissed off at what happened and decided to avenge his death. They got Drane drunk, led him to a small compartment in this room, chained him to the floor, and sealed up the entrance. Imagine the poor fucka soberin' up to find himself suffocatin' to death," says Freney gleefully.

"I swear, it's a true story," claims Freney. "It really happened 'cause in 1905, some workmen were renovatin' the fort. When they knocked down that wall, they discovered a skeleton dressed in an old military uniform."

"There's more to this story," Freney goes on. "Did ya ever hear of Edgar Allan Poe?"

"Wasn't he a writer?" I says.

Freney tells me this story. "Poe was an enlisted man named Edgar Allan Perry in the Third Regiment of Artillery at Castle Island in 1827. He later took the name Edgar Allan Poe and wrote a famous short story called *The Cask of Amontillado*. Poe changed the settin' from Castle Island to Europe. It's a story of an Italian feud. The owner of this huge wine cellar wants revenge for the murder of one of his relatives. So he invites an unsuspectin' friend, who he thinks is the murderer to join him in the cellar to sample the various wines. Lured in by the promise of betta' tastin' wines, the friend becomes more and more drunk. When they reach the depths of the cellar and the final cask — *The Cask of Amontillado* — the victim collapses in a stupor. The owner then bricks up the wall of the cask and leaves the man to die."

As I follow Freney out of the room onto the parade grounds, I'm thinkin' what's the message of Freney's stories. Yah, it's about revenge. But ya know? I think he's sayin' more than that. It's about the power of fear, about buildin' fear in people. Fear leads to respect. My uncle use to tell me this old Irish sayin:'

'Dear God,
*May those who love us love us.*
*And those who don't love us may You turn their hearts.*
*And if You can't turn their hearts,*
*May You turn their ankles,*
 *So we may know them by their limping.'*

I watched Freney exit through the big gates of the sally port, jog down the slope toward the causeway that leads out into the bay and disappear into the mist.

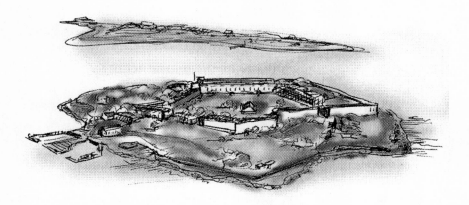

## CHAPTER III GEORGE'S ISLAND

George's Island lies right at the "throat" of Boston Harbor. It faces the main shipping channel, making it the most important strategic point in the harbor. In 1833, the U.S. government sent Sylvanus Thayer, the Father of West Point, to oversee the construction of Fort Warren on George's Island. The project, which began in 1833, took almost two decades to complete. Each block of Quincy granite used to build the fort was cut and faced by hand, a process taking a single laborer two days to perform. But when it was finally finished, with walls ten feet thick, endless labyrinths of dungeon chambers, officers' quarters, a sweeping interior parade ground, and massive parapets overlooking the sea, Fort Warren was indeed a formidable defense — a five-bastioned fortification that one newspaperman called "Boston Harbor's Rock of Gibraltar."

When World War II started, the U.S. Army garrisoned the island. They modernized Fort Warren, transformed its old casement quarters into contemporary officers' quarters, built new mess halls and war rooms, and expanded and upgraded its twelve-inch "disappearing" artillery guns. Fort Warren was also the command post for the harbor's mine system — a network of mines that were laid in the southern channel. Except for one close call when a German U-boat was detected nearing the harbor, the fort saw no real action during the Second World War. After the war, the Army decommissioned the fort and abandoned the island.

But for all its advanced weaponry, soldiers throughout the wars dreaded being sent to George's. There was another history to the island, told in alehouses and madhouses, of the deadly silence in the depths of the mine plotting room, and the aching of souls who were doomed never to find their way out.

Local historian Edward Rowe Snow chronicles some of these stories in *The Islands of Boston Harbor*. Snow wrote that "Fort Warren has more memories of the Civil War days than any other place in New England." It was the place where John Brown, a soldier in the Massachusetts Tiger Battalion with the same name as the abolitionist who was hanged after the famous raid on Harper's Ferry two years earlier, wrote the lyrics about his namesake — *John Brown's body lies a moldering in the grave* — to the tune of a popular hymn of the day. The song quickly spread through the ranks and caught on as the most stirring of Union marching songs, so much so that, according to several accounts, when President Lincoln heard it while visiting a Massachusetts regiment camped in Washington, he asked Julia Ward Howe to write a patriotic poem to the same melody. Thus, *The Battle Hymn of the Republic*, the most famous Civil War song outside of *Dixie* was born."

George's Island was the last piece of land many Union soldiers saw before pushing off to war, never to return. It was a place where one thousand Confederates were imprisoned, including Confederate General Simon Bolivar Buckner, who after receiving the famous message from General Ulysses Grant, "No terms except an unconditional and immediate surrender can be accepted," surrendered Fort Donelson. Also imprisoned there were the Vice President of the Confederacy, Alexander Stephens, and two Confederate commissioners, James Murray Mason, a former U.S. Senator, and his colleague, John Sliddell. The two men were sailing in the British mail steamer *Trent* to Europe, seeking aid for the Southern cause, when a Union warship, the *San Jacinto*, intercepted the emissaries and brought them to George's Island. The event quickly boiled over into a heated national debate, and President Lincoln, fearful of an international incident which would push England into war with the Union, arranged for Mason and Slidell's release.

It was George's Island where *The Lady in Black* took place. As the tale goes, there was a young Confederate naval officer named Samuel Lanier who was captured by General Burnside's troops at Roanoke Island and imprisoned in Fort Warren's Corridor of Dungeons. In a daring rescue attempt, his bride of a few weeks disguised herself as a man, and packing a pistol, rowed across from Hull to George's Island one stormy night. Although she managed to rendezvous with her husband in the Corridor of Dungeons, the two were discovered trying to escape through the winding, dark tunnels. Desperate, the wife aimed her pistol at the fort's commander Colonel Dimmick, but it exploded, killing her husband instead. Our would-be heroine was sentenced to death as a spy, and chose for her hanging dress a robe made from the fort's black mess hall drapes.

Ever since, The Lady in Black is said to haunt Fort Warren, frightening away soldiers from their sentry duty during the long, lonely night. There are actually recorded court-martial cases of men who have shot at a ghost-like figure while on sentry duty. One poor lookout deserted his post, claiming he had been chased by "the lady in black robes."

## FRENEY THE TEENAGE PHANTOM, 1949

Freney first discovered George's Island when he was a teenager. He already had a reputation in Southie as a flamboyant street fighter, known for getting into vicious fights and wild car chases. He was skinny and tough-looking, and wielded a knife that earned him the nickname "Jimmy the Blade" by other gangs. But his most fearsome attribute was an icy cold stare, which like a war drum announced his deadly intentions.

Freney was first charged with larceny when he was thirteen years old, and soon after, branched out into assault, battery, and robbery. But somehow he avoided reform school. He ran with the Shamrocks gang, but, in truth, he was a loner, a teenage phantom who seemed to appear and disappear magically from one place to another.

When Southie soldiers stationed on George's Island returned home after the war, they told many stories about their wartime experiences on George's. Stories about Fort Warren, with its Corridor of Dungeons; the officers' quarters with its elegant décor of sconces and woodwork, marble mantel pieces and chandeliers; the beautiful murals in the chapel where the song *John Brown's Body* was written during the Civil War; stories about those anxious hours tracking the approach of the German U-boat — about the strange and disturbing things that happened while on sentry duty.

Freney belonged to the generation of boys who grew up right after World War II, who acted macho and swaggered around like tough guys, picked fights, and looked for trouble, as if to make up for the war they had missed and to show their older brothers and friends who had served in the war that they were as tough as them. Freney was a restless guy, loved adventure. He joined the Barnum and Bailey Circus as a roustabout when he was a teenager. He was always looking for an opportunity to plunder, vandalize, and booze it up without getting hassled by the police. Listening to stories about this deserted island just forty-five minutes from Southie, he became curious.

Mike Finnegan, a Southie bar keeper at Triple O's, tells this story:

One day, Freney and a few of his gang "borrowed" an outboard motor boat from the South Boston Yacht Club and, motorin' past Thompson's and Spectacle Islands, 'round Long Island Head, then turnin' southeast past Gallop's, landed at the wood and concrete dock at George's. From the dock, they made their way to the north wall of the fort, crossed over a wooden bridge spannin' a dry moat, through a huge medieval-looking iron gate called the sally port, and onto a parade ground. Lookin' up Freney saw surroundin' him massive walls thirty feet high, capped with a steep fifteen-foot grassy parapet.

From the parade ground, Freney found an entrance into the interior wall and climbed up the windin' stone steps that led to the ramparts and a concrete observation post that looked out over Boston Bay — over Boston Light, the Brewsters, and in the far distance, The Graves. Descendin' the steps to the parade ground, Freney found another entrance that took him through windin' passages to a series of dark rooms — the "Corridor of Dungeons," he later learned it was called. Gropin' his way through the maze of rooms, guided by shafts of light from narrow openin's in the walls, he found himself in the daylight outside the fortress' east wall.

Freney then went back through the main gate and wandered into a room, where to his surprise, he saw someone standin' on a ladder, takin' down a gold chandelier from the ceilin'.

"Who the fuck are ya?" commands Freney.

"What's it to ya?" retorts the figure.

Freney, who needed little provocation to pick a fight, kicks out the ladder from underneath the guy, pounds him on the ground with his fists, and gives him a few kicks in the ribs.

"This is my territory, punk," snarls Freney. "Get out of here and off the island while ya can still walk."

Freney picks the guy off the floor, throws him out the door, and then proceeds to take down the chandelier. It wasn't long afterwards that the gold chandelier was spotted in the window of a South Boston pawn shop.

A few weeks later, Freney was at Triple O's shootin' pool when he heard Johnny Duggan, sittin' at the bar, talkin' to anybody who would listen to his George's Island stories. They say Johnny, known to be a nice, quiet boy, was never quite the same ever since he returned from George's Island where he soldiered during the war.

"I tell ya, I know she was there," Duggan said agitatedly, looking up from his beer glass, which he was tightly coddling. "It was a cold, wintry night. The winds were howlin' all around, blowin' the snow into deep drifts. I'm climbin' down the ladder that leads to the Corridor of Dungeons when I hear this voice, sayin' *'Don't come in here!'* I stop, turn around and climb up the ladder and then up the steps to the observation post. There on the fresh snow I see five footprints of a girl's shoe leadin' nowhere and comin' from nowhere. Then I hear a voice callin' me — *'Johnny, Johnny. I'm coming to get you'*. I see this ghost, it's her. She's wearin' a long black dress. I run for the steps, stumble and fall down them, landin' at the bottom unconscious. When I woke up in the infirmary, my leg was broken. I saw her, I tell ya, I saw her. She's still there in the fort — The Lady in Black."

"Hey, Jim, there's a phone call for ya," I yells over.

"Who is it?" asks Freney, puttin' down his pool stick.

"I don't know, he wouldn't say."

Freney goes over to the bar and picks up the phone.

"Is this Freney, Jimmy the Blade Freney? My name is Vinny T. from the North End. I'm not very happy about what ya did to my cousin a few months ago on that island. Rememba the kid ya knocked off the ladder, broke his ribs? Who the fuck are ya to beat up a little kid? Who the fuck are ya to claim the island is yars? Ya're some kind of Mussolini?

"Let's see who owns that island, mick. Ya bring fifteen of yar Irish apes and I'll bring fifteen of my boys and we'll meet you in the fort on Monday, October fourteen at 4 pm. No guns, no chains, no bats — and no knives. Just fists. Agree?"

"We'll be there wop head," answers Freney.

October fourteen was a warm, humid day, Indian Summer they call it around here in New England. Freney's Shamrocks, fifteen strong, march through the sally port gate onto the parade ground. At the other end of the grounds, Vinny T. and his gang are lined up.

Just when the two gang leaders begin to approach each other to signal the start of battle, whistles are blown, and police appear everywhere on the ramparts. They swarm through the entrances of the fort onto the parade ground. Swingin' their billy clubs, they wade into the thick of the two gangs, who flee in all directions.

Freney, realizin' they're surrounded, dashes toward the entrance leadin' to the Corridor of Dungeons. Gropin' his way through the dark, windin', dimly lit rooms, he makes his way through a tunnel runnin' from the dungeon cells under the fort's north wall and into the underbrush outside of the wall.

From there, he runs to the dock where his gang's three boats were tied. Seein' nobody around, neither his gang, the Italians, nor the police, Freney jumps into one of the boats, starts the engine, and motors away.

But as Freney makes his escape, the skies darken, lightenin' flashes and thunder rumbles. A cold front moves through, droppin' temperatures and bringin' howlin' winds and sheets of rain. The sea becomes furious. Waves churn with white caps and fifteen feet swells. Then the engine konks out. Freney tries to restart it, but it won't turn over, he's out of gas. The boat dips and dives, and tosses helplessly over the waves when suddenly a big wave hits the boat, flippin' it upside down. Freney clings to the hull for dear life as the winds and rain slash at his face and body.

It was nightfall when he awoke and found himself on a beach, his overturned boat restin' a few yards away. The storm had passed.

By the light of the moon, Freney could see a row of cottages beyond a seawall. As he walked toward the cottages, he noticed they were all boarded up. Needin' a place to get some sleep, he chose one of the cottages, rippin' open the screen door and with a rock, breakin' open the latch of the door behind. Enterin' the darkened cottage, he could barely make out the room. There were a couple of cots, a few pieces of furniture, and a small kitchen alcove with a wood stove. Gropin' in the dark, he found a table with a kerosene lamp and a box of matches on it. On lightin' the lamp, he saw on the table a dust-covered book titled, *King's Handbook of Boston Harbor*. Openin' up the book where a marker had been placed, he read the chapter title, "Peddock's Island and Its Tragedy."

Freney, exhausted by his ordeal at sea, lay down on the cot and fell into a deep sleep. When he awoke, it was still night. He went out of the cottage and standin' on the seawall, gazed out toward the harbor. Lookin' up into the night sky, he saw the lights of Boston and the twinklin' stars. That night Freney escaped the cops' billy clubs, the frigid waters, and the craggy rocks on the beach where he washed up. If Death himself was watchin', he knew he had met a fierce competitor. And, of course, that was just the beginning.

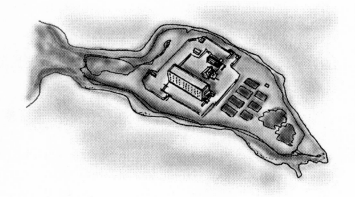

## CHAPTER IV DEER ISLAND

Deer Island is situated in Boston Harbor overlooking Presidential Roads, the main shipping channel from Boston Bay into the harbor. The island got its name from the deer that fled from wolves on the mainland by swimming across Shirley Gut or crossing the ice in the winter. Shirley Gut played a notable role in the War of 1812, when the forty-four gun frigate *U.S.S. Constitution*, 'Old Ironsides', used the narrow passageway to avoid England's naval blockade of Boston Harbor. Deer Island became a peninsula in 1936 when Shirley Gut was filled in, connecting it to the Town of Winthrop.

Today, Deer Island is the site of the Deer Island Wastewater Treatment Plant. The plant consists of a cluster of twelve gleaming, egg-shaped sludge digesters, standing fourteen stories high, looming like a futuristic city over the entrance to Boston Harbor. The island stands in stark contrast to the vegetation-covered drumlins and rock outcroppings of the other islands in the harbor. In Freney's time, the island was known for its prison, the Suffolk County House of Corrections, which was shut down in 1991 when construction of the wastewater treatment plant began.

Back on the streets, Freney was the swashbuckler of Southie, racing around the town in his car with a blonde in the seat next to him, driving off the street and onto the streetcar tracks, waving and honking at the crowd. Then he was gone. His trademark was stealing merchandise from the backs of trucks before they left the Southie docks. But Freney, cocky and self-assured, got too aggressive. The police caught him one day breaking into a warehouse on the docks. The judge sentenced Freney to ten months in the Suffolk County House of Corrections on Deer Island.

The prison was built in 1901 and by the time Freney showed up, the dilapidated brick and cement structure had taken on a medieval ambience. Inside the prison, stagnant and humid air hung over a long, cavernous chamber, an enormous storage room, holding about 340 men convicted of crimes like stealing, drug dealing, and assault and battery. The prison had three tiers of cell blocks, with lights suspended from the ceilings, casting a dull yellow glow over the corridors. Each cell had a few beds, depending on its size and number of inmates, a sink and toilet, which were usually broken. A naked light bulb hanging by a cord from its socket illuminated the graffiti scribbled on the walls, which exuded a smell of urine. In their cells, prisoners played cards, watched television, and talked and talked and talked….about lice, mice, cell thieves, lousy food, lack of shower facilities, boredom, broken plumbing, time left, drugs, ruin, madness — and escape.

The prison grounds were surrounded by a high chain-linked fence with barbed wire on the top. But outside the walls, the sunlight, the openness, the sea breeze, made life more bearable. To kill time, Freney lifted weights, gazed out at the other islands, dreaming of the day he would be free again, and listened to Brendan O'Donovan tell his stories.

O'Donovan was a senior corrections officer, a real old-timer from Charlestown, who looked and acted as if he had been a guard at the prison ever since it was built. O'Donovan fancied himself the unofficial historian of Deer Island, and liked nothing better than to have an audience of Irish boys like Freney sitting around the wooden picnic tables, listening to his stories or his fatherly advice for newcomers.

"Most of yar lads are here for stealin," O'Donovan starts his lecture. "That's no big crime. You'll probably be out of here in less than ten months if yar behave yarself. When yar get out, stay smart, stay clean, else next time yar'll end up in Walpole. That'll make yar time at Deer Island feel like a day at Revere Beach compared to what goes on down thar. I wouldn't be advisin' tryin' to escape. I've seen dozens of men over the years drown tryin' to swim across the gut. The only man to succeed made it by powerboat. These days guys try to smuggle themselves out in garbage trucks, but they usually get caught in a few weeks and end up back here."

"Yar know, Deer Island has always been a place of banishment," says O'Donovan solemnly, casting his eyes on the Irish boys at the table. "Yar probably have ancestors that came over in the Great Famine in the 1840s. Deer Island was the landin' point for thousands of Irish. Many of 'em came over sick and poverty-stricken in boats called 'fever' or 'famine' ships, hopin' to reach the port of Boston. The Yankee blue blood city officials quarantined the people from these ships on Deer Island, where malnutrition and disease spread and four thousand died, accordin' to the unmarked graves, which have long since been paved over.

"Go back in history even further," O'Donovan continues, "to a time when Deer Island was Boston's Devil's Island. Not many people know much about King Phillip's War. King Phillip's War started in 1675. It was the bloodiest, cruelest of all the Indian wars in New England. King Phillip, his Indian name was Metacomet, was the king of the Wampanoag Indians. Seein' the white man takin' their lands, King Phillip called other Indian tribes to unite and fight back together to regain their lands. Battles raged all over eastern and central Massachusetts and Rhode Island as the Indians massacred white settlements and white settlers viciously retaliated, burnin' and razin' the Indian settlements. A year later, 1676, the war was over. The white man had won. The Indian captives were forced to march in shackles to the Charles River, where they were transported on vessels to Deer Island. Over one thousand Indians were imprisoned on Deer Island. It was a concentration camp. Half of them died of starvation, exposure, and lack of medicine. Many of those who survived were sold into slavery."

The group of men that had gathered to listen to O'Donovan were transfixed. O'Donovan looked at them and laughed.

"Thank yar luckies ya' got a roof," he said, chuckling. "This here's a resort, nowadays."

35

Freney considered trying to escape, but eventually he didn't need to. He was paroled after serving three months at Deer Island. After his release, Freney went from stealing merchandise off the docks in Southie to robbing banks across the country — Massachusetts, Rhode Island, Indiana. Big heists like $60,000 from a Medford, Massachusetts bank and $42,000 from an Indiana bank. It wasn't long before his friends were caught, but Freney dyed his blond hair black and eluded the FBI for months. He was finally arrested coming out of a Revere nightclub in March of 1959.

On a fall day later that year, James Freney, his hands and feet shackled in steel, crossed the foggy bay in a prison ferry to his new home on Alcatraz Island.

## THE ROCK, 1959

Alcatraz lies on an island in the middle of San Francisco Bay, 3,105 miles from Boston Harbor. The prison is called the Rock, an impregnable fortress, standing rigid, silent, isolated, on the stone cliffs of the island. The water surrounding the island is frigid, criss-crossed by treacherous currents, and shark infested. There was little chance of anyone escaping from the Rock by swimming. If the sharks didn't get you, most likely the icy cold water and treacherous currents would exhaust and numb your body, and swallow you without a trace.

The U.S. Army built a fort on the island in 1853 and six years later turned it into a military prison for deserters, Confederate prisoners in the Civil War, and later, Spanish prisoners in the Spanish-American War. The Army imprisoned nineteen Hopi Indians on Alcatraz Island in 1895 for resisting government policies that were destroying their religion and language. Following the San Francisco earthquake of 1906, hundreds of civilian prisoners were transferred to the island for safe confinement.

During the Great Depression, the gangster era was in full swing as the country witnessed a violent crime wave brought on by Prohibition and the mob's control of the cities. A public outcry swept the country to take back America's cities and lock up the public enemies. So, in 1934, with Alcatraz becoming too expensive for the army to operate, military control passed to the Justice Department, and Uncle Sam's Devil's Island was born. It was a prison for the most hardened criminals in America's penal system — kidnappers, spies, bank robbers, and murderers — designed to imprison and isolate them from the rest of humanity, with no chance for escape. Al Capone, Doc Barker, the last surviving son from Ma Barker's gang, George "Machine Gun" Kelly, Robert "The Birdman of Alcatraz" Stroud, Floyd Hamilton, a gang member and driver for Bonnie and Clyde, and Alvin "Creepy" Karpis, a flamboyant bank robber and Public Enemy No.1, were among the prison's most notorious inmates.

Freney's cell was cramped and narrow, barely wide enough for a bunk, toilet, sink, and some book shelves. It was on the second tier of B Block. Each day was the same regimen, the same routine. At 6:30 am, a whistle was blown, waking Freney and the other prison inmates. They were given twenty-five minutes to wash up, tidy their cells, and stand to be counted. At 6:55, the whistle was blown again, the cell gates automatically opened, and the prisoners were marched in a single file through a corridor the inmates called 'Broadway' into the mess hall. They were given twenty minutes to eat and then marched out to line up for their work assignments. Inmates typically worked in the laundry, clothing, furniture, or metal shops. Freney worked in the laundry and also the prison library.

A whistle signaled the end of the work period. The inmates were lined up and marched through the snitch box (metal detector), up the stair walk into the recreation yard for body counts before lunch. The afternoon was the same routine. Whistle blows, inmates line up and march to work assignments. Whistle blows, work period stops, prisoners march into the recreation yard for a brief period. Whistle blows, line up, march back to work areas. Whistle blows, march to supper. Whistle blows, end of supper. Whistle blows, march to cells for a body count. Whistle blows, lights out at 9:30 pm.

For two thousand nine hundred twenty-two days, this was Freney's life, except for the nineteen days he spent in D Block, the Treatment Unit, otherwise known as "The Hole," for inciting a work stoppage. The Hole was a dark steel enclosed cell with a sink, toilette, and a low-wattage light bulb hanging from the ceiling. Freney's mattress was taken away during the day to enforce his boredom and isolation. A guard would open the narrow window slit cut into the solid steel door to allow in a little light and serve him his meals. Freney kept his body alive by constantly doing pushups and sit-ups, and his mind alive dreaming of ways to escape.

## BROWN'S STORY

Augie Brown was a bank robber and escape artist who did time with Freney on Alcatraz. Augie, who now lives on Boston's South Shore, recalled that Freney was a different person when he came out of The Hole. "Before he went down there, he always thought he was the toughest guy in the world, always spoilin' for a fight. Couldn't control his temper. Flyin' off the handle if you even looked cross-eyed at him. Real cocky, like the way Jimmy Cagney plays a gangster in the movies," Augie said. "After he came out he was very quiet. I never found anything bad about him. Never got in any trouble. He didn't talk about The Hole, but I felt here was a guy who had survived Hell. It was as if he went into a blast furnace as iron and came out as steel.

"Freney was workin' in the library where I got to know him. He would show me around and tell me about the books he was readin'. There was one book he would show me by an Italian guy, Machiachelli? Machiavello? Or somethin'. I think the book was called *The Prince*. He would open up the book and show me pages where he underlined these, what would ya call 'em, maxims? I rememba Freney callin' 'em "laws of nature." Believe it or not. I wrote 'em down, thinkin' one day they may come in handy. Carried 'em around on a piece of paper in my wallet for years. Umm! Let's see if I still have 'em. Ya, here they are. They're still in my wallet.

> 'It is necessary for a prince wishing to hold his own to know how to do wrong, and to make use of it.'
>
> 'There are two ways of contesting, the one by law, the other by force. The first method is proper to men, the second to beasts. But because the first is frequently not sufficient, it is necessary to have recourse to the second. Therefore, it is necessary for a prince to understand how to avail himself of the beast and the man.'
>
> 'He who has relied least on fortune will become the strongest.'

> *'Once you take over a country and you kill the prince and his family, it is easy to rule. There is no one with power to fear.'*

"Freney liked to talk about military strategy, especially the strategy of World War II generals like Rommel, Patton, and MacArthur," Augie continued. "He was always lookin' for the flaws in the enemy's strategy to exploit. He would pull out this map of the Pacific war that was folded in a book, lay it out on a table, and pointin' his finger at these islands like ya seen in the old war movies about Guadalcanal, Tarawa, Iwo Jima, New Guinea, Philippines, tell me about MacArthur's island-hoppin' strategy, where he would go 'round the Jap strongholds and 'hit 'em where they ain't.'

"Freney had a favorite story he liked to tell. It took place durin' the Korean War. He called it 'MacArthur's Pirate,'" Augie went on. "I think he got the story from some military history magazine the library had. I rememba Freney tellin' the story like this:

"It's Korea, the summer of 1950. The North Koreans are pushin' the U.S. Army down the Korean peninsula. MacArthur has got to find a strategy to stop 'em and turn the war around. He comes up with a plan to land 70,000 troops at this 'ere port of Inchon on Korea's west coast. Then they would drive inland, take back Seoul, the South Korean capitol, from the North Koreans, and sever their supply lines. It was a long shot because MacArthur knew nothin' about its defenses, the harbor's tides, water depths, mudflats, beaches, and islands in the harbor. Knowin' so little about Inchon, would he risk sendin' troops, landin' craft, and supply ships into Inchon harbor?

"MacArthur had heard there was one man who could collect the intelligence needed to pull off the invasion — Navy Lieutenant Gene Clark. When Freney told the story, he was always callin' Clark the 'Barbary Coast Pirate.'

"In the next twenty days, Clark organized a South Korean team and in a motor launch armed with fifty-caliber machine guns terrorized the North Korean boats. 'Drop your sails,' Clark hollered. 'We're comin' aboard.' Once he boarded 'em, Clark interrogated the fishermen and captured any North Korean police or soldiers. At night, Clark led commando raids on islands in the harbor, blowin' up fortifications and communications centers.

"When MacArthur invaded Inchon, he had all the intelligence he needed. Afterwards, MacArthur gave Clark the highest award in the Navy, the Legion of Merit. He said Clark had 'the nerves of a burglar and the flair of a Barbary Coast Pirate.'"

---

Years later, gang members would remember Freney boasting about his Alcatraz experience. "I remember him telling us Alcatraz stories. Telling us how tough the Rock was," recounted Paul Doyle. "We'd be in our office above Triple O's. Jimmy, wearing his fancy belt buckle inscribed with the words 'Alcatraz: 1934-1965,' would be sipping his ice tea — he rarely drank — telling the story of this small white kid who was beaten up by this giant black con.

"'So, the kid fashions a make-shift scythe in the prison machine shop. Then waits for the black con at the top of a dark stairwell. The black guy reaches the top and the kid comes out swinging. Takes his head off with one fell swoop. And the rest of us in our cells, we can hear the head bouncing down each step — *thud, thud, thud*. Later on I hear the kid gets taken out by the California highway patrol, but not before he takes a couple of them with him.

"'Did anyone ever escape from Alcatraz?' I once asked him.

"'Did ya ever see that Clint Eastwood movie, *Escape from Alcatraz?*' Jimmy answered, seein' an opening to tell another good story. 'It's a true story. I was there.'

"'Frank Morris. He's the smart guy, the mastermind of the plan. Then there were the Anglin brothers, John and Clarence. They all knew each other from Atlanta, serving time there for armed robbery. They got shipped to the Rock when they tried to break out from there. They wanted me to come in with them in the breakout, but I said no thanks.

"'There was somethin' about their plan that bothered me. It seemed pretty good at first. They made tools out of spoons and electric fans for diggin' a passageway. Molded plaster heads to fool the guards into thinkin' that they were still in their cell bunks sleepin' while diggin' at night. They built a life raft out of raincoats they collected from the prison clothin' store.

"'On the night of June 11, 1962, they crawled through a ventilatin' duct they had widened and onto the roof, crossed over the rooftop and down a pipe to the ground outside the walls. That's the last anyone saw them. The only trace of them ever found was a wallet belongin' to Clarence Anglin, washed up on nearby Angel Island. A lot of guys like to think they made it. No way! I'll tell you why. Their plan was flawed.

"'The plan called for usin' the raft to paddle to Angel Island, rest there and then swim across Racoon Straights to Marin County. There they would steal a car, rob a clothin' store and split, each man for himself. The problem was these guys had no contacts. No friends, relatives, or money in San Francisco to help 'em. It would cost big bucks to get a boat to escape and they had no way to communicate to anyone outside to set a date and time of their break. They couldn't have made it swimmin'. Either the sharks or the ice-cold water of the Bay would have killed 'em. Just 'cause they found no bodies doesn't mean they made it. Few bodies are ever recovered from San Francisco Bay.'"

"Maybe Jimmy's Alcatraz stories were a way of promoting his reputation as a tough guy or maybe they were delivered as a lesson on the importance of strategy," Doyle said. "Both of these theories are probably correct. His favorite line was: 'If you want to do hard crime, you got to do hard time.'"

Alcatraz was closed in 1965 when it became too expensive to operate. Freney was moved to Leavenworth where he volunteered for a CIA project to find out how people reacted to LSD. Conti said that Freney was selected for the project because of his high IQ. Friends say the hallucinogen gave him nightmares and sleepless nights, but it gave him eleven years of freedom, too. In return for his participation in the project, he was paroled in 1965. Freney went to prison at twenty-seven when Dwight Eisenhower was president. He came out of prison at thirty-six when Lyndon Johnson was president. He vowed he would never serve another day behind bars.

# CHAPTER V   SPECTACLE ISLAND

Spectacle Island is situated in Boston Harbor, four miles southeast of Logan International Airport. When the glaciers receded from Massachusetts 13,000 years ago so much of the earth was locked up in glacial ice that the sea level was about 300 feet lower than it is today. The ancient shoreline stretched well beyond what is now the outer limit of Boston Harbor. As the glacier melted and the sea level rose, the ocean moved inland and slowly flooded the harbor, transforming uplands into islands. When the English settlers first arrived, they saw that one of the islands, consisting of two large mounds connected by a sandbar, looked like a pair of Spectacles, and so went the name.

Native Americans came to the island by canoe as early as 500 AD to spear fish, dig for clams and mussels, and gather berries. They left middens — Indian garbage dumps — filled with piles of clam shells, which over 1000 years mixed with food wastes. Over the years, the wastes broke down and covered the island with a pebbly black and white soil, where the lime of the clam shells neutralized the corrosive effects of the acidic New England soil to preserve the bones of those early Indians buried on the island throughout the centuries.

In 1729, Spectacle Island became a quarantine center. City officials declared that all Irish vessels arriving in Boston Harbor were required to discharge their passengers and crew on the island, since ships coming from Ireland could be carrying smallpox. Most passengers were transferred to the mainland, but many died and were buried on the island, their bones mingling with those of the early Indians.

In the nineteenth century, a businessman named Nahum Ward purchased the island and set up a rendering plant. Slaughterhouse offals and nearly two thousand horses a year were rendered into hides, glues, horsehair, and neat's foot oil. It was a convenient place for the city of Boston to dispose of dead horses. Otherwise the decaying corpses, if left on the streets, would have touched off a plague.

In 1921, the city of Boston signed a contract with a private company to reclaim grease from the city's garbage. The garbage was brought to Spectacle and cooked and compressed to extract grease, which was then sold to a soap manufacturer. The processed garbage was dumped on the island and covered over with rubbish. The market for reclaimed grease declined in the 1930s and the grease plant went out of business. The city continued to dump raw garbage there until 1959, covering the island and filling the gullies with deposits of trash several hundred feet deep. The dump was finally closed in 1965 when a bulldozer moving refuse on the island sank into a trash gully.

But over the decades, the dump had produced so much methane gas that spontaneous combustion would ignite underground fires, undermining the surface of the dump, causing cave-ins, and bounding the island's rocky shoreline with cliffs of decomposing trash. The only man-made structure that remained was a 90-foot draft chimney that loomed above the ruins of the grease extraction plant like a ghostly smoke stack of a death camp. A burning-dump odor wafted through the air surrounding the island. Spectacle had become a 100-acre hell hole that no one was allowed to land on, except the dead.

All this changed a few years ago when Spectacle Island got a big face lift. Dirt from the Big Dig — Boston's $14 billion highway project to sink the city's central artery underground, along with adding a third tunnel to Logan Airport — was barged out and dumped on the island, covering the mountains of trash and elevating the island 60 feet, making it the highest natural point in the harbor. The dirt and gravel were capped with a layer of clay and covered with six feet of top soil so that the island could be landscaped with trees and shrubs. Spectacle Island was officially opened in 2004 as part of the Boston Harbor Islands National Park Area with docking access for a public ferry and recreational boats, beaches, picnic and recreational areas, a trail system, and a visitor's center.

## IRISH GANGS OF BOSTON

Back in the early 1960s, there were five Irish gangs in Boston. Ed "Wimpy" Hawkins and his two brothers, Walter and William, in Roxbury. Bobby Conti, his brother, Charlie "The Wolf" Conti, and Luigi "Limousine Lou" Farnesse were early members of the Hawkins brothers gang. South Boston had two Irish gangs. The Mulligan gang, led by Donnie Mulligan, who operated out of a Southie beer-and-a-beating joint on West Broadway called the Transit Care and the Keogh gang, headed by Paul Rooney and Pat Quinn. The Crusher brothers, Bernie, George, and Edward, known to all as "The Big Crusher," held forth in Charlestown. They were joined by the Casey brothers, Steve and Connie. The Winter Hill gang in Somerville was the biggest Irish gang.

Back then, Winter Hill was an Italian and Irish blue collar neighborhood with lots of bars, lounges, and clubs along Broadway, the main street of Somerville, a city next to Boston. Buddy Gleason, the first big boss of the Winter Hill gang, held court at the Tap Royal bar on Broadway, where there's an Osco Drug now. Howie Summer was the gang's number two man. The Winter Hill gang sometimes paired up with the Italian Mafia. They collected loan-shark debts, shook down small-time hoods for a share of the pilferage from the docks of Charlestown and South Boston, and took contracts for Mafia hits. Buddy Gleason and Howie Summer made weekly trips to Federal Hill in Providence, Rhode Island, to meet with Carmen Borgia, boss of the New England La Cosa Nostra.

Ever since Prohibition in the 1930s, the Irish gangs had always been subordinate to the Italian Mafia. The Irish tried to take control of bootlegging operations in Boston Harbor from the Italians, but when two leaders of the Kelsey gang out of South Boston went to the North End to dictate their terms, they were murdered. The Irish retreated to South Boston and it would be many years before they again challenged the Italians for control of Boston Harbor. After Prohibition, the Italian Mafia grew stronger, more organized, disciplined, and regimented than the Irish gangs. They had capos, soldiers, and consiglieres. The Irish gangs were smaller, undisciplined, constantly feuding with each other, and were headed by strongmen — smart and cunning dictators. But if the top man got knocked off, it usually spelled the gang's end.

When illegal gambling replaced alcohol as the prime criminal activity, the Italians remained on top of the business. They controlled the bookies. The bookies, in turn, were protected by the cops, who were paid off by the mob. They say the mob's tentacles extended everywhere, even to Beacon Hill, where a bookie ran an illegal betting line from the Massachusetts State House.

The Irish gangs survived as subcontractors to the Mafia. They became the enforcers, the hitmen, the leg-breakers for the Mafia when the Italians didn't want to use their own guys. They survived because they took money from the Italians, and put it on the street as loan shark money. Other independents survived, too, like Joe "The Animal" Aguirra, the Portuguese Shylock, who ran his gang from the corner of Brooks and Bennington Street in East Boston, operating as a gun-for-hire between the Irish gang lords and the Mafia. And Harry "Doc" Kalinsky, Jewish, a dentist, graduated from Tufts Dental School, and then became one of Boston's biggest bookies. Kalinsky made headlines when in 1941 he loaned $8,500 to James Michael Curley, the legendary major of Boston, and got in return his name as beneficiary of a $50,000 life insurance policy that Curley had taken out as security for a loan. Kalinsky not only paid Mafia boss Dante Massaroni for the right to operate, but he also had to give the action to the Italians.

So here's the picture. The Italians are on top of Boston's underworld. The Irish gangs operate pretty much independently, ruling like princes in their principalities of Dorchester, Roxbury, Charlestown, Somerville, and South Boston, but for the most part minding their own business and staying out of the way of the Italian mob, living in peace among themselves — until Labor Day, 1961.

According to underworld lore, two Irish gangsters from Winter Hill rented a cottage that weekend on Salisbury Beach, a sea coast town in Massachusetts just south of the New Hampshire border. With them were their girlfriends and their buddy from Charlestown, George Crusher. Crusher had been drinking all day and, fully soused, made a pass at one of the gangster's girlfriends, who slapped him back in the face.

"Hey, bitch, where do ya get off slappin' me," yells Crusher, who wasn't used to anyone hitting him back, let alone a female.

Crusher looked at the girl's boyfriend and says, "Don't ya teach her to have any respect?" and drunkenly tried to throw a punch at her, falling onto the couch. The two other men jumped on Crusher, pounding his face and kicking his ribs over and over again until he was a bruised and bloody heap.

"Ya think he's dead?" asks one of the men.

"Naw, he's still breathin'. Let's get rid of 'im," says the other.

So they dump him on the lawn of a hospital.

A month later, George Crusher got out of the hospital and his brother, Bernie, the leader of the Charlestown gang, went to see Buddy Gleason, head of the Winter Hill Gang.

"I want an apology for what yar guys did to George and I want those two guys dead," said Bernie.

"Fuck you! Get the fuck out of my house or I'll break your fuckin' head," Buddy shouted back.

That night Gleason was awakened by noises outside his house. When he looked out the window he saw a couple of men standing near his car in the driveway. He grabbed his revolver, ran outside shouting "what the Fuck is goin' on," chasing away the two men. Then Gleason crouched down to check his car. "Those fuckers, they've strapped god- damned dynamite under my car."

The next day, Halloween, Buddy Gleason tracked down Bernie Crusher near the Bunker Hill Monument in City Square, Charlestown. "Trick or treat, Bernie, baby," and gunned him down.

The Irish gang wars were on.

For the next couple of years, things seemed to settle down. It was the lull before the storm. In 1964, tensions erupted when an ex-con named Frank Hubble drinking at Walter's Lounge, started running his mouth in front of the wrong people. Walter's was a bar in Roxbury owned by Wimpy Hawkins and run by his brother Walter. The Hawkins gang was an ally of Buddy Gleason and the Winter

Hill gang. After having a few beers, Hubble was getting sloshed and he starts bragging: "I'm goin' take down Gleason and the whole fuckin' Winter Hill. Who's gonna stop me? Buddy's fairies?" Over and over again he boozily boasted about single-handily taking down the Winter Hill gang until finally Charlie "The Wolf," Bobby Conti's brother and a friend of the Winter Hill gang, who was sitting at the bar, had heard enough of Hubble's bragging. He got up off his bar stool as calmly as if he was going to the john, walked over to Hubble and shot him point blank in the head.

A friend of Charlie's sitting at the bar said to him: "Charlie, twenty guys saw you shoot 'im."

So what did Charlie do? He burned the bar down. "No bar, no witnesses," he said.

A few days latter, they found Hubble's body stuffed in the trunk of a stolen car in South Boston.

The Charlestown gang struck back, gunning down Russell Burke, an ex-MDC cop and Buddy Gleason's body guard.

The Winter Hill gang retaliated and bumped off Wilfred Corrigan and Harold Lawton, Crusher gang members, dumping them into Boston Harbor.

In September 1964, the body of Ronald Rawlins was found in his car with the motor running at a red light on Mount Auburn street in Watertown. One story had it that Rawlins was in love with a woman named Dottie from Dorchester. Dottie, however, was going steady with another guy. Rawlins went to George Crusher with a proposition: "George, if you kill Dottie's boyfriend so she'll be able to marry me, I'll kill Buddy Gleason for you. And to show you I'm on the level, I'll kill Gleason first."

A few weeks later Rawlins busted into the Tap Royal bar on Broadway on Winter Hill and shot a guy. But it was the wrong guy. Some petty thief named Charlie Reynolds.

It didn't take long for Gleason to figure it out. So he went to his good friend Joe "the Animal" Aguirra, "Take the Fuckin' Rawlins out, Joey."

The killings continued throughout 1964 and 1965. Aguirra gunned down Edward "The Big Crusher," while he was waiting for a bus in Charlestown.

Eleven days later, the Casey brothers, Steve and Connie, members of the Crusher gang shot Buddy Gleason as he was leaving the Tap Royal.

A few months later, Connie Casey was driving on Route 1 in Revere when a car pulls up beside his and Aguirra stuck his caveman face out of the window, saying "Bye, bye, Connie boy," and blasting him to pieces with a sawed-off shotgun.

Not long after that Steve Casey was driving through Porter Square in Cambridge and a car pulled up alongside his, the window rolled down, and the caveman face poked itself out of the window, "Join ya brother, Stevie boy" and blew him away.

When Freney was paroled and returned to South Boston in 1965, the streets were bathed in the blood of Irish gangsters. The back alleys, car parks, and wastelands of Somerville, Charlestown, Roxbury, Dorchester, and South Boston had become killing fields in what some say was the bloodiest gang war in American history. There were already fifty dead and, with Freney back in town, there were more to come.

Freney joined the Mulligan brothers who were running gambling and loan-sharking operations in South Boston. Freney was an enforcer with a reputation of a tough guy before he went to prison, and a tougher guy when he came out. Police files show that the Mulligans had little trouble collecting their debts when Freney went knocking on the doors.

Donnie Mulligan, the second of four brothers, ruled over his turf from the Transit, a bar on West Broadway. Freney and Donnie were close friends. But by the end of the decade, the Keogh gang was challenging the Mulligan's control of the rackets in South Boston. At the same time, Freney had a falling out with Donnie and aligned himself with the leader of the Keogh gang, Pat Quinn.

"Donnie hadn't taken care of Freney the way Freney felt he should have been," recounted Ed McDevitt, a retired cop who covered South Boston back then. "I also think Freney wanted to keep his options open. He went with the flow. When he saw that power on the streets was shifting to the Keogh gang, he joined them."

On May 13, 1972, Donnie Mulligan got a phone call at his home in Framingham, where he moved after two of his brothers were assassinated in Southie's gang wars. The Mulligan family had gathered for the birthday party of their four-year old son.

"Honey, I got to go out. Start the party, I'll be back soon," Donnie told his wife.

As Mulligan was about to get into his wife's Chevy Nova, someone walked up to Mulligan, pointed a .45 caliber machine gun at him, and pumped fifteen bullets into him, riddling his body like a bloody piece of Swiss cheese.

The next day Kenny, the lone surviving Mulligan brother, received a bouquet of flowers with a card that reads: *"Bon Voyage, COD."*

The Boston and State Police suspected Freney was the one who pulled the trigger, but he was never charged for the crime.

With Donnie Mulligan dead, Freney took control of the Mulligan gang, but he still saw that his flanks were vulnerable, that more blood would be shed with the Keogh gang as they jockeyed for power in South Boston. Realizing he needed a strong ally to shift the balance of power in his favor, he hooked up as an enforcer for Howie Summer's Winter Hill gang. That's where he met Bobby Conti, his future crime partner, and other rising hitmen like Bobby's brother, Charlie "The Wolf" Conti, Johnny Greco, and Luigi "Limousine Lou" Farnesse.

With the Winter Hill gang bolstered by Freney and the other new enforcers, Howie Summer moved to take over all crime business in Somerville, Charlestown, Dorchester, Roxbury, and South Boston, shaking down every bookmaker, loan shark, and drug dealer not controlled by La Cosa Nostra.

The message was simple: "You have to pay rent for the right to stay in business."

Jackie Scott, a big bookie, was told to meet Howie Summer at the Holiday Inn on the Charlestown-Somerville line. "I got no problem with this," replied Scott to Summer when he was given the message.

But Scott changed his mind and stopped paying the rent. He was found dead a few weeks after that, his body full of bullet holes, stuffed in a trunk of a car in Somerville. The hit man, most gangsters and lawmen believed, was James Freney.

"Why the fuck should I pay 'em rent?" groused Joseph "Indian Joe" Angelli, a Medford bookie and member of a rival gang of the Winter Hill gang.

Indian Joe was gunned down while eating at a Pewter Pot in Medford by a gunman brandishing a sub-machine gun.

Down goes Michael Mazzini, member of the Angelli gang.

Down goes Al Mitchell, another member.

Down goes William Finney, another.

Down goes James O'Leary, and again another.

And finally finishing off the Angelli gang, down goes Joe's brother, Indian Al Angelli, the gang's leader.

Each one was mowed down in a hail of machine gun bullets, one by one, like ducks in a shooting gallery, from March 1973 to February 1974, in less than a year.

Other rival gangs were served a similar fate. James Cullerton, a member of the Charlestown Crusher gang was cut down on December 1, 1973 and Paulie McCoy, head of the South Boston Keogh gang, was last seen November 20, 1974, heading to a Charlestown housing project. Police found his station wagon four days later submerged off the Mystic River in Charlestown, with his wallet and family photos floating nearby. Divers found no body.

Who knows how many Freney murdered in those days — in the 1960s and 1970s? No one knows. Many of the victims disappeared. Their bodies were never found. Rumors have it that Freney buried some victims in Nova Scotia, others along the banks of the Neponset River in Quincy or in a mob burial ground near the Southeast Expressway. A few years ago they dug up the remains of Paulie McCoy on the edge of Tenean Beach in Dorchester.

Who knows where there are other grave sites? Nicky Silanus, one of Freney's enforcers before he got killed in a botched robbery attempt, once told a story to gang members about going out several times with Freney in a motor launch with corpses in plastic trash bags.

"We're nearin' some island. I don't know the name of it. As we get closer to the island, in the moonlight I see this chimney hoverin' like a ghost over these ruins. There's a glow, like from little fires burnin' underneath the ground. My eyes are waterin' from this garbage smell comin' from the island.

"We land at the dock and lift up a couple of wheel barrows that we brought with us onto the dock. Then we heaved the corpses that we stuffed in body bags onto the dock and wheeled them onto the island. It was like walkin' through Hades. Smoke comin' out of the ground. Rats as big as cats scurryin' around ya, nippin' at your heels. Piles of rottin' wood and rusted metals everywhere. The wheel barrels sinkin' in this sea of rottin' garbage and trash. We dump the bags in a gully and go back to the boat.

"'Hey, Jimmy,' I ask him, 'Where the fuck are we? Why the fuck do we have to come here to dump the bodies?'

"He stares back at me with those fuckin' eyes that pierce through ya like an arrow," and says:

'This is the isle of the dead, Nicky boy,' in a voice hissin' like a Cobra ready to strike. "There's an Irish curse you put on your enemies that goes 'May six horse-loads of graveyard clay lay on top of you.'"

About 1993, the barges started to haul dirt and gravel from the Big Dig to Spectacle. Trucks then spread the dirt and gravel, some 2.7 million yards of it, over the island and capped it with two feet of clay, interring deep in the bowels of Spectacle, along with the fossils of ancient Indians and nineteenth century Irishmen, the bones of who knows how many of Freney's victims?

Who knows how many Freney murdered? Nobody knows, except Freney. One Southie old timer, who crossed paths with Freney, tells the story of the time Freney summoned him to go for a ride in his car.

"He tells me he'd walk right into the BayView Pub in the middle of the afternoon and put a bullet in my ear, in front of all my friends. He even named them all."

"Trust me," he says. "No one will say a fuckin' thing. There'll be no witnesses. Don't think I wouldn't do it. I've already killed twenty-six people. Now step out of the car. I'm lettin' ya go this time."

By 1974, Freney, at forty-five, was the underworld boss of South Boston. "If you owned a bar in Southie," one long-time resident of Southie recounted, "you had no choice. You dealt with Freney, or else. That's just the way it was. He had a piece of everything — the booze, the bookies, whatever."

For Freney, Machiavelli's dictum held true: *'Once you take over the country and kill the prince and his family, it is easy to rule.'* Now there was only one more prince to go after — Howie Summer, the head of the Winter Hill gang.

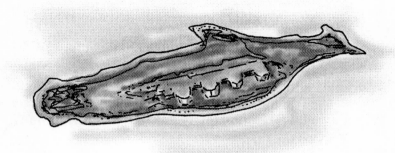

# CHAPTER VI     LOVELL'S ISLAND

Lovell's, an island about three-quarters of a mile long and one-quarter wide, is located in the middle of Boston Harbor. To the north in the foreground lies Broad Sound and Deer Island with the North Shore coast line in the distance. To the east are the Brewsters, Boston Light and the open waters of Massachusetts Bay. To the south are The Narrows, George's Island, the Nantasket Roads anchorage, Hull peninsular, Peddocks Island and the towns of the South Shore, with the Blue Hills in the distance. To the west are Gallops Island, Rainsford and Long Islands, President Roads anchorage and the Boston skyline.

Edward Rose Snow described Lovell's as a romantic island, full of tales of buried pirate treasure, ill-fated lovers who froze to death in each other's arms on the island, and a secret tunnel leading to a mysterious fort. Then there is the wreck of the *Magnifique*, a French man-of-war that sank off Lovell's in 1782. Snow claimed that in the twentieth century, gold and silver coin — perhaps, that said to have gone down with the *Magnifique* — was found on Lovell's. And, maybe, he said, some of that treasure is still on the island.

The island's recorded history is much more ordinary. It was named after Captain William Lovell, an early settler of Dorchester. For most of its early history the island was farmed until it became a training camp during the Civil War. The hidden tunnel Snow referred to was, in fact, an elaborate submarine defense system built after the Civil War. It consisted of a tunnel constructed under the channel between Lovell's and Gallop's Island. Explosives, placed in the tunnel, could be set to go off when an enemy ship passed through the channel above.

The high point of Lovell's military role came in 1900 with the establishment of Fort Standish. Lovell's Island was considered a strategic site due to its location near the junction of two main channel entrances — President Roads and Nantasket Roads — into the harbor, one leading into Dorchester Bay, the other, into Quincy Bay.

The fort was named for Myles Standish, the early *Mayflower* arrival who was military leader of Plymouth Colony from 1620 to 1656. Only the gun battery emplacements, bunkers, and guard house of Fort Standish in World War II remain standing today, the ghostly ruins of Boston's chief role in the nation's history.

## THE GUNS OF BOSTON HARBOR

Ever since the Massachusetts Bay Company, a band of Puritans headed by John Winthrop, landed on Blaxton's Peninsula in 1630, renaming the settlement Boston, the harbor and its islands have played a major role in local and national defense. Settlers were originally attracted to Boston by its large, well-protected harbor, islands, peninsulas, and hills, which offered easily defensible locations for communities around the harbor.

The first fort, Fort Hill, was built in 1634 on the mainland on a site near where Rowe's Wharf on the waterfront is located today. Fort Hill commanded Boston's inner harbor and passage from the outer harbor. A seawall, known as the "Barricado" was erected in 1681 to defend the port against an enemy fleet equipped with "fireships."

"Fireships were ships loaded with inflammables and explosives," wrote Gerald Butler, a local historian, in his book *The Guns of Boston Harbor*. "They were sailed by skeleton crews close enough to a port or an anchored fleet to drift in on tide and wind after their crew lit fuses and abandoned them. The blazing fireships would lodge against wharves, and the fires would spread to the wooden wharves, buildings, and yards of the waterfront, or to other ships that they collided with. Since they were difficult to sink quickly and dangerous to grapple and tow, the best defense against fireships was a barricade or staggered seawall outlying the immediate port area. Any vessel entering a port protected by such a barricade would have to navigate, not drift, through its gaps."

The general line of the port of Boston's 'Barricado" followed Boston's waterfront along what is today Atlantic Avenue.

As eighteenth-century Boston became a booming port, merchants and ship owners realized the need for a powerful beacon at the harbor's entrance to guide incoming ships. So the city built Boston Light on Little Brewster, the oldest lighthouse still operating in North America. Boston Light began to play a strategic as well as a navigational role. Throughout the colonial period, Boston Light would raise the Union Jack to signal military authorities at Castle Island of approaching vessels. Castle Island would then alert the city to prepare its defense.

During the Revolutionary War, British and American forces vied for control of Boston Light. In 1775, the Redcoats captured the light and blocked entrance to the harbor. American troops counterattacked, at first unsuccessfully. Then a Major Tupper, commanding three hundred Continentals dispatched by General George Washington attacked and put the lighthouse out of commission — but not without suffering heavy casualties. As the Continentals prepared to leave the island, they found their boats were stranded on the outgoing tide. Finally, they got their boats free with the British in hot pursuit. It wasn't until American cannons on Nantasket Head zeroed in on the British craft that the Continentals managed to make it back to Boston.

Soon after, the British evacuated Boston in March 1776. British marines, smarting from American offensives, blew up Boston Light. But because of its strategic importance, in 1783 the State of Massachusetts rebuilt the light — the very same structure you see today. In 1790, the federal government took possession of both Little Brewster and the lighthouse. The US Coast Guard operates the 98-foot-high granite lighthouse now. You can hear the blasts of its foghorn as its beacon, flashing every 10 seconds, shines 16 miles out to sea.

When the Civil War began, the islands' forts were converted to Confederate prisons and Union training grounds. Shortly after the shots were fired at Fort Sumter in Charlestown Harbor on April 12,

1861, marking the opening of the Civil War, four companies of the Massachusetts 2^nd Infantry — the Tiger Battalion — landed at Fort Warrren on George's Island to guard against a possible sea attack on Boston by the Southern rebels or their European allies.

As the war effort grew, more and more boys from Massachusetts towns and farms arrived at George's Island to be trained for a few weeks or months before being sent South to their fates at the front lines. They drilled on Fort Warren's parade ground, in summer cooling off with a swim in the harbor, or freezing in winter during snow patrols when icy winds lashed the island. There were complaints about the inevitable Army bean soup, but the soldiers were able to dig clams along the shore for 'chowda.'

By the fall of 1861, however, the Federal Government decided to use Fort Warren for war captives. Overnight, six hundred prisoners landed on the island. Many of them were suspected Confederate sympathizers from the border state of Maryland as well as from places closer to home. The people of Boston rose to the occasion and helped meet the needs of the new arrivals with gifts of food, beds, and other supplies. Humane treatment of the prisoners was the policy of the fort commander, Justin E. Dimmick, a deeply religious old soldier, admired by Northerners and Southerners alike.

With the outbreak of the First World War, the predominant use of the islands was once again for defense. Immediately following President Wilson's declaration of war in 1917, sentinels were posted on the ramparts of Fort Independence. Battery F, 55^th Coast Artillery Regiment, in addition to regular Army and state militia units, garrisoned Fort Strong. The harbor's defense was modernized as forts Andrews and Standish installed submarine detectors and the latest mortars and coastal cannons, such as long-range 12-inch guns mounted on revolutionary high-angle carriages.

During World War II, nine islands in the harbor — Castle, Long, George's, Lovell's Great Brewster, Middle Brewster, Outer Brewster, Calf, Peddocks — were fortified and the entrance to the harbor was heavily mined and fenced off by an underwater torpedo net. Radar-controlled coastal batteries, which could hit an enemy ship thirty miles away, were set up, and anti-aircraft batteries, along with those at Portsmouth, New Hampshire and Providence, Rhode Island, could blanket the skies above the entire Massachusetts coast.

After the war, the guns were dismantled, fortifications abandoned, and the remaining installations became overgrown with thick brush and weeds.

There's a final postscript to the island's military history. A Nike missile base was set up on Long Island in the early 1950s during the Cold War. The Russians never came, and the underground silos housing the missiles were abandoned a number of years ago. But since that time the silos have been used to provide temporary storage space, for of all things 700,000 volumes from the Boston Public Library. The harbor's coastal defenses, however, were obsolete well before the Second World War was over, replaced first by aircraft and then by missiles.

## THE BATTLE OF DORCHESTER HEIGHTS

Hal Shaeffer, a local historian and photographer, told me a story about Freney.

"I first met James Freney while conducting a tour of the Dorchester Heights Monument located in Thomas Park, situated at the top of the highest hill in Southie, a short walk south from the intersection of Broadway and G Street," he said. "The monument is a white marble Georgian Revival tower commemorating George Washington's victory at Dorchester Heights in 1776. Freney was in the small group of people who had assembled to listen to my talk.

"The story of the Battle of Dorchester Heights begins in November 1775. Washington had the British bottled up in Boston, but he lacked the fire power to drive them out. Washington had an idea. Send Henry Knox, a twenty-five year old Boston bookseller-turned-artillery-officer to Fort Ticonderoga to fetch the cannons that Americans had captured from the British. Knox had just become an artillery officer, despite having no formal experience. He learned about artillery from the books he sold as the owner of the London Bookstore on what is today West Street, just off Washington Street in downtown Boston. The British officers would come in to buy books and Knox would ask them 'How do you do this?' 'How do you do that?'

"Aided by oxen, hired hands, and farmers, Knox's men pulled and pushed sixty tons of artillery on sledges across frozen rivers, snow covered fields and woods in a 250-mile trek from eastern New York to Boston.

"Can you imagine what they did? Dragging iron cannons ranging from 100 to 5,500 pounds in weight with some eleven feet long, 250 miles in the winter on roads that were little more than rutted, poorly marked paths, up through the Berkshires, trudging with their feet wrapped in bloody rags because their boots had given out, leaving a trail of red on the white snow.

"When Knox and his men neared Boston, they faced a new challenge. How could they get the cannon to Dorchester Heights without tipping their hand to the British?

"On the night of March 4, 1776, Knox and his men, joined by 2,000 colonial militia and local volunteers and bolstered by 400 oxen, crossed Dorchester Neck, a marshy area near present-day Andrew Square, that linked the peninsula of Dorchester Heights to Roxbury. They had to be silent because they were about 150 yards from the British positions on Boston Neck.

"To move in silence, they put hay on the road and wrapped straw around the wagon wheels to deaden the sound, pulled the cannon up the hill, and entrenched them on Dorchester Heights. Then Washington ordered an artillery barrage from the other cannon positions as a diversion. The plan worked. British General Howe believed Washington was about to overpower him and pound his army into submission. Howe planned a counterattack, but a violent storm prevented his soldiers from landing on the shore. Within a few days, Howe, his troops, and a thousand colonial loyalists set sail for Nova Scotia, abandoning the city to Washington's forces and its jubilant citizens.

"At the end of my talk, I asked the group if there were any questions. There was silence, except for one person in the group. James Freney, who challenged me and asked: 'What's so important about the Battle of Dorchester Heights?'

"'Well, it was a bloodless success. It gave the newly appointed Commander-in-Chief George Washington his first major victory. It galvanized his leadership and raised the morale of the embattled colonists,'" I answered. "'Washington drove the British out of Boston for good. With his troops freed up, he could now move them down to New York and concentrate on fighting the British there. This victory shifted the whole strategy of war. If Washington had not won the Battle of Dorchester Heights, I doubt whether the Revolution would have continued.'"

"Freney and I met a few times over the next year or so," Schaeffer told me. "Sometimes we met at Castle Island, sometimes in the park in Copley Square across the street from the Boston Public Library. We talked about the forts on the harbor islands. I suggested books he could read like Wilbur Hoxie's *Boston Harbor Forts* and Gerald Butler's papers on military fortifications in the harbor. Freney was particularly interested in maps of the islands' fortifications and I showed him maps that I had collected over the years, many of them made by the U.S. Army Corps of Engineers.

"Freney seemed to be especially curious about two forts — Fort Standish on Lovell's Island and Battery Jewel on Outer Brewster.

"Freney liked to explore the ruins of Fort Standish. He would come back from Lovell's and ask me all kinds of questions about the fort, especially about the gun batteries — the tunnel-accessed concrete gun line of the 6 inch disappearing-gun emplacements of Battery Terrill (they were called disappearing guns because the guns were visible over the parapet when firing, with the recoil causing it to 'disappear' into a recessed area behind), the low, earthen parapet, concrete magazines, and fixed-mount gun emplacements of Battery Williams and Battery Whipple, and the deep, extensive concrete 10-inch disappearing-gun pits of Battery Burbeck and Battery Morris. I don't know how many times we talked about the bunkers below these batteries — the reinforced concrete rooms, connected, like a maze, by a series of passageways. Plotting and operations rooms; a chemical warfare service room equipped to purify the air supply in case of a poison gas attack; a power room with emergency generators, heating and air conditioning systems; storage rooms for water, fuel, and ammunition and trap doors that led to underground escape hatches. All were designed and connected to enable a person to live underground for an extended period of time."

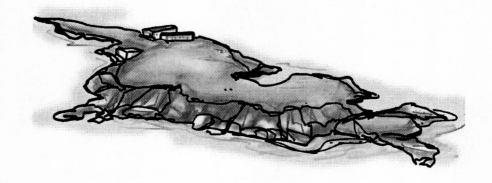

## CHAPTER VII    THE OUTER BREWSTER

The Outer Brewster is the most easterly of all the harbor islands. The island, seventeen-and-a-half acres, is also the largest outcropping of solid bed rock in the harbor. Its rugged terrain contrasts dramatically with the more protected and placid islands in the harbor. Several acres of grass and brush grow on the island, but nary a tree. On the northwestern side of the island stands Pulpit Rock, named for its shape and the sounds made by winds sweeping over its flat top, reverberating like a minister's powerful, mournful sermon.

Nathaniel Austin purchased the island in 1799 and it remained in the family for many years. One of Austin's sons, Arthur, quarried granite on the island for building purposes. Several roads and buildings still extant in Boston are believed to have been constructed with Outer Brewster granite. According to one report, Austin intended to use the quarry site as a small boat harbor. A cave on the northeast end of the island marks the site of the old quarry for the proposed harbor.

The Army took over the island in 1941 and built Battery Jewell, a completely self-sufficient installation. The battery consisted of two 6-inch radar-controlled guns, operated by 125 men. Personnel were housed in three reinforced concrete barracks. The battery itself, which was bomb-and chemical proof, was built into a man-made hill containing tunnels and ammunition storage rooms. The installation even had its own desalination plant for fresh water supply. The Army called the bunkers "The Corregidor of New England."

Shaeffer and Freney also talked about the Outer Brewster.

"I remember Freney telling me how tricky it was to navigate his Boston Whaler up to the rocky shoreline of the island, the difficult climb up the rocks to the top of the island where he could see hundreds of gulls nesting on guano-capped rocks. Trudging through the thick underbrush to find the barracks, down to the entrance to the battery's bunker, into the maze-like series of bare concrete rooms, some of them as small as vaults, abandoned nearly fifty years ago, the walls and ceilings now crumbling from the pounding of wind and rain over the decades.

"How many times did Freney visit Lovell's and the Outer Brewster? I'm not sure. My best guess is he went there several times. For a long time, I could never figure out his fascination with these two islands. It was more than just an interest in military history, in ruins of fortifications, in coastal artillery of a bygone era that beckoned him to these islands. No, it was something more. It was as if Freney were possessed by them."

## THE WINTER HILL GANG, 1975

After Buddy Gleason got bumped off, Howie Summer took control of the Winter Hill Gang. Howie rose to the top by doing what his boss, Gleason, and sixty other mobsters failed to do during the Irish gang wars. He avoided getting killed.

On taking control, Howie consolidated his operations. He mediated a truce between the two warring South Boston gangs — the Mulligans and the Keogh gang. At the same time, he expanded the Winter Hill gang by recruiting more enforcers from those two gangs. Hit men like Johnny and Jimmy Greco, Billy Garniski, Brian Howard, James Boone, Fred Flynn, and two rising players in the underworld — James Freney and Bobby Conti.

By 1975, the Winter Hill Gang was the second largest criminal organization in Massachusetts — second to La Cosa Nostra. That meant Howie Summer was still a Mafia subcontractor, still operated where the Mafia let him operate, and still had to go every week to the Nautica Café in the North End and pay $2,000 tribute money to Mafia underboss Dante Massaroni.

Howie never liked these visits to the North End. He didn't like groveling in front of Massaroni. He resented Massaroni even more when, with his sports betting business off, he had to borrow $200,000 from the Mafia underboss to cover some short-term obligations. Howie had to figure out some way to boost his sagging profits and generate a better cash flow. His solution was to expand the gang's horse race gambling operations, start placing more bets, thousands of dollars more bets, at Suffolk Downs and extend control over Boston area bookies. The money started to flow in, but not for long. Howie's strategy got thwarted by the "master fixer" Fat Harry Fontana, a hulking, bearish 30-year old hustler, who bribed a jockey to hold back his horse in a race Summer's bookies had put down big money to win, place, or show.

Howie's temperature was boiling. He called for a meeting with Fontana at Chandler's, a restaurant in the South End, co-owned by Summer. Fontana recounted the meeting.

"Howie's sittin' at a table at the back of the restaurant when I come in. At first he seems cordial, askin' me what I'll have to drink. I tell the waiter I'll have a 'Gansett. Howie orders Irish Whiskey on the rocks. When I raise my glass to say 'cheers,' he sits there motionless, his drink on the table in front of him, sayin' nothin', just glarin' at me.

"Then he says real soft-like: 'Fontana, you're a dead man. Who the fuck you think you are to mess with me, screwin' me and my associates out of our money?'

"'Howie, I apologize,' I says, sweatin' like bullets. 'I made a mistake. It won't happen again. I promise.'

"'You're damn right,' he says. 'It won't happen again 'cause you're goin' to be dead.'

"'Give me another chance, please, Howie,' I says beggin', shakin', and feelin' like I'm goin' to piss in my pants. 'I'll make the money you lost back for ya.'

"Thinkin' like a bandit, I says, 'Look it, Howie, let's cut a deal. We can work together as partners. I know the jockeys to bribe and the horses to dope — dope 'em with 'but'. That's a painkiller. Lets the horse run faster. We can fix a race either way. We can bribe a jockey ridin' an odds-on favorite to lose. Or we can dope a slow horse to jack up his speed. We place our bets on the long shots. You guys run the bookie operations. Spread their bets around at the tracks and with the bookies out of Las Vegas. I guarantee ya, Howie, we'll clean up.'

"'How do we share the profits?' Howie asks.

"'Fifty-fifty,' I says.

"'No,' he says. 'Seventy-five percent goes to me and my associates. You take twenty-five percent. Agreed?'

"'Agreed,' I says, feelin' I just stepped out of my grave.

"'Waiter,' Howie orders. 'Let's have two filet mignons.'

"'How do you like them, sir?' asks the waiter.

"'Rare, bloody rare,' says Howie like he's celebratin' somethin'. 'And Waiter, bring me another Irish whiskey. Make it a *Jameson*. Oh, waiter. Better yet, change that to a *Black Bush*.'

Starting in 1975, the money came rolling in, estimated by law enforcement officials to be over $8 million in a year's time, as Fontana and the Winter Hill gang fixed horse races up and down the East Coast. Suffolk Downs in Massachusetts, Rockingham in New Hampshire, Lincoln Downs in Rhode Island, Pocono racetrack in Pennsylvania, Atlantic City and Garden State in New Jersey.

Then one day the horse race fixing scheme blew up. A jockey in New Jersey talked to the state police and fingered Fontana as the fixer. Fontana was busted, convicted in 1976, and sentenced to serve four to six years in the New Jersey state penitentiary. But Fontana was not happy about doing time. The feds, for their part, were looking to fry bigger fish. So they cut a deal to get Fontana out of prison and into the federal Witness Protection Program if he told all about his collaboration with Howie Summer and his gang. Fontana would have to name everyone involved in the horse racing scheme — including Howie Summer, James Freney, and Bobby Conti.

Freney got a call from Bill O'Donnell. "Jim, something's up. I got to talk to you. Meet me tomorrow at Castle Island. I'll be in my car waiting for you. Make it in the afternoon at 2:00 pm."

The next day O'Donnell and Freney met at Castle Island.

"Harry Fontana is spilling the beans about the Winter Hill's role in the East Coast horse race fixing scheme," O'Donnell said. "He's telling how you guys put your money down on the long-shots and then directed the bookies to take bets on races not knowing that they were fixed. He's singing about the bookies being more indebted to the Winter Hill gang, and more controlled by the gang after they've suffered big losses. Fontana's naming names — Howie Summer, you, Bobby, the whole gang.

"But Jim, don't worry. I think I've got everything under control. I've talked to the chief prosecutor Jeremy Fitzpatrick. I've told him you and Bobby were my TEs. That if they indicted you two for fixing horse races, I'd lose my best informants and the FBI's best chance to take down the Mafia. I think I've convinced him to keep you and Bobby off the list of those indicted. Howie and the others have to stay on the list."

"Fuck, Howie," Freney said. "It's his tough luck."

"Jim, like I say, it won't happen, but just in case something goes wrong and your names appear on the list, both of you make sure you're out of town so they can't nab you."

On February 2, 1979, the Boston newspapers carried front page stories of the horse-race-fixing scheme. Howie Summer and nearly all the members of the Winter Hill gang were charged, along with three Las Vegas casino executives, three jockeys, and two race horse owners. Two men were not on the list — James Freney and Bobby Conti. Both were ghosts. Conti was in Montreal and Freney was on Peddocks Island, staying in the little cottage he discovered there many years ago.

From the cottage, Freney walked along an asphalt path to Fort Andrews, a cluster of crumbling red brick buildings — guardhouse, quartermaster storehouse, stable, gymnasium, fire house, barracks, and mess hall — surrounded by a dense forest. During World War II, Fort Andrews was garrisoned by coastal artillery, anti-aircraft guns, and an observation station. The fort was also used to hold over a thousand Italian POWs. On the wall of the collapsing POW mess hall, Freney discovered a mural depicting prison life on Peddocks, painted by the POWs in the style of the Italian Renaissance. "Christ!," Freney said to himself. "Who would have ever thought you'd find a beautiful painting like this on an island in Boston Harbor."

I remember seeing the mural many years ago. It's long gone now. Either stolen or crumpled into plaster pieces and dust. The victim of time and neglect. What a pity the MDC didn't do anything to protect this treasure from destruction.

Howie Summer spent six years in prison. When he got out, he took a $250 a week job as a used car salesman. It wasn't long after that he started dealing in drugs, but he got caught in a cocaine sting. The feds told him that if he rolled, that is become a government informant, he could avoid going back to prison for another ten years. But Howie Summer wouldn't rat. He sold drugs, but not his friends.

Like the guns of Boston Harbor, Howie Summer had become obsolete. His power diminished after he came out of prison the first time. Clinging to a code of honor that was no longer shared by everyone. Passed over by time. Superceded by a man more cunning, more wily, and more ruthless than he. A man who followed Miachiavelli's dictum: *"He who has relied least on fortune will become the strongest."* James Freney had become the prince of princes. Yeah! the king — king of the hill, the Winter Hill.

## CHAPTER VIII    NIX'S MATE

Nix's Mate was at one time a sizable island where cows were known to graze. Today, it is little more than a channel marker, dominated by a black and white-shaped cement pyramid, as its shifting sands have washed away over the centuries.

No one knows how Nix's Mate got its name. One theory is that nearby Gallop's Island was once owned by a man named Nix and the smaller island, also owned by Nix, came to be known as Nix's Mate.

There is another explanation. Legend has it that a Captain Nix was killed at sea and that his mate was charged with the crime. When he was about to be executed on the island, Nix's mate protested his innocence and prophesied that the place which witnessed his judicial murder would be washed away by the angry sea.

*Old Nix was a captain, hard and bold,*
*And he reaped the sea, and gathered gold:*
*He gathered gold, but one windy night,*
*They found him dead 'neath the gunwhale light,*
*And his mate stood near him, dumb and white.*

*And his mate they seized, a young sailor he,*
*And charged him with murder upon the sea,*
*And brought him here where the island lay,*
*Where the gibbet rose o'er the windy bay:*

*'Twas more than a hundred years today.*

*Here lay the ship, and the island there,*
*And the sun on the summer oaks shone fair,*
*And they took him there 'mid the chains to die,*
*And he gazed on the green shores far and nigh,*
*Then turned his face to the open sky,*

*And he said, "Great Heaven, receive my prayer:*
*The shores are green, and the isle is fair,*
*To my guiltless life my witness be:*
*Let the green isle die 'mid the sobbing sea,*
*And the sailors see it, and pity me.*

*"O Heaven! Just Heaven! My witness be,*
*Let the island beneath sink into the sea.*

*"Let it waste, let it waste in the moaning waves,*
*Till it lie on the water's black and bare,*
*The ghost of an isle 'mid the islands fair,*
*Where bells shall toll, and beacons glare!"*

*He died, and the island shrank each year.*
*The green trees withered, the grass grew sere;*
*And the rock itself turned black and bare,*
*And lurid beacons rose in air,*
*And the bell-buoy rings forever there.*

Bull Tavern was distinguished by a swinging sign in front displaying the beefy animal on either side. The tavern was found on the water's edge at the head of Bull's Wharf, which juts into Boston Harbor. With the addition of landfill into the harbor over the centuries, Bull's site today would be further inland, near South Station at an intersection of streets forming Dewey Square.

Back in the "Golden Age of Piracy," roughly 1630 to 1730, Bull Tavern was a raucous place of merriment where seamen, waterfront denizens, and pirates flocked to drink, carouse, and tell tales of the high seas — tales of daring buccaneers who plundered merchant vessels for their cargoes of gold and silver, jewels, silks, sugar, and furniture, and who smuggled these cargoes to merchants for great profits, tales of buried treasure and of hangings on the gibbet.

Boston was home port for many pirates. Some were home-born like Joseph Bradish, who was born in Cambridge, Massachusetts on November 28, 1672. Some were home-bred, like Ned Low, who lived in Boston in 1719. And some were transient, like William Kidd, who took up residence in Boston for a brief time around 1696.

Like New Englanders of today, the pirates wintered in the Caribbean. But unlike the latter day snowbirds from the north, who travel to the Caribbean to relax in the sun, the pirates preyed on Spanish, Dutch, French, and English ships laden with gold and silver from Central and South America, rum and sugar from Barbados and Jamaica, wines, furniture, and finery from Europe.

With the coming of spring, the pirates cruised north along the coast of the Carolinas, Virginia, and up to New York, raiding coastal communities, capturing small vessels to obtain provisions and marauding larger craft bound with merchandise to and from England. As spring turned into summer, they proceeded around the tip of Long Island, then in a northerly direction again toward Martha's Vineyard, the Elizabeth Islands to Buzzard's Bay on Cape Cod. There they would wait with some certainty of capturing a vessel sailing through these waters. With their hulls stuffed with rich cargoes plundered in the Caribbean and booty stolen from vessels along the Atlantic Coast, the pirates headed for Boston, where they could fetch good prices for their contraband cargo.

The northerly route from Boston to Portsmouth, New Hampshire to Halifax, Nova Scotia was also favorite hunting grounds for pirates. Notorious pirates like William Kidd, Edward Teach, nicknamed Blackbeard, Samuel Bellamy, and John Quelch roamed Boston's North Shore, known then as the "gold coast." And many of them are said to have buried their treasure on the Isles of Shoals — seven islands located about ten miles southeast of Portsmouth — and on the islands of Boston Harbor.

Boston was also the place where many pirates met their sorry end. The Stone Gaol, where pirates were held awaiting trial, was on the site of today's Boston School Committee headquarters on Court Street. The place of execution is now the North End Park on Commercial Street. The Old North Meeting House, where Cotton Mather preached his execution eve sermon, was torn down for firewood by British troops in 1775.

There were two islands in the harbor where the bodies of executed pirates were left hanging in chains until they rotted away, as a warning to local seamen. One of them, Bird Island, was over time reduced to tidal flats and covered at high tide. It's now buried under the runways of Logan International Airport. The other island was Nix's Mate.

There are many legends about these infamous pirates who sailed from Boston. There was Ned Low. "If ever there was a man who deserved to be hanged and gibbeted in chains, it was Ned Low," it was said. In 1719, Low, a Boston ship rigger, went to sea with his brother, embarking on a pirate career, sailing as far as the Azores and East India. In a few months time, he was said to have captured nineteen ships in succession between the Leeward Islands and the Florida coast. For over a decade, Low sowed fear from Boston down the Atlantic coast to South America.

So bloody and cruel was he that even his own men described him as a "maniac and a brute." When he captured the Spanish galleon *Montcova* in the Caribbean, Low personally slaughtered fifty-three officers and made one Spaniard eat the heart of another before killing him.

Low was finally captured off the island of Martinique. As he was about to be hanged on the gallows a man standing in the crowd before the scaffold shouted "You monster!" Ned Low looked down coldly into the face of his own brother.

There was William Fly. In April, 1775, he seized a slave ship in Boston Harbor, preparing to leave for Jamaica. Renaming the vessel, *Fame's Revenge*, he set sail in his pirate ship, plundering ships from New England to the Carolinas, cursing his captives and whipping them mercilessly with a hundred lashes.

Fly was captured onboard the *Fame's Revenge* when the ship was back in Boston Harbor, anchored off Great Brewster Island.

After he climbed the gibbet and stood on the scaffold, Fly reproached the hangman for not knowing his trade. He remade the noose, which had been poorly tied, and placed it about his own neck with his own two hands.

For many weeks, silhouetted against the sky, the body of Captain Fly could be seen hanging in chains on Nix's Mate. His pirate career had lasted only one month.

Then there's the most notorious pirate of them all.

Long after sunset on the evening of June 13, 1699, there came riding over Boston Neck a weary horseman who inquired his way to the Blue Anchor Tavern, and after a hasty supper was directed to the fine brick house of Mr. Peter Sargeant. There, the Governor, the Earl of Bellomont, lately arrived from New York, was lodging.

The courier was carrying a letter for the governor from Captain William Kidd, saying he had accepted Bellomont's offer to come to Boston. The governor had written that he would pardon Kidd if he would bring his sloop and treasure to Boston — a treasure said to be sixty pounds weight of gold, a hundred weight of silver, and a number of bales of East India goods valued at 30,000 pounds.

It was just three years earlier that Kidd, with a commission and financial backing of Bellomont, the Lord Chancellor, the First Lord of the Admiralty, and other secretaries of state, had sailed from New York in the newly refitted ship *Adventure Galley,* a two hundred eighty-four ton vessel equipped with thirty cannons. Its avowed mission was the suppression of piracy along the American coast and elsewhere. The unstated purpose of particular interest to Lord Bellomont and his associates were "the goods, merchandise, treasure and other things" taken from the pirates.

Before shipping out, Kidd thought his ship could use a more hardened crew, so he recruited a gang of cutthroats in New York and sailed for Madagascar. Once there, a goodly number of his new crew left Kidd's ship to join pirate ships that sailed from that island off the African coast. The remaining number of Kidd's crew threatened him with mutiny unless he would attack any and all ships.

Kidd refused. Mutiny was close at hand and a fight between him and the ship gunner, William Moore, erupted. Kidd killed the man and the crew did not pursue the revolt further. However, after that incident, Kidd was a changed man. Plundering ships of all kinds along India's Malabar Coast, Kidd had become a pirate himself.

The holds of the *Adventure Galley* were already full when Kidd decided to plunder the *Qedagh Merchant*, a huge treasure ship of 400 tons, larger than the *Adventure Galley*. As the pirates approached the *Qedagh,* the captain of the ship gave the sign of surrender. However, the captain was secretly preparing for battle.

Sails were trimmed. Sand was poured on deck for better footing. Ammunition readied and buckets filled for fire fighting.

As the *Adventure Gallery* neared, the *Qedagh* fired its cannon, but the shot missed its mark. The pirates immediately threw their grappling hooks, bringing the two ships together. The pirates boarded the ship and Captain Kidd was in possession of one of the greatest pirate treasures ever.

Kidd headed for New York, believing all his plunder had been taken only from the French and other pirate ships. However, he was mistaken. Two of the ships and most of the booty he seized belonged to the Great Mogul, with whom Britain's East India Company desired to remain on friendly terms.

Bellomont had sprung a trap. Upon his return to Boston, Kidd was arrested, placed in the Stone Gaol, and kept in irons. From Boston, Kidd, clapped in chains, was shipped to England where he was tried for piracy and sentenced to be hanged at Execution Dock in London on May 23, 1706.

After sentencing had been pronounced, Captain Kidd said:

"My Lord, it is a very hard sentence. For my part, I am innocent, only I have been sworn against by perjured persons."

Indeed, he told the truth.

Kidd's death was terrible, for the hangman's rope broke twice. Finally, Kidd was hanged and his body dipped in tar, wrapped in chains, and placed in an iron cage on the riverbed. For nearly twenty years, his body remained gibbeted along the Thames River to serve as a warning to all would-be pirates for years to come.

Decades after his death, amidst the carousing, clinking of beer steins, and singing of sea chanties in taverns at water edge in ports around the globe, you could still hear the mournful refrain of *The Ballad of Captain Kidd:*

*My name was Captain Kidd, when I sailed, when I sailed.*
*And so wickedly I did, God's laws I did forbid, when I sailed,*
*when I sailed.*
*I roam'd from sound to sound, and many a ship I found,*
*There I sank or burned, when I sailed, when I sailed.*
*I murdered William Moore, and laid him in his gore,*
*Not many leagues from shore, when I sailed, when I sailed.*
*Farewell to Young and old, all jolly seamen bold,*
*You're welcome to my gold, I must die, I must die.*
*Farewell to Lunnon Town, the pretty girls all around,*
*No pardon can be found, and I must die, I must die.*
*Farewell, for I must die, then to eternity, in hideous misery,*
*I must lie, I must lie.*

## PIRATE OF THE HARBOR

A hand reached up and brought down a book from a top overcrowded shelf of the Brattle Book Shop, the venerable old bookstore established in 1825, located on West Street off Washington Street in downtown Boston. Holding the book in two hands, the person looked at the cover: *The Pirates of the New England Coast — 1630-1730*. By George Francis Dow and John Henry Edmonds. First published in 1923.

The person opened the book to the table of contents:
*Thomas Pound, Pilot of the King's Frigate, Who Became a Pirate and Died A Gentleman*
*William Kidd, Privateersman And Reputed Pirate*
*John Quelch And His Crew, Who Were Hanged At Boston And Their Gold Distributed*
*Samuel Bellamy, Whose Ship Was Wrecked at Wellfleet And 142 Drowned*
*William Fly, Who Was Hanged In Chains On Nix's Mate*
*Ned Low of Boston And How He Became A Pirate Captain*
*The Brutal Career And Miserable End of Ned Low*

The person closed the book and went over to the sales counter.

"How much for this book?" he asked.

The clerk looked up and saw a man with a black bandana tied around his head. He had a scruffy Van Dyke beard, a gold hoop earring dangling from his left ear, and a black eye patch over his left eye, leaving the right eye peering out in a cold, menacing stare.

"It will be $12.95," answered the clerk in a trembling voice.

The clerk couldn't understand why this customer gave him such a sense of dread. He had seen plenty of 'hippies' and weirdoes in the book store before. Perhaps, he would have understood his fear and trembling if he had known that the man standing before him was none other than James Freney.

It was a typical loud and rowdy night at Triple O's — a lot of boisterous chatter, hollering, and boozing it up. A Red Sox-Yankee game was on the TV screen above the bar. A chorus of cheers broke out when the Red Sox tied the Yankees in the ninth to send the game into extra innings, only to turn soon after to jeers of 'the friggin' Red Flops' and 'fire the fookin' managa,' as the Yankees won it in extra innings. Someone at the bar threw a glass of beer at the TV and a fight broke out. Amidst the brawl, the heads of the old timers slumped on the bar as they cried in their beers.

Upstairs on the second floor of Triple O's, Freney was talking business to several of the gang members.

"I want the message to come 'cross loud and clear. Anyone who wants to do business in Southie either pays Jim Freney or ya don't deal here or ya dead," proclaims Freney, throwing a punch at the metal gas pipe running from the ceiling to the floor. "Nothin' moves in this town — angel dust, mescaline, valium, speed, marijuana, heroin, coke, every fuckin' gram of 'Santa Claus' — without my O.K.

"If they want to know why they have to pay 'rent' in Southie, tell 'em its for the service we provide — the service is not killin' ya. They got a choice on how they want to pay the rent: either a cash payment or a percentage of their profits.

"Rememba, me and Bobby want to keep a low profile. You guys do the collectin.' But if any of yar 'mules' get out of hand, me and Bobby will pay 'im a visit.

"Jim, some of the dealers are complaining about the rent we're charging. That we're jacking up the prices," says Paul Doyle.

"They're saying they use to pay $20,000 per kilo before we moved in. Now they're paying $28,000."

"Tough shit," Freney says, liking the pun he made. "I repeat. If you want to deal in this town, pay up or shut up. We're runnin' a business. It's a matter of supply and demand. That's how capitalism works."

"Hey, guys," Doyle continues, "the pushers and junkies are getting quite a chuckle out of our new signs at the liquor mart and Rotary Variety Store — 'Say Nope to Dope.' Isn't that great PR. Makes us look like solid citizens supporting a good cause. 'Say Nope to Dope.'

"I've got another funny story," chimes in Johnny Greco. "There's this mule, Jacky Jackson. He's drivin' a truck from Florida with $60,000 worth of cocaine in it. He turns off the Jersey Turnpike at a truck stop for a leak and a cup of coffee. When he comes out and is about to climb back into his truck, a guy comes up behind 'im and puts a gun to his head and says, 'I'm takin' over yar truck. Now ya tell me where this stuff is goin.' Who's pickin' it up? Tell me quick. No funny business or I'll blow yar fuckin' head off.' We lata find out that the hijacka is a punk named Dicky Looney. They call 'im 'Looney Tunes.'

"Anyway, Jackson tells 'im to go to the *Dunkin' Donuts* off the McGrath Highway in Somerville."

"'Then what do I do?' asks Looney.

"'You'll see a guy sittin' alone at a table readin' a paper,' says Jackson. You go up to 'im and ask 'im 'what kind of donuts does he like — the crellas or the jelly donuts? If he says the jelly donuts, he's ya man.'

"So Looney gets into the truck and drives up to Boston and finds the *Dunkin' Donuts* in Somerville. He goes in and sees a guy sittin' in the corner readin' a paper. He goes up to 'im but forgets the password — was it crellas or jelly donuts?"

"'Ah, ah, excuse me,' he says to the guy. Do ya like da crellas? Ah, ah, maybe ya like da jelly donuts? Ah, Ah, I kinda like both kinds myself. Do ya know what I mean?'

"'The guy looks up from his paper, stands up, and spins Looney 'round and puts handcuffs on 'im.'

"'What the fuck are ya doin?' Looney cries out. 'All I asked ya is if ya liked crellas or jelly donuts.'

"'Neither. Donuts are fattenin,' says the guy. 'You're under arrest.'

"It turns out the guy is a NARC," Greco wraps up the story, bursting with laughter.

All the gang is laughing, except Freney, who said, "Jackson and Looney are fuckups. Let there be a lesson here. I want none of you doin' business at a *Dunkin' Donuts*. Do ya hear me?"

"Why, Jim?" asks a gang member.

"'Cause there's an informer called 'Dunkin Donuts,' who makes a livin' sellin' information to the government while sellin' heroin, coke and pot."

"How do ya know this, Jim?" asks another gang member.

"Trust me. I've got my sources," says Freney.

"Jimmy, have ya eva heard about a guy called Joe Morrow from Charlestown?" asks Garrett Neeley. "I'm told he's movin' marijuana, lots of it, out of a warehouse in Southie without our permission."

"How much is he movin'?" asks Freney.

"Rumor has it there's fifteen tons of marijuana stored there."

"I say we'll have to pay Mr. Morrow a visit to collect the rent money he owes us, plus, let's say, $90,000 for operatin' without a permit from us," says Freney.

In the early morning of April 7, 1983, federal agents raided a warehouse at 345 D Street in South Boston and seized fifteen tons of marijuana valued at $6 million. Six men were nabbed inside. One of them was Joe Morrow, but none of them was Jim Freney. The agents later learned that Freney had left the warehouse ten minutes before they had arrived.

By the early 1980s, the DEA and every other law enforcement agency in the Boston area knew Freney was running a big drug operation. But they were suspicious about never getting full cooperation from the FBI in investigating Freney. So in April 1984, the DEA, along with the Boston and Quincy police, the Massachusetts State Police, and the U.S. Attorney's office in Boston, launched "Operation Bean Town" to investigate James Freney's drug operations. One goal of Operation Bean Town was to limit the FBI's knowledge and participation in the investigation.

"Let me tell you what happened to Operation Bean Town," recounted a retired DEA agent.

"We started building our case when a convicted drug smuggler, Arnie Klein, started talking.

"'Nicky Silanus, Freney's advance man, drives into the parkin' lot of the Howard Johnson's restaurant right off the Southeast Expressway in Dorchesta,'" Klein told us. "'He gets out of his car and goes to the phone booth to make a call. A few minutes lata, a black Chevy pulls into the parkin' lot with Freney and Conti. They go to the phone booth, make some calls, and then drive off to the Lancaster Street garage near the North End. At the garage, Frankie Colonna shows up with a suitcase full of drug money. This is money he pays Freney for protection from Mickey Barbarini, the Mafia's drug kingpin.

"'Freney and Conti show up back at Hojos a couple of hours lata and go into the restaurant. Then a gray Mercedes rolls into the lot with Mickey Barbarini and he goes into the restaurant. A few minutes later Sammy Salerno drives into the lot in a blue Lincoln Continental and he goes into the restaurant. About ninety minutes later, all of them — Freney, Conti, Barbarini, and Salerno — come out together, shake hands, and go off in their cars.'"

"Meanwhile," the DEA agent continued, "State troopers are in the fourth floor bedroom of the Howard Johnson's Hotel, photographing and videotaping Freney, Conti, and the Mafia's comings and goings. They put a tap on the phone booth. If we can get a few more pictures, a few more videotapes, a few more phone conversations, we could subpoena the bastards. Days passed but Freney and Conti never showed up again. Somebody had tipped them off. We figured out who that somebody was.

"Despite this setback, we got another break when we caught a drug dealer named Tom O'Brian. O'Brian wouldn't stop talking about Freney's control of the drug trade, how he was the top of the hierarchy of every drug distribution network in South Boston, and how he became involved with James Freney."

"'I was robbed of $125,000 while trying to buy cocaine in Florida,' O'Brian began his story. 'When I returned to Boston, I still owed Freney $40,000 in rent. I go to Freney and tell him I don't have any product now to raise the dough I owe him. Freney tells me to go to a guy named Tim Farrell and ask him for a loan. Farrell, who used to own the Corner Café in Southie and now works for a Waltham mortgage company, says he doesn't have $40,000 to loan me, but would help me get a second mortgage so I could pay off my debt to Freney.

"'When Freney hears what Farrell did for me, he summons Farrell to his liquor mart, Atlantic Wine & Spirits, and him and Conti escort Farrell into the back room.'

"'Who the fuck are ya to get O'Brian the money he owes us'? screams Freney, while pulling out a long knife from a sheath on his leg and stabbing the liquor boxes piled up near him again and again.'

"'Then Freney puts the knife to Farrell's face and says: 'I'm gonna buy ya yar life. The price? It's gonna cost ya $50,000.'"

"With the pressure on him from Freney, we figured Farrell might help us nab Freney," the DEA agent continued. "Farrell agreed to wear a body microphone to catch Freney making incriminating statements. But whenever Freney and Farrell were together they made only small talk, nothing of any importance. Freney once even went into a rendition of *When Irish Eyes Are Smilin,*' sounding as if he were singing directly into the microphone. We later learned that the FBI had tipped off Freney that Farrell was wired.

"We subpoenaed Farrell to appear before a grand jury to tell what he knew about Freney's drug operations. But Farrell never appeared before that grand jury. The federal prosecutor turned him over to the FBI. The FBI told us they were using Farrell for another drug probe and he wasn't available as a witness. We learned later that the FBI Boston office had sent a letter to the agency's Washington headquarters reporting that FBI informant James Freney had been a target in a probe of a 'large-scale cocaine and marijuana trafficking organization controlled by the Irish mob in Boston. But that Freney should not be cut as an informant since, at present, DEA allegations are unsubstantiated and the DEA has furnished no specific information relative to the involvement of Freney in these criminal activities.'

"Even though we lost out on Tim Farrell, by August 1990, we had collected enough evidence from Farrell and other informants to indict fifty-seven persons on drug charges. Frank Colonna, Craig Reed, Stan Moore, and Charlie McGivers were among the lieutenants and soldiers from four South Boston rings we said operated under Freney's authority. None of those guys arrested would rat on Freney, though. Maybe if they had known that Freney had tipped off Bill O'Donnell to Mickey Barbarini and Frank Colonna's drug activities in Maine, they might not have remained silent."

Operation Bean Town eventually petered out. And once again, with a little help from his friends in the FBI, Freney was in the clear. He ruled alone as the invisible drug lord of Southie. But what law enforcement agencies didn't know, even the FBI, was that Freney's drug operations extended far beyond South Boston

## OPERATION SEA LORD

Bobby Conti tells a story of a meeting with Freney at Castle Island.

"It was one mornin' in mid-May. Me and Jimmy, we sit down at a picnic table on the slope risin' to Fort Independence. Jim unfolds this map showin' the Atlantic coast. With his index finger, he traces a route on the map.

"'Look here, Bobby. The drugs are shipped from Colombia up the Florida coast to Miami, Fort Lauderdale, and Hollywood. Some of the drugs are carried by cargo freighters up the east coast. Some of the drugs are transferred at the Florida ports to pleasure yachts. They then carry the stuff up the coast. The big drop-off points are Savannah, Charleston, Cape Hatteras, Norfolk, Baltimore, New York, and Boston.

"'Do ya rememba Richie O'Rourke? He used to work out of Southie. Now lives in Florida. 'Been there for a few years. He's our contact in Florida.

"'The way it's set up is Richie will make the deals in Florida and tell us what boats will be bringin' the drugs into Boston and when they're comin'.

"'We'll know that the goods are onboard and ready to be picked up when a black pennant with two white chevron stripes is hoisted on the ship's mast.

"'Our job is to round up a fleet of small boats to pick the stuff up and bring it back to the docks.

"'Find out the owners of small boats who might be interested in pickin' up and deliverin' the merchandise for us. Offer 'em $75,000 to work for us. That kind of money should also attract the fishermen. They're always needin' for cash.

"'My strategy is if we can control the harba, we will control the drug trade. The Italians have controlled it since Prohibition. They still got alotta influence with the longshoremen's union. But they haven't recognized the potential of shippin' drugs through the harba. They're too focused on flyin' or truckin' the stuff in from Florida.

"'By shippin' it in, we can cut out some of the middlemen. We can transfer tons of the stuff — cocaine, marijuana — and control prices betta. Betta profit margins. I'm talkin' profits for ya and me, Bobby. Don't worry about the other guys. There's plenty of money for 'em in Southie.

"'Ya know what we can call this strategic campaign, Bobby?" How 'bout callin' it 'Operation Sea Lord.'

"'If any fucka tries to fuck up Operation Sea Lord, they'll pay a price — a big price.'"

A black and white trimmed speedboat, *The Phantom Pirate* printed in black and gold-trimmed letters on the stern, leaves the South Boston Yacht Club and cruises past Thompson and Spectacle islands. James Freney is at the wheel. Bobby Conti is riding shotgun. Conti occasionally takes pot shots at low flying seagulls.

"Hey, Bobby! Look over towards Deer Island," says Freney, nodding his head in that direction. "The freighter there. It's flyin' a black pennant. Do ya recognize the boat next to it?"

"Naw, Jim. Can't say that I do," answers Conti.

"Let's take a closer look," says Freney, pulling on the throttle.

Freney steers his boat toward the freighter and when they come closer, they can see bales being lowered from the deck of the freighter onto the boat. Freney cuts the engines, drifting closer, and holds up a megaphone to his mouth:

"Hello, thar. Identify yourself. We're harba patrol."

No answer.

"If ya don't identify yarself, we're comin' aboard."

Still no answer.

Then they hear an engine start and the boat pulls away, heading toward the Outer Harbor and Massachusetts Bay. Freney opens up the throttle in pursuit. Conti is firing away with his shotgun. Freney stays on their port side, forcing the fleeing boat to the starboard and Hypocrite Channel that runs between Little Calf and Calf islands. Suddenly, the fugitive boat runs aground on the shoals submerged in the channel. As Freney veers his boat away from the channel, they see the fugitive boat sink into the water.

"They ain't goin' nowhere," shouts Conti over the roar of the engines.

"Yah! When the harba police come to rescue 'em, they're goin' to have to do a lot of explainin' about those bales," hollers Freney, laughing along with Conti.

The luxury yacht, *Paradise Found*, moored off Rainsford Island, was owned by a Florida sportsman named Willard Tucker. "Slick Willie," he was called, both for his weasel ways and weasel looks.

After Freney handed over $500,000 to Tucker for 2,500 pounds of cocaine, Tucker gave him and Conti a tour of his luxury yacht, showing them the bar, mahogany paneled dining and living quarters, and the safe where he stowed the money transacted in the deal, as well as expensive jewelry Tucker liked to lavish on women.

The good will from the deal quickly disappeared when, back at their warehouse, Freney and Conti opened up the crates to find that many of the bags contained flour, not cocaine.

"That Tucka Fucka," screams Freney. " He thinks he can get away with this two-bit trick? I'll tell ya what we're goin' to do.

We're gonna give Slick Willy a little Boston Tea Pa'ty. One he'll neva forget."

What does Freney do? He sends a high-class prostitute to Tucker for an evening of entertainment onboard his yacht. So Tucker will have his privacy, the crew is invited to dine at Jimmy's Restaurant, compliments of James Freney. During the evening, the prostitute slips a Mickey Finn into Tucker's drink and he passes out. Freney, Conti, and Dicky Hudson, the safecracker expert, come out in *The Phantom Pirate* and climb aboard the *Paradise Found*. Hudson breaks open the safe and they take out $500,000 and jewels said to be worth another $100,000.

The next day, the harbor police pick up Tucker, naked, shivering in a dingy drifting in the middle of Quincy Bay. They book him for drunkenness and indecent exposure.

The Boston Boys were two guys, Fred Reilly and Thomas O'Malley, both of them graduates of Boston College. During the 1980s, they imported marijuana by the ton directly from Colombia to Boston Harbor. From the boat, the marijuana was loaded onto large rental trucks and driven back into Boston to Horticulture Hall, where an employee let them in after hours. In the hall, Reilly and O'Malley would weigh the marijuana, noting who was taking what amount of drugs out of there, so they would know how much they would be paid. Celebration and cash payments took place later outside the *Bull & Finch* bar. That was where *Cheers* was filmed.

The Boston Boys' operations in Boston came to an end shortly after Freney heard about them. It seems one night, a creaky old cargo freighter, *The Calypso*, arrived in Boston Harbor and docked at a pier near Anthony's Pier Four Restaurant. *The Calypso* carried ten tons of marijuana arranged by the Boston Boys. During the night, a small boat headed toward *The Calypso*. When the boat was a few hundred yards away from *The Calypso*, two figures jumped into the water. Flames broke out on the boat as it drifted toward *The Calypso*, colliding with the docked freighter and setting it on fire. By the time the harbor police and fire engines arrived, *The Calypso* was a burning hulk, wafting over it the strong, sweet smell of marijuana.

Who knows how many other stories there are about the fates of those who got in Freney's way?

I remember one fisherman who told a real dandy.

"It was a foggy mornin'. We were passin' by Nix's Mate. I couldn't see it clearly in the fog, but I swear I saw a body chained there to the cement, black and white pyramid-shaped marker. We reported it to the MDC harbor police, but when they arrived there the next day, they told us all they found were a couple of chains and manacles screwed into the cement."

*He died, and the island shrank each year.*
*The green trees withered, the grass grew sere;*
*And the rock itself turned black and bare,*
*And lurid beacons rose in air,*
*And the bell-buoy rings forever there.*

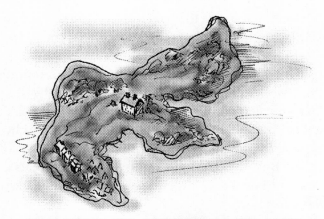

# CHAPTER IX  NODDLES ISLAND

Noddles Island doesn't exist anymore. It was joined by landfill to East Boston in the 19th century. The island, which covered about a square mile, lay a mile and a half north of South Boston, across the inner harbor. It got its name from William Noddle, who settled on it in 1629, before Boston was founded.

Samuel Maverick was the island's first permanent settler. He erected a small, fortified mansion with artillery to defend it and became the first New England slaveholder when he bought a ship filled with slaves from the Tortugas in 1638 and sold them in Boston.

At one time, Noddles was heavily forested. But Indians of the Massachusetts tribe cleared acreage to plant corn and later colonists used the plentiful timber for fuel. As they cut trees, the colonists created pastures and farmers began to ferry cattle from the mainland to graze on the island.

The first naval conflict and the second battle of the Revolution (after Lexington and Concord) was called the Battle of Noddles Island and Chelsea Creek. On May 27, 1775, General John Stark and three hundred colonial militiamen were sent to take possession of the livestock on Noddles. They clashed with British marines on the island, but were driven back when reinforcements of British regulars crossed over from Boston.

Meanwhile, British General Thomas Gage sent a schooner armed with sixteen small guns and eleven barges full of marines up Chelsea Creek to cut off the raiders. Commanding officer Israel Putnam of the Continental Army came to the rescue of the colonial militia with three hundred men and two guns.

In a fight that lasted all night, despite British reinforcements from Boston, the Americans forced the crew of the schooner to abandon her and flee and drove back the other vessels. They took the artillery from the captured vessel and beached and burned the British schooner (at the site of the Meridian Street Bridge connecting Chelsea to East Boston). The fight was over. The colonials evacuated the livestock and burned Noddles, leaving a scorched earth for the British occupying Boston.

In the 19th Century, Boston became a leading shipbuilding center. During the "golden age of sail" (1850-1854), the finest clipper ships were built in the shipyards of East Boston. *The Flying Cloud, Stag-Hound, Westward ho!, Romance of the Seas, The Great Republic*, built by Donald McKay (his monument is located on Castle Island), were launched from the docks of East Boston. The Yankee Clippers — their sharp bows and sleek hulls, and tall masts supporting eight hundred yards of white canvas — "cut their way through turbulent seas, which in bygone days never dreamt of such speed." They 'clipped' days off the sailing record of every journey they undertook — to Liverpool and Newcastle, to San Francisco, around Cape Horn to Hong Kong and Fuchow, China.

Before the Yankee Clipper ships made their debut, there were the Yankee traders, many of them Boston and New England-based, who built their families' fortunes on the China trade. They sold porcelain, tea, and silks at home in the United States — and smuggled opium from Turkey into China to pay for these desired goods. The who's who of 19th century Boston Brahmins — Cabot, Bacon, Coolidge, Cushing, Forbes, Weld — all invested in the China trade. As Julian S. Cutler wrote in 'The Old Clipper Days':

*When we sold the Heathen nations rum and opium rolls,*
*And the missionaries went along to save their sinful souls.*

John Perkins Cushing (1787-1862) was a China trader and opium dealer, who served as an agent for respectable Boston families and firms from 1816 to 1831. He returned from China to Boston a millionaire, kept a grand house on Summer Street, complete with

Chinese servants, and built a beautiful summer estate and gardens on top of a hill in what is now Belmont, Massachusetts. Cushing Square in that town is named for him.

Cushing helped set up J&T.H. Perkins Co. The first Perkins cargo of Turkish opium, onboard the brigantine *Monkey*, arrived in China in 1816. When the transaction proved profitable, the firm dispatched an agent to Leghorn, Italy, to set up an opium-buying operation. It was the beginning of a thriving, if illicit commerce for the house of Perkins.

In 1818, Perkins Co. merged with Bryant & Sturgis, another Boston firm, to become what was called "the Boston Concern." The newly formed partnership held a virtual monopoly on Turkish imports to China. In 1829, the monopoly expanded as Russell & Company, a firm set up with the encouragement of Cushing and other prominent New England families, merged with the Boston Concern.

William H. Russell, who was from a wealthy Connecticut family, was an early director of Russell & Company. While a student at Yale, Russell set up "The Order of Skull & Crossbones," a secret society that "worshipped the goddess Eulogia, celebrated pirates, and covertly plotted an underground conspiracy to dominate the world," according to historical records. The Skull & Crossbones Society still exists today. And, yes, many of our leaders and statesmen, who were graduates from Yale, are known to have been members of Skull & Crossbones.

By the mid-1830s, the opium trade had become "the largest commerce of its time in any single commodity, anywhere in the world." Opium smuggling didn't just make money. At times, opium was money.

As one historian remarked, "Smuggling was and is New England as a boiled dinner — and its history is at least as salty."

## SMUGGLING, 1984

It was the night of October 13, 1984. The Quincy police had just arrested John MacAllister for trying to break into his estranged wife's house. The police file showed that MacAllister was a 32-year old college dropout, joined the Army and had a pretty good record in intelligence, but got busted for possession of marijuana. When

MacAllister started jabbering about dope and gun-running and saying he needed help, the Quincy police called the DEA office.

"How can we help you?" asked the DEA agent.

"If I can tell you what happened, cooperate with the government, can you get me out of this jam?" pleaded MacAllister, noticeably nervous and shaking. "I just want to straighten out my life and start living a normal life. I just sometimes feel like I'm trapped in this whirlpool and I can't get out of it. It's almost like living with a knife in you. I didn't start out in life to end up like this, you know."

"O.K., son, tell us your story," said the DEA agent.

"I was working the docks and boats, smuggling marijuana," MacAllister began. "I was an engineer on these boats. Each boat was carrying anywhere between two to three thousand bales of marijuana. I had made about a half-a-dozen trips when Joe Morrow, he runs a drug operation out of Charlestown, and Garrett Neeley and Pat Quinn, drug operators out of Southie, call me into their office, and ask me if I would be interested in helping out in a smuggling operation of a different kind. They told me to go up to Gloucester and ask for Karl Peterson, captain of the *Aphrodite*.

"I found Peterson on the docks, working on the *Aphrodite*, a seventy-seven foot fishing trawler. He told me he was putting together a crew and would I be interested in working on the boat as an engineer. 'We're plannin' on goin' swordfishin',' he says. 'We could use an experienced engineer.'

"So, in September, we left Gloucester, but instead of heading out to George's Banks to fish, we go down the coast to Boston Harbor. We dock at Pier 7 in South Boston. We're met by three guys waiting on the pier. They introduce themselves as Charlie, Huey, and Jimmy. They're wearing scally caps and Adidas jumpsuits. You could see by the way they carried themselves that they don't know the first thing about boats. Later, when we were out to sea, they lazed about the boat, flossed their teeth, and took a couple of showers a day.

"Anyway, they start unloading these wooden crates from six vans that were on the pier and carrying the crates onto the boat. I see Garrett Neeley and Pat Quinn on the pier, supervising the transfer of the crates onto the boat. Beyond them, I see a figure in the shadows, his arms folded, watching the operations. I couldn't see his face clearly, but I knew it was James Freney.

"When we're out to sea, this other guy on the boat, whose name is Sean, tells me he's with the IRA. He tells me what's in those crates. There's ninety-one rifles, eight submachine guns, thirteen shotguns, fifty-two handguns, 70,000 rounds of ammunition, and a rocket war head, worth over a million dollars. He tells me these guns are for the IRA.

"About 200 miles off the Irish coast, we rendezvous at a point called Porcupine Bank with a fishing trawler called the *Morrigan*. It wasn't easy offloading the crates. The sea was rough and the *Aphrodite* kept bashing against the side of the Irish boat. But we finally got the job done.

"Shortly after we pulled away, an Irish Navy boat appears. We see it shoot a warning shot across the bow of the *Morrigan*. We hear some shouting and see these Navy men climbing aboard. No one came after us. So we headed home to Boston. We docked back at Pier 7 and everyone high-tailed it in different directions from the boat, even Captain Peterson. I learned later that U.S. Customs had seized the *Aphrodite*.

"A couple of days later, Morrow, Neeley, and Quinn call me and the other guys who were on the *Aprhodite* to their office. 'One of you is a rat,' charges Morrow, scowling at us. Fuck it! Let's move on. There's more grass where that came from.'"

"Morrow takes me aside and says: 'Hey, Johnny! How would you like to become an investor in our marijuana trade rather than just a lumper. That's a laborer,' he explained.

MacAllister paused and continued talking to the DEA agent: "You get this thing squared away for me and like I say I could straighten out my life."

"John, go in with their plan. We'll give you $10,000 to show them you're interested in becoming an investor in their operations," said the DEA agent. "If you can help us get these guys, I think we'll be able to set you straight again."

On November 14, 1984, MacAllister and several associates took a boat out of Quincy to meet the *Ramshead*, a freighter carrying thirty six tons of marijuana buried in its hole. As the *Ramshead* entered the harbor, federal authorities boarded the ship, seized the cargo, and arrested the captain and crew.

No one's quite sure what happened after that. Did the FBI get wind of the DEA's plan? And did it pass this information on to Freney?

MacAllister left his parents' home saying he was going to meet with Pat Quinn. He was never seen again. His truck was found early in December in the lot of a Dorchester lounge. His wallet and un-cashed veteran's disability check were on the dashboard. John MacAllister, the man hoping to turn his life around, had vanished.

## GOVERNOR'S ISLAND
Is there pirate treasure buried on the islands of Boston Harbor? According to Robert Kidd, a descendent of William Kidd, Captain Kidd buried two chests on Conant's Island, containing from fifteen to twenty thousand pounds sterling in money, jewels and diamonds. Conant's Island was renamed Governor's Island in the Eighteenth century.

Captain Kidd's treasure chests were said to be buried on the northwest corner of the island about four feet deep with a flat stone on them. A pile of stones was erected nearby as a marker. But over three hundred years, the tides and winds have radically altered the island; later it was leveled and joined with East Boston as part of the construction of Logan Airport in the 20th century.

Kidd's treasure may still be out there. But who knows where? Is it buried under the runways of Logan? Or offshore, under the silt and sediment that now covers the harbor's bottom?

## FROM MADAGASCAR TO GALLOP'S ISLAND
Captain John Avery, known as "Long Ben" Avery, was one of the most infamous of the Madagascar pirates. His most famous capture was a ship carrying a daughter of the Great Mogul on a pilgrimage to Mecca. Booty on the Mogul's ship was immense and consisted of diamonds, pearls, and valuable jewels; and, also, great sums of money intended to cover the cost of the pilgrimage, an amount said to have been over 325,000 pounds.

Avery ravished the young princess and eventually took her in his ship to Madagascar, where he had a child by her. When the Great

Mogul learned what had happened, he became furious and vowed revenge against the English whom he believed Long Ben Avery served. The Mogul's fury was appeased when the British government sent two ships from the East India Company to protect the Mogul's ships carrying further pilgrimages to Jedda and Mecca, and offered a large reward for Avery's capture.

With the British Navy, as well as every other bounty-hunter on the open seas seeking to capture him, Avery retreated to Madagascar and established a fort on the island. From the fort, Avery organized a crude form of government that exacted a tenth of the value of all captured booty brought to Madagascar and required tribute from the native princes on the island. The tribute commodity took the form of their daughters and other young girls who were added to the harem of the pirates.

When Captain Woods Rogers went to Madagascar in the *Delicia* in 1722 to buy slaves to sell to the Dutch at Batavia, he landed at a part of the island where he met some pirates who had been living there for more than twenty-five years and were surrounded by a motley collection of children and grandchildren.

Avery ruled his little kingdom for some time, but at last wearying of it, he left Madagascar with some chosen pirates to make his way to America. His plan was to settle in Boston. But when he arrived in Boston, Avery found that this Puritan town was no safe market either for the display or sale of his store of diamonds and gold.

So he buried his gold and diamonds on two islands in Boston Harbor and sailed for Ireland, hoping to retrieve his treasures at some later date. Eventually, he reached Biddeford in Devonshire where he changed his name and lived quietly. But he needed money and asked a friend to deliver his ill-gotten fortune to him in Bristol. Alas, neither the gold nor diamonds were ever delivered and Long Ben Avery died on June 10, 1714, not leaving enough money to buy a coffin.

The Great Mogul was said to own two brilliant 189-carat diamonds. One of them was the Orloff diamond. Some historians think this diamond disappeared in 1739 and ended up in India where it was stolen from the eye of a statue of the Hindu god Sri-Ranga in 1750.

According to a Sri-Ranga story, a French soldier fighting in the Carnatic wars in southern India deserted and stole the diamond described as the size of an egg. The soldier then sold the gem to an English sea captain, who in turn, sold it to a Persian merchant named Khojeh. In 1775, an Amsterdam firm sold the diamond to Prince Gregory Orloff for $450,000.

Orloff, a former lover of Catherine the Great, gave the diamond to the Russian empress in the hope of regaining her favor. Catherine accepted Orloff's gift, but never reinstated the count to her court. She had the diamond mounted on top of the eagle of the imperial scepter, and it remains in the same setting in the diamond treasury at the Kremlin.

The other diamond — referred to as Orloff's mate — was among the Great Mogul's prized possessions captured by Long Ben Avery. Edward Rose Snow says that when Long Ben Avery came to Boston he "buried his money at Point Shirley [then on Deer Island, now part of the Town of Winthrop] where it was later dug up. But his diamonds, including the mate to the famous Orloff diamond, are yet to be found where Avery buried them — on Gallop's Island, centuries ago. Perhaps, the diamonds will still be discovered."

## THE WHYDAH

Samuel "Black Sam" Bellamy was a pirate for less than a year when he and his buccaneers captured off the coast of Cuba, the *Whydah*, a 100-foot, three-masted English slave ship. The *Whydah* was packed with African slaves, indigo, and thousands of silver and gold coins worth more than 20,000 pounds sterling.

The *Whydah* had sailed two voyages as a merchant galley, following the course of the "triangular trade," which brought manufactured English goods to Africa and the American colonies, captured Africans to the New World, and colonial commodities — sugar, indigo, cotton — back to England, where they would be processed into manufactured goods.

After inventorying the *Whydah's* books, Bellamy is said to have told his men: "Lads, we've gotten enough. It's time to go home."

The *Whydah* headed back to Cape Cod and back to Maria Hallet, a local beauty to whom Bellamy had promised he would return in a ship laden with gold and silver.

By April, 1717, the *Whydah* was off Cape Cod when it was struck by a nor'easter with seventy mile winds and forty-foot high waves. The *Whydah* was top heavy and highly vulnerable to the driving winds blowing her ever closer to the shore and the rocky coastline. The driving winds and waves smashed the *Whydah* against the rocks, capsizing and breaking her back with a piercing cry heard above the howling winds and crashing surf.

Of the 145 men on board the *Whdyah*, including Black Sam Bellamy, all but two perished. One survivor was an Indian pilot who disappeared into the mists of history. The other was Thomas Davis, a Welsh carpenter, whose vivid account of the shipwreck was passed from generation to generation through Cape Cod folklore. According to local legend, Maria Hallet, accused of having an adulterous relationship with the notorious Bellamy, was condemned as a witch to be burned at the stake. Even to this day, her spirit is said to walk along the cliff tops of Wellfleet overlooking the sea under which the *Whdyah* is believed to lie.

## THE ARAPAHO

Captain Bill McGinty operated the Harbor Tow and Salvage Company from his tugboat, the *Arapaho*, an old World War II Navy "rust bucket" with rubber tire strips for bumpers. The *Arapaho* was tied up to an old crumbling wooden dock near the Meridian Bridge, which spans the Chelsea River near where the river and the Mystic River meet to flow into the Inner Harbor. It's the confluence of all the flotsam and jetsam from the two rivers — a floating junkyard of rotting wood pilings, tires, barrels, cans, bottles, garbage, rags, and animal carcasses — suspended in the oily waters of the Inner Harbor.

McGinty was tall and rangy, and had a face like a barnacle — crusty, furrowed and lined. A faded scar cut like a rip-tide across his cheek, caused perhaps by the whiplash of a breaking tow line. But his sparkling, humorous eyes and jovial manner belied the menace of his scar.

McGinty's partner was Davy Jones Guillet, a heavy-set, beer-bellied ex-Navy diver, who gained his stripes working on the crew that salvaged the *Oklahoma* at Pearl Harbor and a German U-boat wrecked off Cape Hatteras during World War II. But booze and the bends had taken their toll on Guillet and he ended up drifting into Boston Harbor and hooking up with McGinty.

If ever there were a pair of sea dogs who scavenged the harbor looking for business, they were McGinty and Guillet. When the *Peter Stuyvesant,* a passenger ship, sank off Anthony's Pier Four restaurant during the Blizzard of '78, they were low bidders to break up and salvage the vessel's parts. They were first to get to the *Olive Branch* and salvage its cargo when the freighter smashed against the treacherous rocks of the Devil's Back in Broad Sound during a storm. And many a time they salvaged and towed boats and barges wrecked off the jagged and submerged rocks of Harding's Ledge in the Outer Harbor.

McGinty was on his tugboat when James Freney paid him a visit. "As I recall, it was in the early summer of 1984," McGinty began his story. "Freney came aboard carrying a nautical map under his arm."

"'I heard you might be interested in undertaking a job I have in mind,' says Freney, unfolding the map on a table in my cabin. 'Have ya ever heard about the *Whydah,* pirate ship that went down off Cape Cod?'

"'Sure have,' I answered. 'The *Whydah* was carrying a lot of silver and gold. People bin lookin' for that sunken ship for years. Nobody's eva found any traces of it, though.'

"'Well, I think I know where the *Whydah* is,' says Freney, pointing to the area off Wellfleet on Cape Cod on the map. 'Would ya be interested in lookin' for the ship and findin' any treasure? I'll make it a sweet deal. How about $1000 a day for rentin' yar boat and services and ten percent of any treasure we find? Agreed?'

"'Agreed,' I says. 'Davy, come out and say 'hello' to James Freney. He would like to avail himself of our services.'

"So the followin' week we head out across Massachusetts Bay, around Providence town, and anchor a quarter-mile off the coast of Wellfleet. We're workin' the area for a few days, each day movin' the boat a few times and makin' dives, when, I'd say on the fourth day, Davy gives us the signal that he's found somethin' and wants to come up."

"'Man, I found somethin' down there that looks like a wooden hull of a ship,' Davy is jabberin' while we're tryin' to get his diver's helmet off. 'Give me a few minutes to have a little nip, get me a brighter light, I'm goin' down again for a betta look.'

"But just as we're puttin' on Davy's helmet, we see this boat comin' towards us," McGinty goes on. "When they're in shoutin' distance, I hear a voice comin' from the boat, sayin' 'Ahoy, there. May I inquire what you are doing here?'

"'None of your fuckin' business,' shouts back Freney.

"'Well, it is our business if you're searching for sunken ships in this area,' replies the voice. 'This is a restricted area. We have a permit from the US Army Corps of Engineers, giving us exclusive rights for exploring this area. I'm afraid you will have to leave this area, or otherwise we will have to report you for violating the law.'

"'Why don't you come aboard and we'll see who has the right to explore this area?' yells Freney, as he reaches down to pull out a long knife sheathed under his pants leg.

"'No, no, Jim,' I call out, tryin' to calm him down. 'I don't want any trouble. I don't want to lose my operatin' license. The law's the law.'

"Freney stares at me with those cold, piercin' blue eyes and mutters, 'Possession is nine-tenths the law.'

"I'm thinkin' hard how to calm him down. I knew Freney's reputation for cuttin' down anybody or anything that stands in his way. So I says, 'Jim, forget about the pirate ship. There's probably nothin' down there. Probably nothin' more than an old schoona that broke up years ago. There's plenty of shipwrecks in these waters.

"'Besides, I got a betta idea. How would you like to find a German submarine? Chances of findin' one of 'em is greata than findin' *Whydah's* gold. Think of it, Jim — your own German U-boat! Probably fetch a pretty good price, too.'

"'Davy, tell Jim about the sunken U-boat in Boston Harbor.'

"'Sunken submarine in Boston Harbor? Oh, yah, of course, Bill. The German sub U-130. I was lookin' through Navy archives and

I came across this U-boat that disappeared off of Nantasket in 1942. Records showed the U-130 was on a mission to land some German spies on Nantasket Beach in Hull. The U-130 never returned to base. There's no mention to what happened to the spies. Did they eva reach the beach? No one knows.

"'Anyway, one day, me and Bill were lookin' for a wreck off of Harding's Ledge. The water was pretty murky, but I swear I saw what looked like the connin' tower of a sub layin' on the bottom. Neva went lookin' for it again, but I bet it's the U-130. My thinkin' is it was either tryin' to surface or dive when it hit the underwater rocks around Harding's Ledge. Ripped a hole in the sub, took water, and sank. No one has eva found 'er cause no one has ever looked for 'er. But I know she's thar.'

"'Alright,' says Freney, who seemed to calm down and become intrigued by the prospects of findin' a German sub. 'Let's start lookin' for the U-boat.'

"So a few weeks later we began our search for the U-130. We drop anchor off Harding's Ledge, about one-and-a half miles off Point Allerton in Hull. For three days, we're movin' the boat around, makin' dives and then on the fourth day, Davy signals to bring 'im up.

"'I found her. I swear I saw her friggin' connin' tower,' Davy is yellin,' and boucin' up and down in his diver's rig like he's an astronaut walkin' on the moon.

"'Give me time for a little nip, give me a betta' light and lowa me down for anotha look.'

"Meanwhile, I see the winds are startin' to shift to the northeast and the sky is startin' to darken. About twenty minutes later, sheets of rain come down, the waves swell up, tossin' the boat from side to side.

"'Let's get goin' home,' I yell ova the howlin' winds. 'If we try to ride this storm out, we'll end up crashin' against the rocks.'

"We made it back to the dock. But the storm raged on for three days and three nights before it blew out to the Atlantic. When the weather cleared, we headed out to Harding's Ledge. For a week, we searched the area where Davy said he saw the German sub's connin' tower. But we couldn't find her. The sea must have covered her with silt and sediment and buried her once again.

"'It's no use,' I said to Freney. 'You can't force the sea.'

"'It was a silent voyage home. Freney didn't say a word. He seemed to be resigned to his fate of neva findin' pirate treasure or a German U-boat.

"I wonda if Freney would have accepted his fate so calmly if he had known what was discovered in that area off Wellfleet where Davy was divin.' Not long after we left the area, they discovered a thirty-foot piece of wood, believed to be a section of the *Whydah's* powder room. It was covered with tin to keep explosives dry. Since then, explorers have found the ship's bell inscribed with '*The Whydah's Gally 1716*,' along with more than 100,000 artifacts from the site, like a sword-sharpenin' wheel, cannons, lead shot, thousands of coins, even the remains of a pirate leg, still encased in silk stockin' and a leather-dress shoe. Though the underwater search continues, most of the *Whydah's* gold and silver is still missin.' Maybe it's lyin' on the ocean floor buried under the sand?"

## TAPS FOR NODDLES

Noddles Island disappeared many years ago. Noddles was transformed from an island into part of the mainland to open more land for commercial and residential development. In 1801, when Boston's population was 25,000, Noddles Island boasted but one mansion, a mill pond dam, and a wharf. Thirty-two years later, General William Sumner (The Sumner Tunnel is named after him.) paid $80,000 for the island and founded the East Boston Company. The goal of the corporation, which owned East Boston, was to develop a trading center and a vacation resort.

Landfill operations began at once. The East Boston Company graded the island by leveling its hills and dumping dirt into the surrounding marshes. Then it divided the land into four sections, fashioned streets in a grid pattern, and sold house lots.

The company also saw the great potential for developing East Boston's waterfront. While commerce flourished in the 1830s, Boston lacked piers. So the East Boston company built wharves, obtained a freight terminal of the Eastern Railroad, and encouraged shipbuilders to locate their yards along East Boston's untapped waterfront.

By 1835, 697 people were living in fifty private homes on the island; ten wharves lined the waterfront; and the Maverick Hotel, an elegant eighty-room resort hotel opened that year.

In the next twenty-five years the population exploded, spiraling from 1,400 to over 20,000 people. First came the Irish, fleeing the potato famine in the 1840s. They formed the bulk of the unskilled labor force that built East Boston's piers, extended its railroad system, and worked as stevedores on the docks. After the Civil War, the wooden-shipbuilding industry collapsed and East Boston's economy went into a tailspin. The Irish turned elsewhere for work, moving to South Boston and the recently opened "street car suburbs."

Then came the Italians and Russian Jews. East Boston's population, which had been declining for years was reversed, doubling from 1885 to 1915. By 1905, the Jewish community was the largest in New England. On Chelsea and Porter Streets, there were kosher markets and restaurants, dry good stores, and chicken houses. The community supported three synagogues. The first Italian immigrants came from the North End, but after 1905, they were joined by "paisani" and relatives from Italy. By 1915, Italians formed the largest part of East Boston's population.

The waves of immigrants put the pressure on for more housing, more development, more landfilling. Land speculators bought abandoned estates and middle class houses and, after subdividing them, rented them out to the immigrants; the East Boston Company filled in more flats to make room for even more dwellings.

No one is quite sure when Noddles' existence as an island actually ended. In 1882, M.F. Sweetser still referred to Noddles as an island in the *King's Handbook*. Suffice it to say that it was sometime during the latter half of the 19th century, through one landfill project or another, that the geography of Noddles changed from island to mainland.

The construction of Logan Airport was the final taps for Noddles Island. After World War I, it was decided Boston needed an airport to serve the new mail service as well as other commercial and military interests. On June 4, 1923, Logan Airport was officially opened. The airport was constructed in East Boston on land created by filling in the Noddles Island flats and joining it with Governor, Apple, and Bird islands. Thus, Noddles Island passed into history. For Noddles, geography was fate.

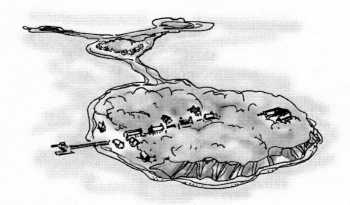

# CHAPTER X   PEDDOCKS ISLAND

Peddocks Island is the third-largest island in the harbor and has the longest shoreline. It is comprised of four drumlins, or heads, connected by sand or gravel bars called tombolos. The 188-acre island lies across Hull Gut, a quarter of a mile from the town of Hull.

Some years before the Pilgrims landed on Plymouth Rock, a French trading vessel was riding anchor off the shores of Peddocks Island (so named for Leonard Peddocks, who was the first white man to land there), when the Indians massacred all the men, except five whom they saved to exhibit before the various Massachusetts tribes.

There is a story in the *King's Handbook of Boston Harbor* called "Peddocks Island and Its Tragedy" that tells what befell those Indians. It seems a Captain Dermer, who paid a ransom for the surviving Frenchmen, asked the Indians why they had killed the others. When the Indians failed to give Captain Dermer a satisfactory answer, the Captain cursed the Indians and swore that "God will destroy you for your bloody deeds."

A short time later, smallpox savaged Peddocks Island. The "Red men" died by the hundreds "in heaps and their carcasses lay unburied, left for crows, kites, and vermin to prey upon them." A visitor to Peddocks many years later described the piles of skulls and bones looking like the "field of Golgotha."

Smallpox was called the "speckled monster" in the 18th century. The disease appeared suddenly, like a minister of death, afflicting its victims with high fever, chills, swelling in the brain, back and muscle pain, prostration, nausea, and vomiting. After two to four days, the fever relented and a rash appeared on the face and inside the eyes. The rash would subsequently cover the whole body. Then purplish skin lesions evolved into blisters and pussy pimples, and finally dried into scabs that fell off after three or four weeks, leaving those who survived disfigured, and in many cases, blind.

Smallpox epidemics broke out in Boston in 1690 and 1702. The most lethal outbreak occurred there in 1721. Boston was a prosperous port city of 11,000 residents when in April of that year, the British vessel, *Seahorse*, arrived in Boston Harbor from Barbados, bearing several passengers and crew who were infected with smallpox. Although Governor Samuel Shute ordered the ship quarantined at Spectacle Island, crew members had already come ashore and the infection spread.

By early May, more seamen showed evidence of acute smallpox. Despite frantic efforts to quarantine the latest victims on Spectacle Island, cases were now appearing among the residents of Boston. On May 26, the Reverend Cotton Mather entered the following in his diary: "The grievance calamity of the smallpox has now entered the town…. Because of the destroying angel over the town, a day of prayer is needed that we may prepare and meet our God."

About one thousand Bostonians immediately fled the community. Of those remaining, about 6,000 were ultimately stricken with smallpox. Nearly 850 died of the disease, before the epidemic ran its course by the following year. Doctor Zabdiel Boylston (who, during the epidemic, introduced the technique of inoculation, which eventually lead to the eradication of the disease in the 20th century — or has it?) mourned the plight of Boston: "Parents being left childless, children without parents, and sometimes parents and children being both carried off, and many families broken up by the destruction the smallpox made."

In 1737, the quarantine station was moved from Spectacle Island to Rainsford Island, a small, eleven-acre island off Long Island. One of the hospital buildings, ambitiously constructed in 1832 in the style of a Grecian temple, was a smallpox facility. Hundreds of those who died from smallpox and other diseases were buried on the island. Before the tombstones were removed to Long Island some years ago, Edward Rowe Snow noted a number of their epitaphs. Two of these grim reminders of the mortality of man:

*"Nearby These Gray Rocks*
*Enclosed in a Box*
*Lies Hatter Cox*
*Who Died of Smallpox"*


*"Behold And See You Pass By*
*As You are now, So Once Was I*
*As I am now So You Must Be*
*Prepare For Death And Follow Me"*


Ever since the 18th century, the Boston Harbor Islands had been a popular destination for recreation. Wealthy Bostonians would sail their yachts to the islands for sightseeing, nature walks, bathing, and fishing parties where they would catch and cook cod on the beaches of the Brewsters, Long, and Peddocks islands. In the 19th century, Augustus Russ, who operated the Boston Yacht Club and sponsored boat races in the harbor, built a summer villa on Middle Brewster, where "the patrician yachtsmen and other guests enjoy ease with dignity during the dog-days, and are entertained with free hospitality at the Russ villa."

With the advent of the steamboat in 1803, the islands became more accessible to the masses in Boston. As one contemporary writer described it: "Numerous steamboats ply between the city and the places of resort in the harbor and just outside it. For reasonable fees one may steam in and out between the several islands, and enjoy, in the most sultry of days, a cool and refreshing breeze, together with the most delightful and ever-changing scenery."

Splendid and luxurious hotels like the Colonel Mitchell House on Long Island and modest eating establishments and boarding houses like Newcomb's on Gallop's Island were built to accommodate the growing number of vacationers to what was called in those days Boston's "green isles of romance." Gallops was a particularly popular attraction as excursionists visited the island to search for the Orlov diamond and other pirate treasure believed to be buried there.

Even Rainsford, the site of the smallpox hospital, was a popular summer resort. The Old Mansion House on Great Head was allowed to take on boarders whenever no communicable diseases were reported at the hospital. One can imagine the pall that descended on the island when an outbreak occurred, followed by carousing and the clinking of ale tankards when the all-clear signal was given.

The Civil War brought a temporary halt to recreation on the islands as many of the islands were used for military purposes. After the Civil War, recreation resumed on the islands, but it was of a different nature. Wealthy Bostonians were now searching out more distant and exotic destinations, abandoning the islands to illicit pleasure-seekers who took advantage of the islands' seclusion and its proximity to Boston to watch unsanctioned boxing matches and baseball games, gamble, take drugs and have sex as prostitution rings set up on the islands. Fishing parties were replaced by "Chinese picnics," the euphemistic name for opium parties. Romantic strolls on island trails were replaced by police chases. Where men once cheered on racing boats, they now cheered on the brutal beatings and brawling of rowdy crowds who frequented the islands.

From the late 19th century through the early 20th century, there were two inns on the island: the Island Inn, owned by John Irwin and the Y.O. West End House, owned by W.L. Drake. Although Bostonians may have patronized the inns for their deviled lobster for 75 cents, clam chowder for 20 cents, French fried potatoes for 15 cents, and a bottle of Guinness for 30 cents, they would have more likely made the trip to Peddocks to partake in a Chinese picnic or watch an illegal boxing match or baseball game.

The Boston Bees (later the Boston Braves) of the National League were prohibited to play baseball in their stadium on Sundays because of Boston's Blue Laws. John Irwin, the proprietor of the Island Inn and a former professional baseball player, managed to circumvent the law by getting the Bees to play their Sunday games on

Peddocks. Boats would typically bring over 5,000 spectators to these Sunday ballgames. The Irish loved the Boston team. After all, the lineup in those days consisted of Carney, Cooley, Delehanty, Moran, Needham, and Malarkey.

## BOSTON STRONGBOY

John Lawrence Sullivan was born in mid-October, 1858 in the Roxbury section of Boston. His father, Mike Sullivan, who immigrated to America in 1850 from Laccabey, Abbey Dorney in County Kerry, Ireland, was a typical Irishman of his day: He worked with his hands for he had few other skills; he was quick in temper, slow in temperance. His son John L. inherited his father's combativeness and fondness for alcohol. John L. became known around town as "Boston's Strong Boy."

Under Massachusetts law, prize fighting was illegal in Boston back then. Always looking to promote business on his island, Irwin, with a little bribing of local officials, organized a number of boxing matches on Peddocks, claiming these boxing matches were for charity. Stepping into the ring on Peddocks on a hot day in June, 1878, was John L. Sullivan and a local tough named Jack Scannell. Scannell landed the first punch at Sullivan's head, but it was his last as John L. knocked him down and out in the very first round. In the audience that day was Richard Kyle Fox, who was to become the biggest boxing promoter in the United States in the years ahead. "If you ever make it to New York, kid," Fox said to Sullivan after the fight, "look me up."

In March, 1881, Sullivan stepped into the biggest boxing stage of all — Harry Hill's Dance Hall and Boxing Emporium on New York's East Side — and announced that he was offering fifty dollars to any man who could last four rounds with him under Queensberry rules. A veteran fighter named Steve Taylor took up the offer, but was pummeled in two rounds. After the fight, Richard Kyle Fox, who was once again in the audience came up to Sullivan and said: "Kid, how would you like to become the next heavyweight-boxing champion of the world?"

On February 7, 1882, in Mississippi City, Sullivan fought and defeated in nine rounds the reigning champion, Paddy Ryan, an Irish-American from Troy, New York. For the next decade, Sullivan, despite chronic alcoholism, held on to his title, defending it nearly thirty times, all of these bouts with gloves and under Queensberry rules. Sullivan's fame grew through his great tours of the United States in 1883-4 and 1886-7; at each stop, John L. made his standard offer of one thousand dollars to any man who could last four rounds, an amount he rarely had to pay out for he could "lick any man alive." It's estimated that Sullivan cleared between eighty thousand and one hundred thousand dollars during his 1883-4 tour of the United States alone, though, unfortunately, he drank away most of his earnings.

In 1887, at the height of his fame, Sullivan went to Ireland where he was received as a conquering hero by cheering crowds throughout the country. After returning to the United States, he stayed out of boxing for the next three years. But finally, he stepped into the ring on September 6, 1892 in New Orleans to defend his title against James "Gentlemen Jim" Corbett. Corbett's victory that day marked the end of the legendary career of the Great John L., whose star was born on Peddocks Island. After that, Peddocks became a testing ground for future boxers and street thugs alike.

## CHARLIE MCGIVER'S STORY, 1985

Boxing was Southie's sport. It beat fightin' in the street where you could get arrested by the bad guys. Ya know, the cops. The best boxers like me, we belonged to the Fenian Athletic Club. We trained at the Muni gym. They called it the Muni gym 'cause it was right behind the municipal court house.

I rememba how I got recruited by the Fenians. It was at Southie Day. I think back in the mid -80s. Southie Day is held every August in Marine Park by the waterfront. There are lot of festivities like Irish music and food. Everyone comes wearin' somethin' green, like a Shamrock, to show Irish pride. They set up a boxin' ring in the park and invite all comers to take a chance with whoever else is brave enough to step into the ring.

I step into the ring with some punk who I deck with one punch. *Pow*! To the kissa. I'm standin' over the punk, who's on the mat pleadin' with me not to hit him again The ref is holdin' me back from killin' the bastard.

When I climb out of the ring this guy, his name is John Taney, they call him Tiger Taney, comes over to me and says: "Hey, kid, how'd ya like to train at the Fenian AC." Now anyone who knows the boxin' scene in Southie knows Tiger's reputation for developin' Southie guys into golden glove champions. I liked the idea of belongin' to the Fenians. Ya feel like someone special. Ya got the look. Ya know, the swagger, the tough-guy image. Wearin' leather sneakers, the barracuda coat with the elastic waist band and plaid linin', with the collar turned up to show ya were from Southie. Man, that's cool.

"Hey, that's great Mr. Taggert. Ya, I'd really like to train with the Fenians. Thanks," I tell him, feelin' already that I'm his next golden glove champion."

It wasn't long after I started workin' out at the Muni gym when I learned who ran the Fenians. It was Jim Freney. I'd see him all the time at the gym, watchin' us train. Every St. Patrick's Day, they held the Baby Golden Gloves tournament at the Muni gym. All the politicians were there, cheerin' like crazy. There was Jim Freney at ringside. The biggest match was the New England Golden Glove Championship. They held that up in Sun Auditorium in Lowell. There's Jim Freney. sittin' in a ringside seat. Watchin', always watchin'.

The Fenians had plenty of Golden Glove champions. There was me, 'Bobcat' Reed; 'My Man' Moore; 'Andre the Giant' McCoullough; Ray Rooney; and Jim's favorite boy, Garrett Neeley. We were all heavyweight champions.

Jim Freney gave rings to the champions. They're solid gold with three clover leaves designed on them with an emerald in the center cupped by a pair of hands. The emerald is suppose to be the heart. Freney had 'em specially made by a jeweler in Southie. Freney wore one of these rings. 'is had a crown on it. Wore it on 'is right index finger. They're called Claddagh rings. They're suppose to be magical. They bring ya good luck. This is the story I heard about the Claddagh ring.

Back in the 1680s, there was a guy called Richard Joyce. He came from Galway and went to sea lookin' for adventure. At sea, he was captured by Mediterranean pirates and sold as a slave to a West Indies plantation owner. He sold 'im to a Moorish goldsmith who taught 'im gold-smithin'. After he got released, he returned to Claddagh, a little fishing village near Galway. There he setup a shop to design these rings. They became real popular in Ireland.

When the Great Famine of 1849 came, people by the thousands left Ireland. These rings were kept like heirlooms and passed down from generation to generation. There's a sayin' behind the ring — "love, loyalty, let us reign."

I also learned after ya join the Fenians that Jim Freney not only owns the club, but he also owns you. You're not only recruited to be his boxer, but his street soldier, his enforcer, his leg-breaker, and drug runner. We was the muscle guys who distributed drugs for the boss and broke the limbs of those who didn't respect his rules.

Freney was a schizoid about drugs. He controlled drug sales, but didn't do drugs 'imself. He was a physical fitness freak, kept 'imself always in prime condition. He didn't smoke and I didn't see him drink much, maybe a beer now and then. "Ya gotta be in top physical condition if you're gonna be on the top of yar game," he would tell us, "and you're not if you're high or drunk."

He expected us to stay in shape. Stay away from drugs and heavy drinkin'.'

Our job was to distribute drugs and police the neighborhoods. Make sure no one broke the rules. That meant operatin' in Southie only with his permission. Bein' in the ring or on the streets, we provided him the power and the protection to rule.

Freney liked to call us 'is "communications men." He knew that any Southie kid arrested for anythin' was likely to be worked over by the cops for information about 'is operations. Our job was to communicate, make sure these kids who were in and out of jail understood that silence was the only way to stay alive in Southie.

Freney was a stickler for details. Even for the way we dressed. He told us to chuck our barracuda jackets for somethin' classier, like full-length coats or maxis as we called 'em in Southie. "Somethin' good for concealin' a shotgun or a .35 magnum snub-nose pistol," he would point out.

Here's a story I once heard about Freney and the Italians, back in '83. You've probably never heard it before 'cause it ain't been told much.

One day, Freney gets a call from Sammy Salerno.

"Jim, Dante Massaroni wants you to come over to Prince Street. He's got some important business he wants to discuss with you," Salerno says.

The next day Freney meets with Massaroni.

"Sit down, James. Sit down and make yourself comfortable. How've you been? We haven't talked in quite a while."

"I'm fine. Everythin' is goin' fine," answers Freney.

"Let me get right to the point, James. There's a problem that's come to my attention — a serious problem. Garrett Neeley, I gather he's one of your top lieutenants. The one who's always bragging how 'the Italians are a bunch of old guys who are no match for the shooters of Freney's Irish gang.' I can excuse his remarks as just braggadocio coming from a young buck with a lot of testosterone in his balls. But I can't excuse him violating the rules. I'm told that Neeley supplied Jerry Esposito in East Boston with a large quantity of coke. When Jerry had trouble paying him, Neeley comes into East Boston and threatens Jerry he'll kill him if he doesn't pay up. Now Jerry's a good boy, maybe not too bright and he shouldn't be dealing with Neeley in the first place. But nevertheless, Neeley broke the rules. He shouldn't be dealing in East Boston. And we can't tolerate him coming into our territory and threatening our people. The rules between my people and your people must be enforced or else our alliance will collapse.

"There's more, James. To add insult to injury, Neeley was over to Polcari's restaurant in the North End with a few of his friends and a girl Laura Bianchi. A good Italian girl, *Bella Ragazza*. She should know better. Stick to her own kind. Neeley is drinking a lot and starts talking about how the Irish are better than the Italians. 'We're better than you in politics. We're better than you in sports. We're better than you in runnin' this city. An Irish potato tastes better than a bowl of pasta. And the men, we're better lookin' than you, else how would you explain this pretty gal by my side goin' out with me instead of one of you wops.'

"There was no further trouble that night, but the next day Laura's brother Dino Bianchi, he's a good soldier of mine, comes here and says that he's been disrespected. His family has been dishonored. I don't have to tell you, James, how important honor and respect are in our family.

"It's very serious, James. I want this matter settled by us. I don't want to have to go up to Federal Hill to ask Carmen to settle this. I want to make sure this doesn't happen again. Neeley must be punished. He must be taught a lesson he'll never forget. If he or anyone of your gang violate the rules again, like I say, our alliance will collapse. That's just what the FBI wants — to have the Irish and Italians fighting each other again.

"Think it over, James. Come back to me in, let's say, a week and tell me your plans for handling this matter. I know you'll work it out. You always do."

So a week later, Freney goes back to Prince Street to meet with Massaroni.

"Here's my proposal, Dante. We'll have a boxing match between Neeley and your best boxer."

"A boxing match? What the fuck are you talking about."

"It would be like a duel. That's how you settle matters of honor. Your best boxer versus our best. Neeley's a golden gloves champion. Who's the 'Italian stallion' of the North End?"

"I don't know, maybe its Frankie Nitti. But he's no Golden Gloves champion. Christ, James, you're still talking nonsense. How's a boxing match which Neeley would probably win be a punishment for him?"

"Because we'll fix it so Neeley will lose."

"Oh, I suppose you're going to tell him just to lay down."

"No, we'll drug him a little. Make him sluggish and to make sure your boy wins, he'll be wearin' 'sap gloves.'"

"What the fuck are sap gloves?"

"They're gloves with iron weights sewed into them. So when you hit somebody, it's like gettin' hit with a crow bar. It's an old Winter Hill technique. Been usin' it for years. I guarantee Neeley will be the loser. His reputation will be shattered. It will be a humbling experience. He'll brag no more about bein' the best boxer in Boston. It'll make it much easier for me to get my message across that he should never again taunt your people, deal in your territory, and look at your women."

"Oh, one thing, Dante. That's where we'll hold the fight. I want it held on Peddocks Island."

"Where the fuck is Peddocks Island?"

"It's in Boston Harbor. You can get there by boat. It takes only about twenty minutes from the North End. I want it there out of sight. If we held it in Boston, Lowell, Worcester, wherever, everybody would be there, including the press. Word would spread like wildfire that the Italians beat the Irish. That would be bad for our morale. You can understand that, Dante. Besides, this is a personal matter between families. We don't want it inflamin' ethnic passions. It's not good for our relationship. This way, we both come out ahead. You get to win back honor and respect and we both get to keep the peace."

On an October day, two boats set out for Peddocks Island. One boat sets out from Commercial Wharf in the North End, carryin' Dante Massaroni, Sammy Salerno, Luigi Faranese, Frankie Nitti, and a couple of their soldiers. Another boat sets out from the South Boston Yacht Club, carryin' Jim Freney, Bobby Conti, Suspenders Doyle, Garrett Neeley, and Tiger Taney.

The ring is set up in a grassy field behind an old red brick buildin' on the East Head section of the island. For three rounds, Neeley is dancin' 'round Nitti, throwin' jabs and hooks, while Nitti is standin' flat-footed, tryin' to land a solid punch. Then in the fourth round, the drug starts to take effect and Neeley is movin' slowa and 'is defense is lettin' down so that Nitti gets in with his lead fists and decks Neeley with a couple of solid punches to the head.

When Neeley regains consciousness, he's lyin' under a tree at the edge of the field. Freney is crouchin' by his side.

"What happened?" asks Neeley. "I could've beaten the shit out of him. But my legs, they started to get rubbery and my head went into a fog."

"We drugged ya, Garrett, and Nitti was wearin' sap gloves" says Freney. "I know ya could have taken 'im with one hand behind your back. But ya had to take one for the gang. Ya had to be my sacrificial lamb. Ya had to lose. The Italians wanted revenge for what ya did. Christ! Where was your head at, Garrett. Ya knew the rules. Ya don't do business with the Italians. Ya stay out of their territory. And ya stay away from their women.

"The Italians wanted ya dead. I saved yar life and I saved our alliance with the Italians by preventin' a war that would have crippled both sides."

Oh, I got another good story. It was on one of, what I call "Jim's fishin' parties."

I rememba goin' out on a fishin' party with Captain Jim, me, Garrett Neeley, and Ollie Brown, a Southie drug dealer.

We pull out of the Southie yacht club in Freney's twenty-foot Sea Ray, *The Phantom Pirate*. Freney's at the helm, wearin' his usual sailin' outfit — a Red Sox cap, shades and a barracuda jacket. We head out the main channel and into the open water of the bay.

"There's Great Brewster ahead of us. I'm goin' to dock the boat there," Freney shouts out over the noise of the engine.

Freney eases the boat up to the dock. "Why are we landin' there?" asks Ollie, who's gettin' a little nervous.

"'Cause this is where we're goin' fishin', Ollie," answers Freney. "You get out of the boat first and we'll bring all the gear."

No sooner than Ollie gets onto the dock, Freney whacks him from behind. *Thud!* With a blackjack, right on the back of his head. Ollie crumples like a sack of potatoes on the dock. Lookin' real dead.

"He's not dead, he's just unconscious," says Freney. "Garrett, tie 'im up and throw a bucket of salt water on 'im."

"When Ollie comes to, blood is tricklin' out of the side of 'is mouth. He's quakin' like a leaf, terrified we're goin' to push him off the dock."

"Ollie boy," Freney says lookin' down at him. "It seems we got a problem. You've been shootin' off your mouth, sayin' you got a ton of information that the FBI would be interested in hearin' about. That's not very smart, Ollie. That's not very smart."

"No, no, Jim, you've got me wrong," Ollie is cryin. "I was drunk. Just makin' a joke. Showin' off. Showin' I was in tight with the gang. Braggin' about how much I know. I didn't mean anythin' by it. Ya know, I wouldn't rat on ya. Please, please. I swear on my mother's grave, I'll never say anythin' like this again."

"There's a long silence. I'm thinkin' that this poor fuck has about as much chance of survivin' as a bleedin' flounda' in a pool of sharks. Then Freney speaks.

"Untie him, Garrett. You're lucky, Ollie, that I think you're better alive than dead — for now. But if ya eva cross me again, if ya eva think of crossin' me again, you're goin' to end up on the bottom of the harbor as fish bait for the stripers."

When we get back to the yacht club, Ollie is dumped into his car and told to get out of our sight. Freney turns to me and says "Charlie, what did you learn from our little fishin' party?"

"I learned ya don't mess with Jim Freney," I says back to 'im.

"No, no, that's not the point I'm tryin' to make. Ya know how I'm always talkin' to ya about fear? Ollie's still alive, as I said, he's better alive than dead. Why? 'Cause if he was dead nobody would know what happened to 'im. Dead men don't talk. But if he's alive, he'll tell others. Word will spread throughout Southie, Dorchesta, Roxbury, all over Boston that somethin' bad has happened to 'im. We've saved a lot of time and energy in gettin' our message across that this is how we deal with stoolies. This is what happens to anyone who breaks the code of silence. I've told ya this before, Charlie. This is how ya build fear and respect."

It wasn't the first or last time I got that message.

## WOMEN OF THE MOB

I met Diana DiPalma at the Jolly Roger. She was sipping a daiquiri, reclining on a chaise lounge at the poolside of one of those palm-thatched, open-air tike bars that dot Miami Beach. DiPalma was wearing a baseball cap, sunglasses, and a black and dark purple-striped bathing suit. She was a deeply tanned, well-preserved woman in her early 50s, who spent her life now jet-skiing, scuba-diving, and lounging in the Florida sun.

"Back in the late 70s and early 80s, I was the unofficial mascot of the Winter Hill Gang," DiPalma began her story.

"I was Bobby Conti's girl, at least one of them. I first met Bobby when I was waitressing at Chandler's restaurant in the South End. That's where a lot of gangsters hung out.

"Bobby was a good-looking guy. He had dark, flashing eyes and was very charming. I was an attractive brunette in my 20s, divorced, with two little kids, going nowhere in life. One night Bobby asked me out and the party began.

"Bobby took me to fine restaurants and nightclubs, lavished me with gifts — jewelry, clothes, and a two-tone blue and white Cadillac. He would regularly pull out a fist-size wad of one hundred dollar bills, peel off a few and say, 'Why don't you go out and buy the kids somethin'?'

"Most of the time, though, we spent in bed. Bobby liked to fuck all the time. I know he had other women who he fucked regularly, but he told me I was the one he really cared for. I knew he was lying, but I pretended to believe him. I guess I really wanted to believe him.

"During the day, I spent a lot of time at the Lancaster Street garage. Jim Freney, Johnny Greco, Bobby, and me, we would sit around gabbing and joking. We talked a lot about sports, baseball, some hockey. The boys were always betting on one sports event or another. I was their errand girl. I'd go out and buy coffee and donuts in the morning, pizzas and calzonis for lunch.

"The three of them. They reminded me of Brar' Bear, Brar' Rabbit, and Brar' Fox. Johnny was a big hulking, teddy bear. He must have weighed 250 pounds. He was the comic, never really serious, always telling jokes. Bobby had the sexual energy of a rabbit. Always had sex on his mind. Jim was the schemer — the fox. Always organizing and planning things. I guess I'd call him the intellectual. I'd remember him, sitting at his desk, pulling out his long knife that he had strapped under his pants leg and picking his fingers with the knife. All the while talking about things, everything from how we should free the American hostages the Iranians were holding to what a great community Southie is and all the good things he was doing there, like giving turkeys to the elderly for Thanksgiving and Christmas gifts to widows and orphans. His obsession was the Red Sox. He was always analyzing the team. How the manager should have made this or that decision. His favorite player was Roger Clemens, who he said would lead them to the 'promised land,' as he called it. But at the end of every baseball season when the Red Sox fell out of the pennant chase, Jim would like to say — 'Ya know, what will be written on my tombstone? *He Never Lived To See The Red Sox Win The World Series — May He Rest in Peace.'*

"The boys avoided talking about criminal matters in front of me. They downplayed their criminal activities and said they had nothing to do with murders or trafficking drugs. 'The North End guys do that,' they said.

"I basically thought they were bookmakers — powerful bookmakers. I guess I chose to believe this because I wanted to. I was too dazzled to really care where the gifts came from, like the diamond sapphire cocktail ring that Bobby gave me. Probably some swag from a burglary they pulled off.

"I first met Annie Jones on the dock at the South Boston Yacht Club. She was waiting with me and Bobby for Jim to take us aboard his boat for a tour of Boston Harbor. Annie was a real good-looking girl, in her mid-20s. She had long flowing red hair, like Rita Hayworth, the movie actress in the 1940s. Nice cheekbones. Blue-green eyes that you'd think would have an Irish sparkle in them, but seemed to me to be sad eyes. Lonely eyes. You know, kind of lost.

"She was wearing jeans and blue sneakers, a short-sleeved, white shirt with epaulettes, like Navy officers wear. A blue sweater wrapped around her shoulders. She wasn't your typical gangster's bimbo. No way. There was something classy about her.

"Bobby told me she was once a dancer. Tried to make it in New York, but it didn't work out. She came back to Boston and was making a living teaching aerobics and giving massages at some fitness club.

"We boarded Jim's boat. It was called *The Phantom Pirate.* I don't know why but to this day the name has always stuck in my mind. We pull away from the dock and pick up speed as we head into the harbor. As we went by these islands in the harbor, Jim would tell us a little story about each island.

"'See that island on the right with all those trees on it? That's Thompson Island. There's a boys' school on it. When I was a kid, the priest in our parish told my father he thought it might be a good idea I go to school there. It would get me off the streets of Southie. Be a betta environment to grow up in. No way was I goin' to any reform school.

"'The next island comin' up on our right is Spectacle Island. It's a dump. Nothin' but garbage and rats on it. Now see that lighthouse further over to the right? That's Long Island Light. Below the lighthouse you can see the crumblin' bunkers of old Fort Strong. The fort was built durin' the Civil War. They shut down the fort after World War II when the six and twelve-inch gun batteries 'came obsolete.

"'Now we're headin' into the main channel. On your left is Deer Island. I spent a little time in the prison there. Hah! That was nothin' compared to my time in Alcatraz. See those three islands comin' up on our right? The first is Gallops. They say a pirate named Long Ben Avery buried some treasure there. People have been lookin' for it for centuries. Rumors have it that some gold coins have been found on the island in the 20$^{th}$ century. But none of the diamonds he's said to have buried there. They found gold and silver coins on the second island over there, Lovell's. They say it may have come from the *Magnifique*, a French man-of-war that sunk off the island. Maybe there's still more coins that will be found someday. The third island, furthest over there, is George's. There's an old Civil War fort, Fort Warren, which I went to when I was a kid.'

"Jim opens up the throttle when we hit the open water of the bay. The air is fresher. The sea gets rougher. White caps are forming. The wind's blowing my hair and the salt spray's tingling my face. I never felt anything like this before. The power. The rush. It was like bounding over the waves in a chariot driven by a god.

"'See those wind-swept islands ahead of us in the distance?' Jim yells out over the roar of the engine. 'Those are the Brewsters. They're the farthest east of all the islands of Boston Harbor. Great Brewster is a drumlin hill. The others are rock outcroppins. You can see Boston Light, the oldest lighthouse in the country, over there to the right. That's Little Brewster.'

"Jim steers the boat away from the Brewsters and anchors off a beach.

"'This is Calf Island,' he tells us. 'The island was named after Robert Calef, a Boston merchant. The guy wrote a book called *More Wonders of the Invisible World*. The book explained the witchcraft hysteria that was scarin' the shit out of people in Boston in the 17$^{th}$

century. Back in the early 20<sup>th</sup> century, Benjamin Cheney purchased the island and built a mansion for his wife. She was a famous actress, Julia Arthur. The mansion was built on a cliff overlookin' the southeastern shore. All you can see today are the ruins of the foundation and two stone chimneys. Some punks from the North End torched the mansion after World War II. Fuckin' wops! They've got no respect for private property. Ha, Ha! Bobby. Just kiddin'. Ya know, some of my best friends are Italians.'

"As we headed back to South Boston, me and Bobby we're sitting in the back seat of the boat. I see Annie, who was sitting next to Jim get up and stand next to him at the helm. She's got her arm around his waist. He's got his arm around her shoulder. They made a nice couple.

"From that day on, Annie and me became good friends. We'd often meet for lunch in Boston and talk about things. We needed each other to talk to. We both needed a confidant. Someone to share the adventures we were having but also the risks of living the life of a big-time mob mistress.

"'Diana, what do you think attracts us to guys like Jim and Bobby?' Annie would ask me.

"'Honey, there are a lot of things. There's the bad boy image. It's exciting, really thrilling being around these guys. They take us places — to restaurants, clubs, sporting events. Give us gifts — clothes, jewelry, cars. Maybe it isn't the glamour like you see in the *Godfather* movies, where you get a front-row seat to a Sinatra concert or a surprise trip to Atlantic City. But I love the attention — the special treatment and the respect — you get when you go with your man to a nice club like Lulu's. 'Good evening, Mr. Conti, Ms. DiPalma. We have a private booth for you away from the dance floor.' Or a restaurant like Anthony's Pier Four. 'Good Evening, Mr.Conti, Ms. DiPalma. We have a window table looking out over the harbor. Can I check your coat for you?'

"'It all comes down to power. Women love power and guys who have power.'

"'I know what you mean, Diana. They have the power to give us everything we want — clothes, jewelry, a condo,' said Annie. 'You know, where Jim buys dresses for me? Not at some 'hot pants shop' in the Combat Zone. He shops for me at Bloomingdale's and those fancy, boutiques on Newbury Street. He buys me classy things, like my Diane Von Furstenberg dresses. He's also given me a ring. He calls it a Claddagh ring. It's like he's given me an engagement ring. He says wearing the ring brings good luck.

"'Tell me about the condo Jim bought you,' I said.

"'It's in Louisburg Square off Wollaston Drive in Quincy. It's a brick-front duplex with two baths, good-size kitchen, living room, master bedroom, and a room Jim fixed up as an exercise room. It also has a view of Boston Harbor from my balcony windows.

"'Jim spends a lot of time at the condo. I know he visits Mary Wright and her family in South Boston. He likes to have supper and Sunday meals there. But he's been coming over here lately. He usually comes in late at night. He's real tired. I cook him some pasta. Maybe give him a massage. It really helps him to relax. A lot of nights he has insomnia and some nights he talks and tosses in his sleep. I can't understand much of what he's muttering about. A lot of times, it's something about an Indian guy. He calls him the Cherokee Kid. Someone he knew in Alcatraz. Something about having to give him a proper Indian burial. Jim tells me it was the LSD the feds gave him in prison that gives him hallucinations and nightmares in his sleep. He says the LSD also caused his angina. It can give him a lot of pain. It gives him high blood pressure. I go out to the pharmacy and get him Atenolol. He takes it to lower his blood pressure.

"'Sometimes I wake up in the night and see Jim standing on the balcony and looking out over Dorchester Bay. The lights at night make the coast line look like some Mediterranean seaport. He seems to be staring at a gas tank that has lights winding around it like a Christmas wreath. You know, the gas tank painted by Corita the nun? There are lights of the planes taking off from the airport and a flashing beacon light. I'm not sure. I think Jim told me it was Boston Light. It's way, way out in the harbor. Standing there on the balcony looking out toward the harbor, Jim seems far away.

"'Come back to bed, Jim baby,' I call to him. 'He gets back into bed, puts his arms around me, and pulls me next to him. That's when I feel I'm in the safest place in the world.'

"'Oh, weren't there some fun times, Diana?' Annie would ask.

"'Yeah, there certainly were. Remember the *Showboat*, Annie?,' Diana asked.

"'Wasn't that the old steamboat they grounded off the water's edge in Nantasket and turned it into a night club? Wasn't that the place you and Bobby, Jim and me, and Johnny Greco and his date went to see those night club acts — the hypnotist and the magician?' Annie asked.

"'Yeah, the hypnotist — what was his name? Dr. Sleep. I think it was.' said Diana.

'He had people in the audience come up to the stage and he would hypnotize them.'

"'You are getting sleepy,' Dr. Sleep would say, directing the guy who was lying on a couch to look at a gold watch he was dangling in front of his eyes. 'Your eyelids are getting heavy. You are falling deeper and deeper into a beautiful sleep. Let yourself go. Sleep. Sleep. You are now in my power. Arise now and follow my commands: Take off your jacket. Take off your shoes. Take off your socks. Take off your pants. Take off your shirt.' The guy peels off each layer until he's standing in his skivvies. The audience is howling and hollering. 'Take it off. Take it all off.' Then before he strips naked, Dr. Sleep snaps his fingers and the guy wakes up out of his trance.'

"'Dr. Sleep asks for another person in the audience to come on to the stage to be hypnotized. Up bounds Jim onto the stage and announces 'I'm your man.' He lies down on the couch and Dr. Sleep dangles his gold watch before Jim's eyes and begins his 'Sleep. You are falling deeper and deeper into a sleep….Jim, meanwhile, is staring into Dr. Sleep's eyes. Those icy-blue eyes of Jim's, staring back into Dr. Sleep's eyes like daggers. Dr. Sleep's voice starts to tail off, he drops his watch, and his head slumps down on his chest. You hear snoozing. Dr. Sleep is fast asleep. Jim stands up, claps his hands and says, 'End of act.' Dr. Sleep wakes up. Everybody in the audience is laughing like crazy.

"'Then the next act comes on. Remember Mandrake the Magician? Among his bag of tricks he had a knife-throwing act, in which he throws the knives one after another at a female assistant who's standing against a board at the back of the stage. The knives strike all around the head of the assistant, giving her a close shave but never hitting her. Bobby tells me it's all a trick. The knives spring out of the board just as the magician appears to throw them, looking as if he did throw them and they strike close to the assistant's head. 'It's all a matter of the hand is quicker than the eye,' Bobby says.

"After the magician goes through his first knife-throwing demonstration, Jim suddenly bounds on to the stage again. 'Hey, let me try this. I'm pretty good with knives.'

The magician says 'Absolutely not. This is a professional act, not some amateur hour.'

"'Oh, so you think I'm some amateur, do ya? Here, gimme those knives.'

"'Give him the knives. Give him the knives,' chants the audience. Someone yells out: 'You'd better let him have the knives. He's Jim Freney.'

"The magician turns white with fright and says to Jim: 'Take them, take them. By all means take them, Mr. Freney.'

"'Alright,' Jim says to the magician, 'you stand up against that board and I'll throw them at you and we'll see if I'm any good.'

"The magician stands up against the board and starts trembling. Jim throws three knives, one right after another. *Swish! Swish! Swish! Thump! Thump! Thump!* They strike what would have been the two eyes and the mouth of the magician if he had not fainted and fallen to the floor.

"As time went by, the fun times were fewer. Things began to change. Annie and me and the guys went out less together as double dates. Me and Bobby would go out alone, mostly to out-of-the-way places where we weren't known.

"Jim and Bobby told Annie and me to carry a gun. They bought us each a blue-and gray revolver to carry in our hand bag. Jim said it wasn't for our protection, but theirs.

"I started doing the driving and began to notice that in certain parts of town, Bobby would slouch down in the passenger seat. 'If anyone gets close,' he said, 'just pull over and duck down and I'll jump out.'

"I started noticing cars following us. It was the Boston Police. I got a telephone call from them saying they were subpoenaing me. I was getting nervous. God forbid, if something happened to me. What would become of my children? I couldn't leave them to my parents. I partied and played all these years and I wasn't giving them any kind of life. Hanging with these guys was getting me nowhere.

"What finally convinced me it was time to cut out from the mob was what happened at the Blackfriars. Blackfriars was a club on Summer Street in Boston, owned by a cocaine dealer named Vincent Salucci from Quincy. I was supposed to meet Bobby and have drinks with Annie and Jim there. I think it was sometime in June in the 1980s. Bobby calls me up during the day and tells me: 'Don't go to Blackfriars tonight. I'll catch up with you tomorrow.'

"Annie also gets a call from Jim, telling her the same thing. They're not meeting at Blackfriars that night.

"The next morning we learned that five men had been murdered, gunned down during a drug money robbery in the restaurant's basement. Bobby insisted he had no idea what was going to happen that night. Rumor has it that Nicky Silanus, one of Jim's enforcers, headed the massacre. The case was never solved.

"I met with Annie for lunch a few weeks later.

"'Annie, I'm splitting. Things are too risky. I've got to think of my kids' future. Hanging out with the mob's just going to lead to more trouble. Friggin' Bobby, he's as loyal to me as a rabbit in a carrot patch. He's got other women in his life to screw. Tells me 'he loves me better than the others.' That's bullshit! He gives his bimbo friend Barbara Bennett a Mercedes and I get a crummy Cadillac, like I'm some suburban housewife.

"'Guys like Bobby are incapable of love. They're macho men. Bobby's a macho Italian man. What they want they get. And if they can keep their women all in order, they're OK. Give them any problem, they'll flip you away like a cigarette butt.

"'I got no illusions about my life with Bobby. There's no emotional involvement with him. If I get possessive, then he'll dump me. So I'm cutting out before he cuts me out.

"'Annie, split with me. Sooner or later you'll get hurt. If you stay with Jim, you could get killed.

"'How about coming with me to Florida? Maybe we could run a restaurant there. You could set up a dance studio. What do you say?'

"I see a tear trickle down Annie's cheek as she says softly, 'I know Jim has Mary Wright and who knows how many bimbos in his life? But he's a loner. He won't let the net fall on him like it will on the others. Sooner or later he's going to have to make a break from all of them — from his other women, from his gang, and from the world he's now in. Where will he go? I'm not sure. But he'll need me to go with him if he's going to survive.'

"I saw Annie one last time before I told Bobby I was splitting. I can remember the exact date — October 25, 1986 — the sixth game of the World Series between the Red Sox and the New York Mets. Jim had purchased six tickets and we had flown to New York that afternoon. Bobby said Jim got these tickets through a connection with the Red Sox organization. There was me and Bobby, Annie and Jim, Garrett Neeley, and Suspenders Doyle. We had box seats on the first base line. Down the line toward right field, I could see some guys waving to us, Bobby said they were with the five families of New York. I guess they were in the New York Mafia.

"We were all in a festive mood, especially Jim. The Sox were leading the Mets in the late innings and it looked like a lock that the Sox would win the World Series that night.

"'Hey, everybody. How 'bout hot dogs and beers?' Jim announces. 'Come on with me, Suspenders. You and me, we'll pick up the food and drinks.'

"I had to go to the bathroom, so I followed them out. I don't think they saw me. For a while, I just eavesdropped.

"'Did ya talk to Doc Kalinsky?' Freney asks while they're walking down the ramp to the food and drink concessions under the grand stand. What's the bettin' line with Las Vegas?'

"'Kalinsky says we should make a cool million if the Sox win,' answers Suspenders. 'If they lose, though, we'd be out five-hundred thousand grand.'

"'They ain't goin' to lose this time, Suspenders' says Jim.

"'Shit, look at the line for food and drinks, Jim,' says Suspenders as they make their way from the men's room to the food and beverage concession stand.

"'We'll just step to the front of the line,' says Freney.

"'Hey, who the hell do you think you guys are, breaking into the line like this?' yells out the customer waiting at the front of the line.

"'Look, pal, it's an emergency,' says Suspenders. 'Our parents, we brought them to the game from a nursing home in Queens. They're really old. Probably their last chance to see a Red Sox game. They're really hungry. You know how they don't feed you much in nursing homes. How about being a sport and letting us get in front of you? Here's a sawbuck for doing us a favor.'

"'What are you guys havin'?' asks the concessions man.

"'Ah, let me see. Give us six beers and twelve hotdogs.' says Suspenders.

"'Why are ya orderin' twelve hotdogs?' asks Freney.

"'A hotdog each for the girls. Two hotdogs a piece for Garrett, Bobby, and you. That makes eight. And four hotdogs for me. That makes twelve,' says Suspenders.

"'Why do you want four hotdogs?' asks Freney.

"'Jeez, Jim. Have ya ever eaten a Shea frank?' asks Suspenders. "'They're shrivlin' weenies. No bigger than a dog's dick. They boil them in dish water. I'm hoping one of the girls won't want hers. I can always eat an extra one. You carry the beer in this tray and I'll carry the trays with the hotdogs. Come on let's get some mustard and ketchup to camouflage the skinny buggers. Things are kind of quiet here under the stands. Do you think anything's going on, Jim?'

"'Excuse me! Excuse me! Coming through,' says Suspenders, as he and Jim make their way back through the aisles to their box seats.

"A loud roar from the crowd is heard. Everyone's screaming: 'The run is scoring. The run is scoring. The Mets have gone ahead.'

"'What the fuck is happenin?' yells Jim, spilling the beers on the heads of people in the row in front and knocking over the hotdog trays Suspenders was carrying, splattering the mustard and ketchup all over the same heads.

125

"'Buckner couldn't bend down to field the ground ball,' Annie explained. 'It dribbled right through his legs and the Mets scored and have gone ahead.'

"I think it was the toughest baseball game Boston has ever lost. They never recovered and lost the seventh and final game — and the World Series. The last memory I have of Jim is him shrieking and raving like a man gone out of his mind — 'The Red Sox are cursed. The Red Sox are cursed. They're never fuckin' goin' to win the World Series.'"

There are many curses and calamities that have befallen the people of Boston over the centuries. But none has caused such misery, such heartbreak, such torment of the soul for the Red Sox Nation — that fanatical tribe in New England who root for the Red Sox — as *The Curse of the Bambino.*

According to the Boston sportswriter, Dan Shaughnessy, *The Curse of the Bambino* was Babe Ruth's revenge for Harry Frazee, owner of the Red Sox, selling him to the New York Yankees in 1920 to raise money to produce the Broadway musical *No, No, Nanette.* Ever since that fateful sale, the New York Yankees have won twenty-six World Championships. The Red Sox last won the World Championship in 1918.

## CHAPTER XI     SOUTHIE

South Boston is an island. Originally, it was a peninsula, known as Dorchester Neck, separated from Boston by a stretch of mudflats and a narrow channel. Over the centuries, the mudflats were filled in and bridges built across the channel, attaching South Boston more firmly to Boston.

Yet, South Boston remains an island, surrounded by the sea on the east and an invisible boundary around the rest of the territory that keeps it separated from the mainland — separated, with its own culture, its own government, and its own history.

It wasn't long after its annexation to Boston in 1804 that South Boston began to experience its "separateness" from Boston. The community felt the Boston authorities, the Yankee establishment, men like Cranston Howe, Samuel Perkins, and Isaac Adams, ignored South Boston. They saw Boston officials refusing financial support for their schools and bypassing the area to construct hospitals, reformatories, poor houses, asylums, and other public buildings in other parts of the city. This feeling of municipal neglect fostered an attitude that still permeates South Boston to this day: the defiant spirit of us against them.

In 1845, a strange fungus attacked the potato crop of Ireland, the mainstay of the Irish diet. By the fall of 1846, the fungus had ruined the country's entire potato crop. Starvation and disease stalked the land. For many Irishmen, the future looked hopeless. One possible road to survival was immigration. By the tens of thousands, the Irish poured into America, landing at Boston and other east coast ports in vessels called "famine ships."

In the 1840s, Boston was receiving about 4000 to 5000 immigrants a year from all of Europe. In 1847 alone, 37,000 immigrants arrived in Boston from Ireland. They were officially classified as "Irish labourers." Most of them came ashore half-starved, disease-ridden, impoverished, and unskilled, which prompted one historian to call them "a massive lump in the community, undigested and undigestable."

By the 1850s, the Irish had grown to nearly one-third of the city's total population, making a clash with the Yankees inevitable. The city's Brahmin aristocracy was made up of WASPS, white Anglo-Saxon Protestants. They detested the "vulgar" culture and religious practices of the Irish Catholics, calling them "shanty Irish." One observer described South Boston in that era as "the roughest, toughest, neighborhood in the city, a spawning ground of politicians and prize fighters, politicians, policemen, and plug-uglies." The plug-uglies were the odious bands of gangsters and ruffians who threatened the security of the Brahmin world.

Above all, the Puritan-minded Yankees detested the Irish immigrants' drinking habits — the grog shops, barrooms, and saloons that popped up in South Boston. In 1846, Boston had 850 licensed liquor dealers; in 1849, there were 1,200 dealers, most of whom were Irish.

The saloon became the center of political activity, where new voters were recruited and newcomers were prepared for eventual citizenship. Alcohol was accepted as an essential part of an Irishman's social and political life. Thomas O'Connor, chronicler of the Boston Irish, said that because the Irish were denied most avenues of economic advancement by the Yankee establishment, they chose politics as the road to power and influence. Politics in South Boston, he said, was dominated by strong men, quick, shrewd and tough enough to seize opportunity; men who ruled their wards with "gentle smiles and iron fists." These "bosses" established themselves as centers of patronage and influence and turned out the votes of "these people" with almost mathematical precision.

In the last decades of the twentieth century, South Boston's population was still 94% white and the large majority Irish Catholic. It was still described as "working class," a community of day laborers, longshoremen, tavern keepers, grocers, construction workers, bricklayers, carpenters, plumbers, electricians, policemen, MBTA conductors, firemen, and letter carriers.

They still lived on streets overlooking the harbor in two- and three-decker, wooden-frame houses, once known as 'Irish Schooners' because the architecture created a maximum amount of space, bringing three or more families together in an extended household, on a minimum amount of land. If they were poorer, they lived in the Old Colony and Old Harbor housing projects off of Old Colony Avenue and Columbia Road.

Faced with discrimination over the years, the citizens of South Boston had built an imaginary fortress around their embattled community, determined to hold onto their own distinctive beliefs, values, unwritten laws and identity — a city within a city in which "outsiders were not welcome and whose citizens were told to stay with their own kind."

Southie is still an island — where history becomes legend and legend becomes myth.

## FRENEY'S DRUG EMPIRE

"James Freney was like a mythic warrior-king," mused Charlie McGivers, "bringin' law and order out of the surroundin' chaos. Rememba the gang wars in Boston when everyone was bumpin' each other off? Things changed when Freney gained control. He kept crime in Southie organized, settin' the rules and makin' sure everyone obeyed 'em. Anyone who didn't would be punished.

"Take the night Freney told me to tail him and Tommy Clancy down at the Black Falcon docks. Tommy was a loan-shark who was welchin' on the tribute money he was suppose to be payin' Freney for permission to operate in Southie.

"So I'm down at the docks watchin' Freney walkin' with his arm around Tommy's shoulder, real friendly-like, when he lifts his finger, the index-finger with the Claddagh ring on it, pointin' it like a king would do in his court when he's passin' judgment. That's the signal for me to come out of the shadows and beat the shit out of

129

Tommy. Not kill him. No, just break a few bones and bloody him up so others will see what happens when anyone breaks the rules. Freney was always preachin' that 'it's betta PR to throw the motherfucka back alive in the streets for the other wolves to see.'"

"'Killin' ain't always cost-effective,' Freney would say, 'cause dead-men don't tell stories and ya don't get that advertisin' bang for ya buck.'

"Freney built his drug empire like a general," McGivers continued, "organizin' it along military lines. He carved up the neighborhoods into war zones, puttin' lieutenants and foot soldiers into each zone to deal and enforce his rules. The myth was he kept drugs out of Southie — ya, maybe heroin and angel dust. The reality was he controlled coke and pot distribution in Southie, Dorchesta, Charlestown, and Quincy and he controlled the price by controllin' the inventory. 'It's good ol' capitalism, Charlie,' Freney would say. 'It's a matter of supply and demand.'"

"Freney liked to work behind the scenes," McGivers continued. "He liked to keep a low profile. Keep up the image that he played no role in drug dealin' in Southie. We would meet in out-of-the way places in Southie, places where he wouldn't be recognized, like the sugar bowl on the causeway that loops off of Castle Island.

"'How're ya doin', Charlie?' Freney asks.

"'I'm doin' OK," Jimmy, I answer. 'How ya, doin?'

"'I'm doin' OK,' he answers. 'How's business goin'?'

'Not bad, Jimmy. I'm not complainin'.'

'Oh, ya, business is not bad?' he turns lookin' at me with a puzzlin' grin like ya see Bobby DeNiro wear on his face in the movies. Then I'm lookin' at him. He's wearin' these Foster-Grant sunglasses. You can't see his eyes, only my reflection in those sunglasses — the reflection of a victim. They say that eyes are the windows to the soul. Well, if that's the case then what I was seein' reflected in those shades was the black soul of the devil's work.

"'Don't ya fuckin' lie to me, Charlie,' he shrieks in my face, his hand grabbin' my sweater and twistin' it into a knot like he was about to strangle me. 'I know what you're pushin' on the street and what your tribute money is suppose to be. Ya been buyin' coke for twenty grand a kilo, cuttin' it up, and nettin' a profit of sixty grand. I know you've bought seven kilos over the last few months. So I figure you're makin' at least three hundred K. My books say you've been payin' in five thousand bucks a week. But accordin' to my calculations, your 'T' money should be ten thousand. What the fuck do ya have to say 'bout this?'

"'I'm, I'm sorry, Jimmy,' I says, barely able to get the words out of my mouth as he twists my sweater tighter in a stranglin' knot. 'I just miscalculated. I didn't mean to screw you. I swear on my mother's grave. Maybe it's the way I've been cuttin' up and distributin' the coke. Maybe I'm not chargin' enough per ounce. But Jesus, Jimmy, I'm not about to bite the hand that feeds me.'

"Freney seems to calm down, lettin' go of his grip on my sweater.

"'Ya know, Charlie,' he says, 'I like ya. You're one of my best enforcers. You're tough, smart, and loyal. I'm goin' to forget 'bout your 'miscalculation' this time. But in the future I suggest your math gets betta, 'cause if it doesn't, you'll end up like Tommy Clancy — a Southie poster boy for what happens if you cross Jimmy Freney.'

"Like I said, Freney ruled his empire like a general. He was always lecturin' me and other gang members about the importance of strategy in winnin' a battle."

"'You guys could learn somethin' by readin' books 'bout the great generals in history — Alexander the Great, Caesar, Napoleon, Patton, Rommel,' Freney would say. 'Rommel was a German general in World War II. He was called the Desert Fox 'cause he was always outwittin' the British in North Africa. He had a 'sixth sense' that enabled 'im to seek out his enemy's weakness.'

"Freney talked a lot about the importance of planning in military operations," McGivers continued. 'The Japs were plannin' their surprise attack on Pearl Harbor as far back as 1905,' Freney told us. 'I rememba readin' in a book by Jack London how they studied little things like the currents and wind directions in the harbor as part of their attack preparation.'

"Ya know, thinkin' back," McGivers went on, "Freney was a big planner. He planned all his moves, like it was a chess game, while the lawmen was playin' like it was checkers. Ya know? I think he even had his escape route planned when he saw his days were numbered. I rememba him tellin' me that 'ya got to be ready to hit the road on a moment's notice when the law closes in.'

"Yeah, Freney was smart. But he was somethin' more, somethin' kind of weird and scary. He liked to dress up in different disguises. Take the time me and some buddies were hangin' around the South Boston Library in Flood Square. We'd come there to look at some of those books Freney was recommendin' we read, like *The Prince, The Rise and Fall of the Roman Empire, The Odyssey, The Art of War.*

"This ol' lady wearin' thick glasses perched on her nose, a long black coat and hat, carryin' a big shoppin' bag, bumps into one of the boys.

"'Hey, sonny, don't you say excuse me?' the ole lady says.

"'I'm sorry lady, but in all due respects you bumped into me,' he says.

"She starts to walk away and then turns around and yells back in a high-pitched voice — 'Why ya motherfucka, you bumped me.'

"While we're standin' there shocked at hearin' this ol' lady swearin,' she disappears around the corner and we hear a voice none other than Freney's.

"'Next time ya don't show any manners, I'll bury ya cocksuckas alive under ya mother's porch,' he says.

"I tell ya, Freney could be really weird," McGivers exclaimed, launching into another story. "I rememba this Russian Jew. 'is name is Boris somethinorutta. He lives in Brighton, but he don't know the rules and he's dealin' drugs in Southie. We tell 'im, 'Ya don't deal in Southie unless you pay your dues to James Freney.'

"Boris just don't speakadaenglish. He just don't get it. So one day Boris is comin' out of the Beth Israel Hospital and this rabbi, ya know with this long beard and hair comin' down like ringlets ova 'is ears, he's wearin' this black hat and long black overcoat, in the middle of the summer. The rabbi comes up to Boris pulls a gun out from under 'is coat, says to Boris, 'Shalom,' and plugs 'im right between the eyes. Boris slumps to the sidewalk. The rabbi walks back into the hospital and disappears. I find out later that the friggin' rabbi is Freney.

"The thing about Freney was he wore different disguises. He was an actor playin' different roles — a quick-change artist who could change himself as quick as a blink of the eye into a pirate, general, super spy, businessman, community caretaker, or killer.

"The eerie thing was ya neva knew what he was doin. Ya neva knew where he was. Even when he was outa town, ya didn't know if he was gone. He was like a ghost. Ya couldn't see him, but ya felt he was always around… watchin'.

"The feds say Freney made more than a hundred million dollars in the drug trade. But I figure if ya add in all the millions he made in bookmakin' and loan-sharkin', he made a hellava lot more than that."

## DAN FRENEY

The elder James Freney, the union organizer who took the blows from a cops' club, had a second son, Dan. Like his brother Jim, Dan grew up in the Old Harbor housing project of Southie. He was five years younger than Jim, shorter in stature, and known to be a "good kid." He was a bright student, an altar boy at St Monica's Church, and an athlete — his favorite sport was baseball and his favorite position second base. His heroes were Red Sox second baseman Bobby Doerr and left fielder Ted Williams, and James Michael Curley, the legendary mayor of Boston. While other kids in the neighborhood read *Penthouse* and sports magazines if they read at all, Dan read *The Purple Shamrock*, Curley's biography.

He went to Boston College and studied Greek, Latin, and English literature, becoming known to teachers and students for his classroom recitations of the speeches of Demosthenes and Pericles. After BC, he went on to BC law school (considered around Boston as the Irishmen's Harvard Law) with his mind set to enter politics.

Jack Kirby was Dan Freney's early campaign manager and longtime trusted advisor. Sitting in the parlor of his Victorian home on South Boston's Telegraph Hill, I listened to Kirby narrate the story of Dan Freney.

"It was back in the early '60s when Dan decided to run for a seat in the Massachusetts State Assembly. His opponent was Mike

Hogan. Dan called him a 'grinigog.' That's an old Elizabethan term for someone who was always smiling, even though there was nothing to smile about. Underneath that petrified smile, though, he was an alley cat, clawing and scratching away at Dan.

"Hogan ran a smear campaign, always pointing out in his speeches that Dan belonged with his brother in Alcatraz. He claimed that Dan wasn't even Irish. That he was Polish or Lithuanian.

"But Hogan's negative campaign back-fired. Dan won the election by a narrow margin. He did it by going door-to-door, to church meetings, nursing homes, veterans' groups, standing on the corner, pressing the flesh, charming the ladies — always sticking to bread and butter issues like jobs, housing, welfare, rent control.

"I think the way the media covered Dan's campaign soured him permanently toward it. It was painful for Dan to talk about his brother. But every time he was interviewed, he was invariably asked something about him. 'Do you know where your brother is now? What's your relationship to him? Is it close? Do you talk to him or see him often?' He really hated some reporters, thinking they were just hacks for Hogan, spreading lies and innuendoes about his brother.

"I remember Dan talking to one reporter who was interviewing him. The question of his relationship to his brother came up. 'I don't know what my brother is doing now,' Dan said. 'I have no way of knowing. His life is his business.' When the reporter pressed him further, Dan cried out — 'Look he's my brother and I love him.'

"With me, Dan was more open about his relationship to his brother. He liked to reminisce about the old days growing up together."

"Here are some of the stories Dan told about his brother.

"Ever since Dan could remember, Jim was a rebel. What he was rebelling against, he never was sure. As a kid he was always defiant. He was stubborn. Wouldn't give an inch. When he got in trouble, he always talked back to the police. The police hated his defiance. It seemed to get under their skin. They would beat him up savagely. It seemed like the entire Boston police force had it in for Jim.

"Jim was never home much. His mother was always asking where he was. Dan couldn't answer. He didn't know. Jim was just out.

"Dan always said he thought Jim had a quicker mind than him. But Jim was restless and found school boring. His teachers were always calling home to ask why Jim had been skipping classes. Sometimes for weeks. Of course his parents thought he was at school. Once he was gone for several months. It turned out he had left town with The Ringling Brothers and Barnum & Bailey Circus. He had joined up as a roustabout — that's sort of a gofer — when the circus was in Boston.

"Jim didn't drink or smoke. He abhorred drugs. He was a physical fitness nut. He kept himself in great condition. He was concerned with impurities in the environment, telling his mother not to use Spray Flit or other insecticides around the house.

"Jim had a funny sense of humor. Like the time he brought home a pet ocelot called *Prince*. His mother was scared to go into the boys' bedroom for fear the ocelot was there. Finally, she read the riot act: 'Get that beast out of the house. Don't you know pets aren't allowed in the project?'

"'Ma, read the rules,' Jim said. 'It says dogs and cats are forbidden. Where does it say you can't have an ocelot in the house?'

"The ocelot grew up pretty fast and much to their mother's relief, Jim and Dan's dad had Jim take *Prince* to the Franklin Park Zoo where the animal could live out the rest of his life in a cage.

"Jim drifted further away from the family as he grew up. As a teenager he began dating a burlesque queen named Belle Starr at the Old Howard. Remember the Old Howard in Scollay Square? It was Boston's hot spot. The best strip joint in town, where all the sailors went on shore leave. Scollay Square was torn down in the 1960s to make way for the Government Center, Boston's first urban renewal project.

"After he finished trade school, Jim joined the Air Force. Knowing Jim, I'm sure he couldn't stand all the rules and regulations of the military. So he went AWOL. Then it seems he compounded his misfortune by falling in with some bad people. He fell to robbing banks with them, got caught, and was sent up to Alcatraz.

"When Jim got out of Alcatraz, Dan got him a job in the custodial department at the court house. But he quit a short-time after, saying he couldn't stand the job. He was bored sick.

"Dan told me he would see Jim on the holidays, like Thanksgiving and Christmas. Jim would show up usually in his jogging clothes, bringing gifts for the family.

"But you never saw the two brothers together publicly. Even at their mother's funeral at St. Monica's, Jim stayed in the shadows of the sanctuary during the ceremony. I think Jim thought it was best to keep a low profile, not wanting to hurt Dan's public image.

"Why was Dan such a good politician? I think because he had two educations. He got one education in the streets of Southie and the other in the Jesuit classes of BC. He knew the laws, knew how to make the laws, and how to apply them to meet the needs of those he favored.

"In the Assembly he was a good soldier — loyal, hardworking, and popular. He pushed the leadership's agenda, campaigned for other Democrats, and posted himself in the public limelight of most major events in Boston. There was nary a St. Patrick's Day parade where he wasn't at the head of the parade, wearing a neatly pressed dark, pin- stripped suit, shamrock in his lapel, shillelagh in his hand, marching down Broadway to the tune of *McNamara's Band*.

"The pols liked to hang out at the Golden Dome Pub across from the State House on Beacon Hill. That's where the pols schmoozed about Boston's four great passions — politics, sports, real estate, and revenge. That's where deals were cut and favors exchanged.

"There was Tom Monahan, a judge over in South Boston. Tom had an enormous ego. He was known to collect honorary degrees. He had degrees from Suffolk Law, New England Law, and how many more schools I couldn't imagine. He would hang them up on the walls of his private chambers in the court house. One day Dan's at lunch with Tom at the Golden Dome when he asks the judge if he'd like to get an honorary degree from BC law. Tom is, of course, flattered. Both of them lift their glasses to toast the future occasion. Dan smiles at Tom and delivers that old Irish proverb — 'It's better to know the judge than the law.'

"But it's with the common folk that Dan was at his best. He loved to go down to Connolly's Tavern in Andrew Square and sing along with the crowd songs like "Shall My Soul Pass Through Ireland," "Southie Is My Home Town," and his favorite "Danny Boy." He frequently checked into a bar called Wave Cottage at 6th and P streets and schmoozed with the bar tender 'Knocko' McGrath. McGrath was like a guidance councilor, dispensing advise for the forlorn as well as markers promising a job in exchange for helping Dan out in his campaigns.

"Dan's annual Christmas party in the State House offices was a much-anticipated event, providing lots of gossipy amusements until the following year's Christmas party. Everybody was invited — from assembly men, members of the executive and judicial branches, prominent business men, clergy, local celebrities, the janitor Harry 'the broom' Harrigan, who also doubled as an in-house bookie on Beacon Hill, and the State House mailman Johnny McBride.

"Oh, I'll always remember ol' Johnny McBride. Every Christmas, Dan would present Johnny with a Christmas-wrapped bottle of Jameson Irish whiskey. And every year Johnny would accept the bottle, fondling it and holding it out like he was the proud father of a newborn baby. His eyes would be closed and you could just see dancing through his mind the savory thoughts of those first sips. Then he would nod his head in a knowing way, the nod seeming to summarize the fate of the whole Irish race and say — 'Ya know? I think God invented whiskey to keep the Irish from takin' over the world.'

"Dan's favorite story — he would tell it to any audience at any social gathering — went like this:

"'Do you people know of Katie Fox? She lives over on Logan Way. Well, one day I'm over at the Hibernian Club and I ask Katie if she has ever seen a leprechaun — one of those little people who are said to run about the Irish countryside doing magic.'

"'Well, I'd known a woman from County Cork who had an evil eye,' Katie said. 'If I hadn't known her myself, I'd suppose you'd be tellin' me the evil eye is just a fairy tale.'

"'Well, Katie, there are many who say it is just a fairy tale,' I said.

"'Well, that's just what Father McGonigle the priest said," Katie countered. 'So one day he came a ridin' into the village and that woman cast her eye at him and his horse fell right out from under him.'

"'Did Father McGonigle ever ride a horse again?' I asked.

"'Oh, only ignorant people think a curse lasts forever,' Katie replied. 'That's just a superstition. If you take a scrap of a witch's clothin,' boil it and drink the water, the curse is gone.'

"Dan's rise to Head of the Massachusetts Assembly was quite rapid and unexpected. Ed "Duke" Donahue was the Head of the Assembly. The "Iron Duke" had held the position for a decade. But the Duke began to lose his grip on the position. They say an Irishman forgets everything but the grudge. Well, that was true for the Duke. The problem was Duke had so many grudges to settle that he was picking fights indiscriminately. His enemies had begun to outweigh his supporters.

"His office smelled of corruption. Each passing day brought new allegations that he was involved in shady real estate deals, kickbacks, bribes, extortion. His life style was out of control. He was known to buy a new Cadillac each year, owned a home on the Irish Riviera in Scituate, and chartered extravagant fishing parties in Massachusetts Bay. In short, he was living high-off-the-hog — all with taxpayers' money. He was a philanderer and made no attempt to hide his relationship to a high-class call girl named Lulu Kelty. He was often seen with her, riding around in her red convertible and hitting the night spots in Roxbury.

"But it was booze that ultimately did the Duke in. It all started with a fund-raising dinner for Duke at Locke-Ober restaurant. It was a $100 plate dinner with lobster Savannah (that's lobster stuffed with lobster) as the entrée. After the meal was concluded, Duke, who was getting tipsy, got up to the speaker's rostrum, cigar in one hand, brandy glass in the other, and started telling jokes.

"'People ask me if I ever worry,' he said. 'Well, I tell them I never worry as long as I get up in the morning and don't find my name in the death notices of the newspaper.'

"'The other day I was asked if I were on my death bed would I renounce the devil. Certainly not! I answered. This is not the time to make new enemies.'

"'Seriously, though,' his words slurred out, 'I want to thank all of you — judges, legislators, friends, and all you other suckers who have donated $100 this evening.'

"Then as Duke, dropping his cigar and brandy glass, slumped drunkenly to the floor, he belched and cried out — 'Thank God, now I'll never have to be on welfare.'

"The final chapter of Duke's fall took place one summer night on Nantasket Beach in Hull. Duke and Lulu had driven down to Nantasket to get away from Boston's stifling heat wave. Duke, drunk as usual, decided to go skinny-dipping in the ocean. The MDC police see this guy running nude on this public beach, singing some ditty — 'I don't want to be a millionaire. I just want to live like one' — and arrested him.

"When the police went to book the Duke, they found out who he was. The desk sergeant then called somebody on Beacon Hill who got back shortly to the sergeant, directing the police to let Duke go on his own cognizance when he sobered up.

"The party leadership had had enough. If the press had found out about this incident, the Democrats would become the laughingstock of Beacon Hill. So Duke Donahue was quietly shipped off to the detoxification center (They called it the Irish pol's country club) on Long Island in Boston Harbor to dry out. The search for Duke's successor was underway.

"Although there were others who ranked ahead of Dan in terms of service, Dan was selected to become head of the Assembly because he was the brightest, most loyal, and hard working Democrat on Beacon Hill. He also had the approval of the Four Horsemen. I can't say more about this except for you to know that the Four Horsemen were the liaison between the Fenian Brotherhood in Southie and the IRA and Sinn Fein in Ireland.

"Soon after he became Head of the Assembly, Dan seemed to change. When he first entered politics, Dan was the idealist, the populist who championed the poor, the elderly, the unemployed, the disenfranchised. Now, while it still appeared he was championing the little guys, in truth, he was cutting deals with the big guys — the big realtors, the big bankers, the big contractors, and the big unions. Politics for him had become more a blood sport than a public service.

"The word on Beacon Hill was 'Don't mess with Dan Freney.' Dan was a practitioner of the politics of revenge. Anyone who crossed him, anyone who defied his political agenda, anyone who attacked his reputation was certain to suffer.

"Judge Carter Nelson had his pay frozen and his staff cut for refusing to carry out an appointment that Dan had tried to secure for a friend. When judicial court clerk Ralph Edwards eliminated James Freney's job as a court house custodian from the payroll seven years after James had quit, Dan froze Edwards' pay. And I can't count the number of assembly people who failed to get key committee appointments like Ways and Means and Finance and Budgetary because somewhere along the line they failed to carry out Dan's bidding.

"But Dan giveth more than he taketh. More than anything else Dan had the reputation that 'he cares for people.' He gained this reputation by controlling patronage. In our war room in the State House, we had a list of every agency, authority, board, bureau, committee, council, court clerkship, department, division, office, and quasi-public agency in the Commonwealth. We had every field covered — business/economic development, children, consumers, community action, education, arts, employment, environment, energy, health, housing, licenses, permits, records, public safety, law enforcement, recreation, senior citizens, administration/revenue/taxes, transportation, utilities, social services — you name it. We had listed over 280 public organizations. Not only did we have virtually all of them listed, but we also knew which ones had job vacancies to fill.

"We had a great intelligence network feeding us information where job openings were. If a job vacancy occurred in the Office of Employee Relations, the Workers Compensation Litigation Unit, the Massachusetts Strategic Environtechnology Partnership, the Alcoholic Beverages Control Commission, the Victim/Witness Assistance Program, the State Racing Commission, the State Lottery

Commission, Registry of Motor Vehicles, the Massachusetts Police Accreditation Commission, the Office of Refugees and Immigrants, the Division of Public Housing and Rental Assistance — Bingo! We could fill the vacancy with our person. You can see that it wasn't surprising that South Boston had the highest percentage of public service jobs in the city and state. But in fact, our 'other welfare system' provided jobs to loyal party workers well beyond South Boston to the entire Commonwealth.

"Dan's greatest challenger to political supremacy in the state was Governor William Woodbridge. Dan detested everything Woodbridge stood for. Woodbridge was a Yankee, whose ancestors came over on the *Mayflower*. Dan's ancestors were called the 'Niggars of Europe,' who fled Ireland on famine ships like the *Jeanie*. Woodbridge was a suburban WASP. Dan was an urban Catholic. Their worlds collided. Their battles were fought in the political arena.

"In the early rounds, Dan seemed to be winning passage of our bills. But then things turned around. We started losing by close votes after thinking we had everybody in line. The Governor seemed to anticipate our strategy. He seemed to be one step ahead in knowing what we were going to do. I remember Dan thinking we had sowed up the votes to pass legislation that had buried in it a provision enabling South Boston's trash to be hauled to the incinerator in the town of Belmont, where the governor resided. Dan was salivating at the thought of having Southie's garbage passing right under that 'blueblood's nose.' But at the last minute, the provision was dropped and the bill was passed into law, leaving South Boston literally holding the trash bag.

"Dan was worried at what was happening. Why were we being outmaneuvered? It all came to a head with the Massachusetts Port Commission (MPC). The commission had five members who voted on projects undertaken by the MPC. The big issue was the budget. The governor supported spending most of the budget on expansion of Logan International Airport. Dan supported spending more for development and cleanup of Boston Harbor. Dan thought he had the votes on the commission to get his harbor budget passed. Once again, though, we were foiled. The Governor's budget was passed over ours.

"'Jack, the governor keeps beating us to the punch,' Dan said to me in an emergency meeting in his office. 'I smell a rat. There must be an informer in our ranks who's feeding them information about our operations. Find out who he is and find out fast before our organization is crippled.'

"It wasn't long before I reported back to Dan. I'll always remember what happened next.

"Three of our most trusted aids — Brad Coleman, Dave Harris, and Shelby Kirk — were ushered into Dan's office. The office was dimly lit. A shaft of sunlight poured through a window on the three men, standing as if they were in a spotlight. Dan sat in his chair behind his large desk and spoke."

'We Irish have a fatal flaw. We are our own worst enemies. The devil tempts us whether for money, power, or position to spy and inform our adversaries. Our folklore bleeds with the names of informers who have sold out their brethren to the hangman and worse.

"'We loath informers.  They are the lowest of humanity. In *The Divine Comedy*, Dante wrote of the ninth circle, the innermost circle of hell, as that place for those who betray. Irish history and literature is filled with stories of in which we betray ourselves. The informer is a cancer that that lies in our Irish soul.

"'One of you standing before me is an informer. One of you is a Judas who has betrayed us. One of you is a spy — an informant for the governor, tipping him off, feeding him information about our strategies and organization.

"'One of you be brave, shed your cowardice, come forth, and confess.'

"The three men stood frozen. You could see fear in their faces. Silence.

"Then Dan lifted his finger — the finger with the Claddagh ring on it — and like the Grand Inquisitor, pointed it toward Dave Harris.

"'You, Dave Harris, are the informant. It is you who has betrayed us.'

"'No, no, Dan, it wasn't me,' cried Harris. 'I wouldn't rat on you. I owe everything I have to you — my job, my home, my family.'

"'You're lying,' Dan said, staring coldly at Harris. 'We know it is you. We had your phones tapped. You were the only one who had made phone calls to the governor's office and to his residence in Belmont.'

"'Oh, oh, alright. Maybe I made a few calls to them,' Harris stammered. 'But it wasn't anything really important. That's the truth. Give me another chance, Dan. Please. I'll make it up to you. I know. I can spy on them. They'll never know it. For God's sake! Have mercy.'

"'It's too late, Dave,' Dan said. 'You've made your bed and slept in it. You are banished from this office. I don't ever want to see you again — either in the State House or in Southie.'"

Jack Kirby relit his pipe and resumed his narrative: "They say there were three extraordinary periods in Boston's history — the Revolutionary War, the abolitionist time before the Civil War, and busing.

"South Boston became, not just in Massachusetts but nationally, the symbol of resistance to busing. The media characterized South Boston as the 'barbarous outpost of racial bias, 'the home of hate,' and branded Dan, as Southie's leader and the voice of anti-busing, a racist, bigot, and reactionary.

"The truth was that busing represented the state and federal government's fight for the power of the lawmaker to regulate society. Dan fought for the rights of parents to supervise the care and education of their children. The issue of busing was a microcosm of the classic clash of positive versus natural law, a clash as ancient as Antigone and as modern as Mandela.

"School segregation had been found unlawful by the U.S. Supreme Court in the landmark case of Brown v. the Board of Education, Topeka, Kansas. In 1974, a federal court ordered the busing of black students from Roxbury to South Boston High and white students from South Boston to Roxbury in order to achieve racial balance in the city's segregated public schools.

"Southie turned defiant. 'What right does the federal government have to supervise the education of our children? What right does the federal government have to tell us how to run our affairs?'

"Banners went up all over the town, graffiti was scrawled on buildings — 'Stop Enforced Busing,' Stick To Your Guns, Southie,' 'Don't Tread On Me,' and 'ROAR, Restore Our Alienated Rights.' An American flag was hung up on the Muni building, with a poster underneath. It read 'George Wallace for President.'

"Dan was an implacable foe of forced busing. But he was not a segregationist. At anti-busing rallies held throughout Southie, Dan would argue that busing is not an answer to desegregation."

"'Even if busing could rescue black children from schools they didn't want to attend. Wouldn't it also drive the white children of the poor into schools they did not want to attend? And wouldn't it do so on the basis of their skin color?' he asked, rhetorically.

"'Yes, moving children to a safer area makes sense. But does busing children from a safe community like Southie into a high-crime area make sense? Does it make sense to break down our old neighborhoods whose schools our people have attended for generations?

"'No, busing is not the answer to desegregation. Busing will bring danger to our children and to our cultural identity. It will bring nothing to Southie but misery.'

"I think what Dan really hated the most about busing was the hypocrisy of the governor and those white liberals in the suburbs like Belmont, Wellesley, and Winchester, who preached integration in the schools. But, God forbid! Not in their schools.

"To enforce busing, the federal government put Judge Edmund Garth in charge. People in Southie called him 'Garth Vadar.' And they sent in 1400 policemen for school duty, 100 federal marshals, 50 FBI agents, and 600 National Guard reserves. Southie was a war zone ready to explode.

"It did, on St Patrick's Day, 1975. The authorities figured that all the drinking and celebrating going on would erupt into anti-busing violence. Rumors had it that Dan's brother James was passing out guns to the South Boston marshals, a group of vigilantes who were getting everyone ready to protect the town. And the police warned that snipers organized by James Freney would be on rooftops overlooking the streets.

"Hundreds of National Guard troops, state troopers, and riot police, wearing combat gear and carrying shields and clubs as well as rifles assembled at the Fargo building, an old US Navy structure on South Boston's waterfront. Under the glare of the lights of local and national television, they marched toward Broadway, the route of the St. Patrick's Day parade.

"There were so many mounted police, TPFs, state troopers, and National Guardsmen on the side lines of the parade that spectators couldn't see the step dancers, the people on the floats dressed up as St. Patrick, chasing the snakes out of Ireland, or the posters with the faces of Irish martyrs from the 1916 rebellion and slogans of 'England Get Out of Ireland.' Suddenly, above the sounds of the bugles and bagpipes, there was an explosion. They think somebody had thrown a Molotov cocktail. All hell broke lose. Pandemonium. People, yelling and screaming, scattered in all directions. The mounted police, flailing their clubs, waded into the crowd. Above the noise, you could hear voices chanting *'Fight the Power, Fight the Power, Fight the Power!'*

"Later in the day, after the parade was suspended and order was restored, crowds milled about various public places in Southie, talking about the day's events, becoming more infuriated with the police tactics that had ruined their St. Paddy's Day parade.

"Dan was in Thomas Park on Dorchester Heights, standing next to the statue of George Washington, giving a St. Patrick's Day speech, when police commissioner Robert DiNunzio and a unit of TPF officers approached the crowd."

"'I'd appreciate Assemblyman Freney, if you would cooperate with us and ask your people to go home,' the commissioner said. 'I think it's about time you people start obeying the law.'

"'Look it, commissioner, you don't have to use force, swinging clubs like you're the Gestapo to make your point,' Dan said.

"'Freney, if you had any guts, you'd tell your people to get their kids back into school. My men's job is to enforce the law,' DiNunzio retorted.

"'Sed quis custodiet ipsos custodies?' Dan queried.

"'What's that suppose to mean?' DiNunzio asked.

"'It's Latin for 'Who will watch the watchers,' Dan answered. 'You're a disgrace to this city and to your uniform.'

"'You've got a big mouth, Freney. 'Why don't you learn to keep it shut?' DiNunzio shouted back.

"'Why don't you go fuck yourself?' Dan parried.

"'I've had enough, Freney,' DiNunzio said, shaking with rage. 'Get your God damned hooligans off the streets.'

"'I'll tell them to leave if you get your storm troopers out of here. That's a promise and I keep my promises,' Dan said.

"Dan turned to the crowd and told them to go home. As the crowd dispersed from the park, you could hear them yelling — 'We'll be back.'

"Dan never said anything about the role that his brother played in busing. Most people assumed James was against busing like his brother. As I said before, there were rumors going around Southie that James was organizing armed resistance in Southie. Contrary to popular theories, this couldn't be further from the truth, according to inside dopesters in Southie.

"The fact is that James Freney was instrumental in keeping the hooligans from joining irate parents in the streets. He knew that such a volatile combination would bring more police, which would jeopardize his control of South Boston. James also had a financial stake in keeping the peace. He feared the prospect of a protracted presence of law enforcement in South Boston and the heat it would generate. The word from James Freney to anyone who was thinking about stirring up any anti-busing trouble was 'Knock it off.'

"Dan was a battler and a believer. He said that he would leave paradise to go and fight if the cause were right. As an Irishman he never thought of backing down on the busing issue because 'backing down is even worse than losing.'

"Fifteen years after the troops and police entered South Boston to enforce the order of Judge Garth, forced busing came to an end. The U.S. Supreme Court upheld a California referendum, making it clear that no federal law empowered a court to order busing to achieve racial balance.

"Dan was vindicated. But he was sad, too, for the price of the racial imbalance law was high. Six years after Judge Garth's decision to enforce busing, some 80,000 people had left Boston. Dorchester lost 24,000 people. South Boston lost 8,000. The city's neighborhoods were weakened, many of them destroyed. Segregation in the city was much worse than before.

"I remember entering Dan's office once. He was sitting at his desk, gazing out the window, singing softly an old Irish song.
*Oh, the strangers came and tried to teach us their way.*
*They scorned us just for being what we are.*
*But they might as well go chasing after moonbeams,*
*Or light a penny candle from a star...*

Kirby asked me whether I wanted any beverage — a glass of wine, beer, something non-alcoholic, coffee, tea. "No thanks," I said. "I'm quite comfortable." He resumed his story.

"You've heard of the Big Dig, of course. But I bet you never heard about Dan's role in getting the Big Dig off the ground.

"The Big Dig, officially called the Central Artery/Tunnel Project, is the largest public works project ever undertaken in this country. It's like triple bypass heart surgery, cutting the heart of Boston open and unclogging the city's blocked arteries. The project called for tearing down the old elevated highway over downtown Boston and constructing a third tunnel, the Ted Williams Tunnel, named after the Red Sox slugger, running from South Boston to Logan International Airport.

"Nearly 43 miles of underground super highway are being constructed — over 160 lane miles of super highway in tunnels, bridges, viaducts, and surface roads. The southernmost tip runs from Roxbury and South Boston to the northernmost tip of Charlestown, the North End, and East Boston. By the end of 2004, the Big Dig will have cost nearly $15 billion and it's still at least two years away from completion.

"In constructing the tunnels under Boston Harbor, one of the biggest problems the engineers faced was where to dump the muck that lay on the harbor floor. They call the muck 'the black mayonnaise' because it consists of five feet of polluted sediment filled with gunk and heavy metal — the pollution of five centuries of ship traffic soaked with oil and grease — contaminating the harbor, making it what engineers called the 'poison pit of death.'

"At first, Dan opposed the Big Dig, although the feds were going to foot ninety percent of the costs. Dan saw the project as another step toward the destruction of South Boston — building more roads and bridges, uprooting neighborhoods, destroying homes, schools, and playgrounds and breaking down the barriers that Southie had erected to keep it separated from the rest of the city.

"But when we figured out the economics of the project, Dan realized the Big Dig could be a big bonanza. But we had to get a majority vote in the assembly to approve the project. That meant we had to get our Italian colleagues to vote for it. We set up a meeting with Assemblyman Manny Costa at Joe Tecce's restaurant in the North End.

"'Hey, Dan, it's good of you to come over here to the North End so we can show you a little Italian hospitality,' Costa welcomed us, exchanging greetings and introductions to staff members.

"'Yes, Manny, it's nice to get together again. We haven't had the opportunity for a relaxed, informal chat in quite a while,' Dan said.

"'Waiter, please bring us a couple of bottles of Chianti,' Costa ordered. 'Gentlemen, I recommend the veal scallopini. It's excellent here. But all the pastas are good, too.'

"After we finished our meal, we sipped espressos and discussed the Patriots, Red Sox, Celtics, and Bruins, the runway expansion of Logan and real estate development along the waterfront. Then Dan got down to business.

'Manny, I'd like to talk to you about the Central Artery/ Tunnel Project,' he said. 'It's called the Surface Transportation and Uniform Relocation Assistance Act in Washington. It promises to be the biggest public works project in the history of this nation. Bigger in scale than the Panama Canal or the Hoover Dam. It's going to mean jobs, Manny, 5,000 jobs for the city and state.'

"'Tip O'Neil is sponsoring the bill on Capitol Hill. But he needs our support in the state. He needs us to get the bill approved in the Assembly if he's to get the legislation passed in Congress.

"'Tip needs our help because Reagan opposes it. He doesn't want to give us Commies in Massachusetts anything. The president says that if the legislation is passed it will be the biggest pile of lard he's seen since he handed out blue ribbons at the Iowa State Fair.'

"'Dan, I understand that there will be jobs for the city and the state, but what's in it for me and for my people?' Costa asked.

"'This is how I see it, Manny. 'First, we divide up the city. You get the North End, East Boston, Revere, Chelsea, Everett, the usual. I get South Boston, Roxbury, Dorchester, Charlestown. You know, we divide the area along our old ethnic lines.

"'You award contracts in your area. I award them in mine. Take for example, muck. There's this muck on the floor of Boston Harbor. They call it 'black mayonnaise.' The stuff is contaminated so they have to treat it. Then they have to dump it somewhere. Where? In your district, they want to take the treated material and fill in the mudflats around Governor's Island to expand the runways of Logan. Don't worry, the landfill material is safe. The MBPC has assured me the land fill around Governor's will remain safe there until *the Second Coming*.

"'In my district, they're planning on taking dirt from the Ted Williams tunnel and downtown Boston and barging it to an old dump on Spectacle Island. I'm told they're going to use nearly four million cubic yards of dirt to cover the island's dump sixty feet high and top it with six feet of clay, making it into a nice recreational island.

"'If we gain a majority in the Assembly for the project, it will give the green light to pass the legislation in Congress. Think of it, Manny. All those trucking and barge contracts to hand out.

"'There's more, Manny. Much more. The approaches to East Boston and Logan and in South Boston to the tunnel are designed to be roofed or decked over. If the approaches had remained open, then the government would have to compensate the property owners for air, ground, and sub-surface rights. By decking them over, constructing the approaches underground, the property can be returned to its original owners for open space to develop hotels, office towers, convention centers, and retail stores.

"'All this development will bring in plenty of local taxes. It'll increase Boston's business districts by 1000 acres of seaport, all valuable waterfront property, while the highway passes under the ground — out of way and out of sight.

"'Manny, I'm not finished yet. Here's where we can really control things. To do anything on the project, you need a permit — either from the state, the feds, or both. You supply steel to the project, you need a permit. You clean the streets on the project, you need a permit. You serve coffee and donuts on the project, you need a permit. They're setting up a 'critical issues list' for everything that needs a permit. If you're not on that list, you can't get a permit.

"'Manny, imagine the leverage we'll have in determining who gets on that critical issues list. Imagine the power, the votes, the contracts we can award if the country funds this project.'

"'It sounds great, Dan. You can count me and the Italian contingent in,' Costa said, holding up his glass of Chianti to make a toast.

'Salute!'

'Slainte!' Dan rejoined in his good old Irish brogue."

Kirby got up from his chair and stretched. Then he sat down again, looked at me with a twinkle in his eyes and said,

"Rats."

"What about rats?" I asked, taken back by his abrupt change of subject.

"Do you remember the great rat scare in Boston? It started in 1987. City officials were telling the public that construction from the Big Dig was dislodging millions of rats from deep under the city. Stories of rats swimming up pipes and through toilets and into homes were spreading like wildfire. Rats were falling from the ceilings, leaping out of garbage cans, running up people's trousers. One Boston resident reported she had been bitten by a rat while sitting on her toilet. Rodent Control was claiming the rat population was higher than two rats per citizen in Boston."

## RATS EAT BOSTON

"'Rats Eat Boston,' screamed one tabloid, triggering a media feeding frenzy headlining stories about millions of rats with gnashing teeth, shining, yellow eyes ascending from the underground. The rat scare drew attention of the national media. CBS-TV, *Time* magazine, and *The Wall Street Journal* reported on Boston's rat population. It was a field day for the local media:

"This is Janet King at WBZT-TV. Today we are continuing our coverage of the Boston rat scare. We'll be taking an in-depth look at this scare. Just how real is the rat scare? Are rats really dangerous? Should Bostonians be frightened? What is the city doing to exterminate the rats? These are some of the questions will be asking today. To start off our program, we have in our studio the noted ratologist Dr. Hans Skinner.

"Doctor Skinner, welcome to WBZT-TV. We're glad you could join us today."

"It's a pleasure to be here. It's nice of you to have me, Janet."

"Doctor Skinner, could you first start off by giving us some background about rats?"

"Certainly, Janet. Let me tell you, rats are amazing creatures. They are impressive physical specimens. They can climb up a brick wall and fall off a five-story building and land on their feet. They can jump three feet in the air, burrow underground, walk high wires, and gnaw through steel and concrete. Because they have collapsible skeletons, adult rats can squeeze through a hole the size of a quarter. They can bite with the force of a shark. They're vicious if cornered. I've even heard of cases where adult rats have attacked human babies.

'If you think that's amazing, Janet, let me tell you about their sex life. A female rat averages twenty-two sex acts a day. She can give birth to baby rats every three weeks, with six to twelve baby rats in a litter and get pregnant forty-eight hours after giving birth. A single pair of rats has the potential to produce 359 million heirs in three years.

"Rats carry germs and disease. That's why we use the expression 'dirty rats,' Janet. They urinate eighty times a day and defecate up to fifty times. They carry salmonella, trichinosis, and many other food-borne diseases. A rat bite can give you chills, fever, vomiting, aches and pains. It's like a bad case of flu.

"Rats carry the bubonic plague. You can recognize the symptoms. Egg-size, pus-oozing tumors break out under the armpits and on the groin. Your skin becomes mottled with blue-black splotches. What usually follows is a slow agonizing death.

"There have been no serious outbreaks of bubonic plague in the U.S. since 1924. It was reported that a woman in Cambridge was diagnosed as having bubonic plague symptoms, but I never heard anything more about this case. But we must remain vigilant, Janet. You never know when the bubonic plague can strike again.

"History teaches us that rats are terrorists. Rats have killed more humans than all the world's wars combined. The three great epidemics of bubonic plague killed 150 million people worldwide."

"Wow. Thank you, Doctor Skinner for your informative and insightful analysis of rats."

"It was a pleasure to be here, Janet. Thank you for having me."

"Now for a report on public reaction to the rat scare we go to our reporter in the field Allen Weaver. Allen, can you hear me?"

"Yes, Janet, I can hear you. I'm standing under the elevated subway tracks at North Station talking to Bill about the rat scare. Bill, can you tell us what's your experience with rats?"

"See that alley between those two buildings over there? That use to be my sleepin' quarters. I could bed down in that corner off the alley. Go to sleep peacefully. Every night I would fall asleep with the trains runnin' overhead. Their rumblin' sound was like a lullaby rockin' me to sleep. Nobody bothered me. Then a couple of weeks ago somebody puts a dumpster in my corner. I think it was that restaurant over there. The next thing I know is that rats are crawlin' all over the place. I'm sleepin' one night and I hear lots of scurryin' around. I knowed it was rats. Sure enough, when I woke up in the mornin' I saw a few bones remainin' of a chicken. The rat ate that whole chicken. I can't sleep there any more. I don't want to be eaten by no rats."

"Thank you, Bill, for sharing your experience with us. Now back to you, Janet.

"Thank you, Allen, for your on-the-spot coverage of the rat scare. Now let's go to Lisa Klein at Rodent Control Center. Lisa, can you hear me?"

"Yes, Janet, I can hear you. I'm here at Rodent Control Center talking with Donald Rathbane, chief rat exterminator of the city of Boston. Mr. Rathbane, can you tell me how your agency is dealing with the rat problem?"

"First, let me tell you a little about rats. Rats are smart. They have good memories and good eyes and the ability to solve problems. But rats are evil. They've got these sharp yellow teeth and yellow shining eyes. They lie in wait, then swarm all over their prey, lunging at the throat, burrowing into the eye sockets, gnawing on lips and cheeks, ripping off clumps of flesh, picking bones clean, squealing, scratching, and slobbering in a blood orgy. They're vicious. I've known them to attack human babies.

"We lay traps to catch rats. The traps' jaws are powerful enough to break a man's fingers. The traps break the rats' backs and necks. They mangle them. I watch their pinched little faces wincing in agonizing death. I've seen traps where all that remains is a leg, a shoulder, a mush of flesh, the rest of the rat having been eaten by other rats.

"Rats are cunning, more cunning than men. Your big rats, the dominant rats, never fall for that old peanut-butter bait. More often than not we find the little juvenile rats in the traps. The big rats are still on the loose. The big rats run the show. I've seen them bite off the legs of the little rats, making them harmless and subordinate. The big rats often use their subordinates to scout out a potentially dangerous environment or act as 'tasters' of suspicious food items. To catch a rat you got to think like a rat. But you'll never catch them all. There will always be some king rat that can outsmart you and get away."

"Thank you, Mr. Rathbane. Now back to you, Janet."

"Thank you, Lisa, for your report. I think we have a better idea now of what the city is doing in its war against rats. For up-to-date coverage of Boston's rat crisis turn to Channel 1 — WBZT-TV."

"By 1990, the rat scare had turned into a panic," Kirby went on. "The public was screaming for the state to take some action. Dan called for hearings on Beacon Hill to find someone who could help us combat the crisis. That person was Dr. Harris Bannister, a world renowned 'ratologist.'

"'Gentlemen and women of the Massachusetts Assembly,' Dr. Bannister began, 'it is not the Big Dig that's causing your rat population to grow. It's garbage. You've got to reduce the amount of garbage that rats can find. Garbage is their food source. If you eliminate their food source and habitat, you will reduce or eliminate their population.

"'You begin with surveillance. You got to have intelligence about the rat population. If you watch a rat for a couple of nights, you will find out where it lives, where its colony lives, and where these rats feed. Traditionally, rodent control called for 'see one, kill one.' A complaint comes in. A technician races to the scene and lays a trap. *Snap!* End of story.

"'My approach to the problem is much more systematic. I call it integrated pest control, or IPM. IPM's main principle is to create an environment that is hostile to rats. The main task is to coordinate all departments affecting garbage and trash disposal. The key is to improve sanitation and decrease the rats' food supply. The city should initiate a site cleanliness ordinance with stepped up inspections and increased penalties for sloppy commercial trash disposal.

"'Let me emphasize my point: You have to coordinate all departments. For example, rats love low-lying shrubbery. So you have to coordinate with the parks department to minimize this type of flora. If parking restrictions aren't strictly enforced, then trash removal is hindered. So you have to get the traffic control department in on the act.

"'Boston's a wonderful place to be a rat. You are a waterfront city. You have an active night life. There are lots of bars and restaurants generating trash and garbage. But I believe if you apply the IPM plan, you will have established the necessary coalition to combat rat terrorism.'"

"While IPM was taking effect, the complaints about rats overrunning the city kept coming in, particularly from South Boston, East Boston, the North End, and other communities bordering Boston Harbor," Kirby continued. "What made matters worse was that the rodent control exterminator for Boston Harbor was in jail, serving time on a cocaine charge. No one was killing the rats that were in Boston Harbor. Nor did we know anyone who would want that job."

"But I had an idea," Kirby said.

"'Dan, may I make a suggestion?' I asked gently, knowing the sensitivity my suggestion may imply. 'Why don't you talk to your brother? He knows the harbor. Maybe he knows someone who would take the job.'

"So Dan called his brother and Jim told him that there was someone who might be interested in taking the job. His name was Captain Bill McGinty, the operator of the Harbor Tow and Salvage Company.

"We met Captain McGinty at our state house office."

"'Sit down, Captain. Make yourself comfortable,' Dan said, ushering McGinty into the office. 'I've heard you may be interested in a contract to exterminate rats in Boston Harbor.'

"'Aye aye, Mr. Assemblyman!' McGinty responded. 'You might say I'm the 'Pied Piper' of Boston Harbor. I know where the rats are in the harbor. Me and my partner, Davy Guillet, we'll catch 'em.'

'OK, Captain, the contract is yours. Let's make it for $50,000. Talk to my aides to work out the details,' Dan said. 'And one thing, Captain, make sure you clean up the rats in the South Boston waterfront. Don't worry about the North End and East Boston. They're not important. Do you know what I mean?'

'Aye aye, Sir! It's as good as done.' McGinty said. 'Oh, by the way, I met your brother once. I don't know if he would remember me. He hired me and Davy to look for the pirate ship *Whydah* off Cape Cod a few years ago. I think we found it but someone had claimed it first. Too bad, 'cause I heard there was quite a treasure found there. Told 'im 'bout the U-boat that sunk in Boston Harbor back in World War II. He was interested in that, too. But we had no luck findin' it, either. Too bad. It would have fetched a good price from some naval museum or the Smithsonian.'

"I heard about the adventures, or I should say, the misadventures of Captain Bill and Davy Guillet several months later," Kirby told me. This is the story:

"'Hey, Davy, we got the contract,' Bill said. 'We're goin' to eradicate rats from Boston Harbor.'

"'Bill, we don't know nothin' 'bout killin' rats. How are we suppose to do it?'

"'Don't worry, Davy. It ain't complicated. We'll go where we know the rats are, set traps with poison bait, collect their dead carcasses, and dump 'em in the outer harbor beyond the Brewsters. We'll start with Spectacle Island. It's crawlin' with rats.'

"McGinty and Guillet landed on Spectacle Island.

"'Christ, Bill, this island's smoke is makin' my eyes water and the stench is killin' my nostrils. Let's set the traps and get the frig out of here.'

"'We'll work fast, Davy. Why don't you go down and set some traps in that ravine? See, where those seagulls are hoverin' overhead. Ya figure if ya see seagulls there's garbage and if there's garbage there's rats.

"'*A-i-i-e-ek!*' Guillet screamed from the ravine. 'Bill, come down here. There's a rotted corpse with its bones stickin' out of a body bag. There's rats all over the place, gnawin' away at what's remain' of the flesh. I'm gettin' the frig out of here. This place is spooked.'

"When McGinty and Guillet left Spectacle Island, they vowed never to come back.

"'Contract or no contract, Bill, I'm not goin' back to that island.'

"'OK, Davy, we'll stay away from Spectacle. Maybe the island is spooked. I've heard it's called the 'Isle of the Dead.' Gangland rumors say they're bodies buried here by the mob.

"'Let's try Grape Island. A garbage scow broke up off Grape in a storm a few months ago. I'm sure there's plenty of rats there.'

"'Bill, I'm not goin' to Grape. You could get friggin' shot trespassin' on that island.'

"'Come on, Davy! Who's goin' to shoot us? It's a state island. No ranger is goin' to shoot us.'

"'The rangers aren't there in the winter, Bill. I hear stories that there's a drug operation runnin' out of Grape during the winter months. Remember a guy called Captain Smith who's a drug smuggler in the bayous near New Orleans? I hear he comes north in the winter when everythin' is closed 'round here. Picks up drugs from the big ships in the harbor, ferries the stuff in little boats to Grape. Keeps it on Grape until it's safe to move them to the mainland. This guy's not goin' to think twice 'bout shootin' us if he sees us set foot on his island.'

"'Well, if you're afraid of goin' to Spectacle and Grape islands, Davy, where the frig can we go?'

"'How 'bout Deer Island. They're tearin' down the old prison on the island and puttin' up a new waste treatment plant. There's bound to be plenty of rats scurryin' around 'cause of the demolition.'

"'Naw, the rats on Deer mainly affect the Italian neighborhoods. Let's concentrate on the South Boston waterfront. There's plenty of rats we can catch in Southie. That's what Dan Freney wants.'

"Maybe it was the result of the IMP program," Kirby said. "Maybe it was the Pied Piper of Boston Harbor. At any rate, by the early 1990s, the rat population in the city had declined by ninety-five percent. Boston's rat scare was over," Kirby recounted. Then he reflected philosophically: "You know, rats were here before men. They'll be here after men. As the man said, 'We can catch a lot of rats, but they'll always be some who get away.'"

---

Two brothers. Both born and raised by the same parents, in the same housing project, and in the same neighborhood of Southie. Two brothers. So opposite in nature, yet living in the same "culture of silence" and by the same code of ethnic honor and tribal loyalty. Two brothers. Each took a different road to power: one through politics; the other through crime. One, the law-maker; the other, the law-breaker.

Two brothers. One, Lord of the Middleworld; the Prince of 'Realpolitik' — the governmental policy based on retaining power rather than pursuing ideals, who followed Machiavelli's dictum: "A *wise prince ought to adopt such a course that his citizens will always in every kind of circumstance have need of the state and of him, and then he will always find them faithful."*

The other, Lord of the Underworld, the Prince of Darkness, who followed Machiavelli's dictum: *"It is necessary for a prince wishing to hold his own to know how to do wrong and to make use of it."*

Two brothers. Each ruled his own world with his own 'mystique of power' until there came the time....

# CHAPTER XII     WORLD'S END

From the heights of World's End, you can see rocky beaches, ledges, and cliffs sloping into the sea below, Hingham Harbor melting into Boston Harbor, and beyond that the Atlantic.

As you gaze around the two hundred forty-eight acre peninsula, you can see rolling fields, tree-lined drives, patches of freshwater and saltwater marshes dominated by cattails and bulrushes and grassy fields in various stages of growth — from young meadows to plants and shrubs and finally stands of mature trees.

The peninsula, now called World's End, was once comprised of two islands — two drumlin islands formed by glacial till — separated from the mainland. But in the 17th century, Puritan settlers built the bar, a causeway connecting the furthermost island to Planters Hill, and a dam, serving to reclaim the 'Damde Meadows' (a strip of woods and a salt water marsh), connecting Rocky Neck and Pine Hill to the mainland. Thus, a peninsula was formed.

The area was continuously farmed over the next three centuries, well into the twentieth century. John Brewer purchased the land in 1855 and built a huge wood-shingled mansion and a sprawling farm that included stables, barns, a blacksmith shop, a greenhouse, a poultry house, workers' quarters, and windmills. Prize Jersey cattle grazed in the rolling pastureland. On the hillsides grew fields of hay, corn, oats, sugar beets, alfalfa, and vegetables.

In 1891, John Brewer hired Frederick Law Olmsted, the famed landscape architect who designed Central Park in New York and the "Emerald Necklace" park system in Boston, to draw up a park plan for his estate. Gravel paths lined with oak, hickory, and red cedar trees following the contour of the land were constructed, transforming World's End into a New England Elysian fields. But after the roads were built and the trees planted, the project came to a halt for "reasons unknown."

Today, this diverse landscape of manicured hedgerows bordering old fields, groves and formal tree plantings of native and exotic species lining the gravel paths provides food and shelter for a variety of wildlife, including quail, pheasant, foxes, rabbits, and migratory sea birds. World's End is a fuel stop for birds migrating from the Bay of Fundy to Delaware Bay and to sites further south in the winter.

The Brewer family line died out in 1936. Eventually, the cows were sold and the buildings were torn down. World's End became threatened by development as the land was no longer used for agriculture. The UN considered it as a site for its headquarters in 1945. Later, the area was proposed as a site for a World's Fair. Housing development schemes and in 1967 a nuclear power plant were also proposed. (The power plant went to Plymouth, Massachusetts instead.) In the face of mounting development, the trustees of the estate bought the property from descendants of the Brewer family, preserving the bucolic character of the land.

Few people now remember how or when World's End got its name. Perhaps, it was inspired by the area's graceful topography that juts out then melts into the sea. But there is another account.

The Bible begins with the creation of the world, before time itself began. The Book of Revelation prophesied the Apocalypse — the vision of the end time when wars, plagues, famines, and earthquakes would shake the world. Then, after a final cosmic battle between Christ and Satan at Armageddon, Christ would establish a millennial kingdom on earth for the Just and pass judgment for all the living and all the dead. For all the Just, there would be a heavenly Jerusalem — a new heaven and a new earth.

It is told that two early settlers in this area, true believers in the Puritan religion that preached their theocratic colony was the

New Jerusalem, called this place World's End. The End of the World. The End of Time. The Place of Last Judgment.

**FRENEY'S DISCOVERY**

Freney first discovered World's End while cruising on *The Phantom Pirate* around the islands in Hingham Harbor. Anchoring his boat off a crescent-shaped pebbled beach that settles between two sloping hills, he paddled his inflatable rubber lifeboat to shore. Looking about, he saw a narrow causeway separating the harbor from the Weir River on the other side of World's End. As his eyes followed the landscape from left to right, he could make out what looked to be tree-lined carriage paths looping around the low hills.

Soon after his discovery, Freney found that he could drive to World's End. It took only fifteen minutes by car from Annie Jones' condo in Quincy to the reservation. Freney liked to come to World's End to jog, usually early in the morning when the world was pristine and still. He would park his car at Martin's Cove, where he would see the clamdiggers, silent and motionless in their work. From Martin's Cove, he jogged around the shoreline, over tree-lined paths and Planter's and Pine Hills down across the bar around Rocky Neck and down through Damde Meadows.

In recent weeks, though, as Freney jogged around World's End, something was troubling him. He felt a premonition, a feeling he hadn't had for years, that all was not well. He feared he might be on the verge of losing control of things.

It had been five years now since Bill O'Donnell retired from the FBI in 1990. O'Donnell got the opportunity to take early retirement for his role in taking down the Italian Mafia in Boston, for putting Mafia bosses Lou Farnese, the Massaroni brothers, and Sammy Salerno behind bars. O'Donnell would have been nowhere without the information that he and Conti had provided, Freney thought to himself.

O'Donnell, meanwhile, had taken a six-figure job with Boston Utilities. Within the city's boardrooms, it was accepted wisdom that Boston Utilities hired O'Donnell because of the company president's longtime friendship with his brother, assemblyman head Dan Freney, the most feared politician in the state and the pre-eminent power in the region's Irish-American elite. As a regulated utility, Boston Utilities' fortunes rose and fell on the decisions of state officials.

With O'Donnell retired and out of the loop, Freney felt disconnected and out of touch with the FBI. He was lacking the intelligence that gave him his sixth sense — the intuition he always had relied upon in his decision-making. Freney thought this was how Robert E. Lee must have felt at Gettysburg when Jeb Stuart, his trusted cavalry general, was off riding around northern Virginia chasing Yankees, instead of providing him with the "eyes and ears" on Union troop movements around Gettysburg.

O'Donnell had not only kept other law enforcement agencies off Freney's back, but the agent had provided him with inside information on FBI operations — operations that directly affected Freney. In effect, with O'Donnell gone, Freney had lost his early warning system.

Gordon Smith, a private detective in Boston, once told me a story that illustrated Freney's situation after O'Donnell retired.

"Do you remember the Gardner Museum theft? It took place in the wee hours of March 17, 1990 as St. Patrick's Day came to a close. Two men, disguised as Boston police officers, saying they were responding to a call about a disturbance within the museum, talked their way into the Isabella Stewart Gardner Museum, handcuffed and bound the two guards with duct tape, disarmed the alarm system, and looted the museum of art valued at $300 million. Among the art stolen were five works by Degas, *The Concert* by 17th century Dutch master Jan Vermeer, and two Rembrandts — *A Lady and Gentlemen in Black* and *The Storm on the Sea of Galilee.*

"More than thirty FBI agents were assigned to the case, but despite thousands of leads, the crime is still unsolved. Not a person has been arrested. The art is still missing. The Gardner Museum has offered a five million dollar reward for the safe recovery of all the stolen art.

"I was involved in the case for years and there was one trail I followed that really intrigued me. I found out that one of the disguised policemen was an IRA operative, known as Gypo Nolan, and the mastermind of the theft was none other than James Freney.

"Nolan was gunned down shortly after bragging to an ex-FBI agent that he had information on a major art theft. Who killed Nolan? Where are the paintings? Who's got them? Are they still in good condition? Are they still in this country? Or are they in some other country overseas? Could they be in Dublin, Ireland? Who knows? The trail came to a dead end.

"I've tried to get the cooperation of the Boston FBI to help me follow this trail. But they've never shown any interest. I now think that's typical of the FBI — not wanting to share information, wanting to keep things to themselves. With O'Donnell gone and no contact inside the FBI, I suspect that Freney also had no idea what the FBI was up to. Whether or not they were still even involved in the case. And if they were, God knows, were they following *his* trail? Freney was like a phantom in the shadows, unseen but also increasingly isolated. He couldn't see the dangers surrounding him."

## ESCAPE, JANUARY 1995

As he jogged over the path on World's End that loops around Rocky Neck and the Ice Pond one morning in January 1995, Freney's premonition that something was going to happen, something bad, seemed to be unusually intense. The melting snow and the unseasonably balmy air from the January thaw had an unnerving effect on him. He got spooked when he saw an owl on a branch of an oak tree, watching him — an omen of bad things to come?

This time, it was more than the communications blackout on the FBI's investigation of the Gardner Museum theft that was bothering him. There were rumors circulating that a Grand Jury was seeking indictments of him and Conti. In the past, he could forget about these rumors. Even if they were true, he could count on O'Donnell tipping them off and intervening on their behalf. That was no longer possible. O'Donnell was gone — retired from the FBI.

When Freney jogged back to Martin's Cove, he got back into his car and turned on the radio:

*We interrupt this program with this news bulletin: Acting on Grand Jury indictments of Winter Hill gangsters James Freney and Robert Conti, law enforcement officers have just arrested Conti at a condominium on Commonwealth Avenue in Boston. According to law enforcement officials, Conti surrendered without resistance at the condominium believed to be owned by his girl friend, Barbara Bennett. Freney is still at large. He is armed and considered extremely dangerous, officials say.*

Freney hurriedly drove to a gas station in Hingham Harbor and called Annie Jones on a pay phone. "Annie, listen carefully. Get out of the house now. Don't take nothin', no bags. Do ya hear me? Nothin'. Just what you're wearin' and your winter coat and your handbag. Take a taxi to Chinatown. Meet me at the House of Roy at noon. Make sure no one is trailin' ya. And, Annie, don't call anybody. Just get out of that house."

## PRE-TRIAL HEARINGS, 1998

Reporter Michael Howard covered the hearings for *The Boston Monitor*. This was his account of the proceedings:

The hearings on racketeering and extortion indictments against James Freney and Robert Conti began in May of 1998. Judge Joshua Lyons presided over the hearings, which were held in the federal court building on the South Boston waterfront. Anthony Antonelli was the defense lawyer for Conti. Frederick Cusack and Stanley Pendleton were the government's lawyers.

James Freney was in absentiam — a fugitive from justice.

The government lawyers laid out the charges against Freney and Conti. They described their racketeering and illegal gambling empire, their race fixing, loan sharking, extortion, and money laundering. Then after several weeks of testimony, Conti, who was serving time in prison since his arrest, took the stand.

*Cusack:* For several weeks, we have heard the charges against you and James Freney — charges of racketeering, illegal gambling, loan sharking, extortion, and money-laundering activities that you and Mr. Freney carried out over the course of twenty-five years in Boston, the state of Massachusetts, and throughout New England. Do you deny these charges?

*Conti:* I don't deny these charges. But you gotta understand, there were extenuatin' circumstances.

*Cusack:* What do you mean extenuating circumstances?

*Conti:* I mean we had permission to do these things.

*Cusack:* Permission? Who gave you permission?

*Conti:* The FBI.

*A collective gasp swelled up and crashed like a wave through the courtroom.*

Yeah! Ya see me and my partner Jim Freney had an agreement with the FBI. Kind of you'd call "a gentlemen's agreement." We were TEs....

*Cusack:* Excuse me, Mr. Conti. What's a TE?

*Conti:* Oh, that's a top echelon informer. Ya see, like I said, we had this agreement with the FBI to pass on information to Bill O'Donnell at the FBI's Boston bureau about La Cosa Nostra. In return for our givin' them this information, they promised us "protection" against gettin' prosecuted for anythin' illegal we may have done.

*Cusack:* Tell me, Mr. Conti. Didn't you know that Mr. O'Donnell was breaking the law in his relationship to you?

*Conti:* As far as we was concerned, everythin' was legal. I believe me and Freney was performin' a service as informers for the United States government. We helped the FBI to destroy La Cosa Nostra in Boston. I believe what ever we were doin,' we were doin' it in the interest of the United States government.

*Cusack:* Mr. Conti. Do you think it was in the interest of the United States government to control the flow of drugs to South Boston? Is that what you think, Mr. Conti? I think you had a good deal going. You were committing crimes at will, putting money in your pockets, and, in your view being protected from prosecution.

*Conti:* You're forgettin' one thing, Mr. Cusack. LCN was taken down. That was the FBI's goal. They were satisfied with that. We fulfilled our part of the bargain.

*Cusack:* Do you think, Mr.Conti, that you and Mr. Freney single-handedly took La Cosa Nostra down?

*Conti:* Well, I'll tell ya somethin', Mr. Cusack. We did a hellava job.

*Cusack:* That's what you think?

*Conti:* I think we did. The FBI thought we did.

*Cusack:* And when the FBI did that, you and Mr. Freney were top dogs, weren't you? That was really your goal — to gain control of criminal activities in Boston. Isn't that true, Mr. Conte?

*Conti:* We had a partnership with the FBI. Our goals was the same as their goals. I would say the partnership worked out pretty good.

The news of Conti's testimony sent shock waves across the city and state. My paper's morning edition flashed the headline across the front page:

*FBI AND BOSTON IRISH GANGSTERS*
*IN SECRET DEAL TO BRING DOWN ITALIAN MAFIA*

All hell broke loose in the court building that next day. Lou Farnese was in the court's holding cell waiting to testify. Farnese was serving time in Walpole, along with other Mafia bosses who were brought down by the FBI. When he heard that Conti, his longtime friend, was an informant for the FBI, Farnese went berserk.

Farnese lunged at Conti, who was also in the holding cell waiting to go on the stand again. With both hands around Conti's throat trying to choke him, Farnese screamed:

"You fuckin' rat. You've fucked me good. You've fucked everyone around you. You scumbag. I'll get out of prison someday and I'll get ya, ya fuckin' bastard."

The US marshals grabbed Farnese, pulling him away from Conti and wrestling him to the floor. It was the last time the two former crime partners would ever speak to each other.

Later that day, William O'Donnell's supervisor, Walter Huff, took the stand.

*Antonelli:* Tell us, Mr. Huff, when did this unholy alliance between the FBI and Mr. Freney and Mr. Conti begin?

*Huff:* Back in the 1970s there was a lot of pressure on agents to have informants against the Mafia. Bill O'Donnell had a good track record against La Cosa Nostra when he came to Boston. Since he was from South Boston and came from the same neighborhood as James Freney, we figured he would make a good handler.

*Antonelli:* Did the FBI promise Mr. Freney and Mr. Conti immunity from prosecution?

*Huff:* I personally did not have the authority as a supervisor to confer immunity on the mobsters. Immunity is a very formal process. There's got to be actual documentation. There was none for James Freney, nor for Robert Conti.

*Antonelli:* Do you believe the FBI violated its standards, its rules and regulations, and its integrity in dealing with Mr. Freney and Mr. Conti?

*Huff:* I wouldn't say so. As far as the FBI is concerned, Mr. O'Donnell acted on his own.

*Antonelli:* Did the FBI's crusade against La Cosa Nostra justify Freney and Conti's evil? Did the FBI believe that the ends justified the means?

*Huff:* I'm not certain of that. But I can't speak for Mr. O'Donnell. As James Freney's handler, he would be in a better position to answer that question.

The following day, William O'Donnell took the stand.

*Pendleton:* Mr. O'Donnell, as James Freney's handler, did you think you violated FBI standards, rules and regulations, and integrity?

*O'Donnell:* Absolutely not. Let me explain the difficulty of handling informants. It's like a circus. If the circus is going to work you need to have a guy be there with the lions and tigers. I was the guy in the ring. My job was to get in there with the lions and tigers.

*Then O'Donnell leaned forward and pointed his finger in a gesturing manner toward Pendleton — his right index finger with a ring on it. I think it's called a Claddagh ring. And he said loudly:* Do you think I did a good job? Well, the proof is in the pudding. Look where the New England Mafia is now. It's in shambles.

In November 1998, six months after the hearing began, Judge Lyons issued his ruling. The judge threw out Conti's claim that the deal with the FBI gave him and Freney immunity from prosecution. The judge concluded that the evidence finding Conti guilty of charges of racketeering and extortion was incomplete. Conti's case should go to trial.

The findings of fact about the relationship between O'Donnell and Freney and Conti showed the FBI's deal with them was wrong. O'Donnell's case should also go to trial.

## THE TRIAL OF ROBERT CONTI, 1999

Reporter Peter Schwartz covered the trial of Robert Conti for *The Boston Tribune*. This was his account of the trial:

The trial of Robert Conti began in February 1999. Judge David Barton presided over the trial, which was held in the federal court building on the South Boston waterfront. The lead government prosecutor was Ronald Atwater. Conti's lawyer was Norman Macy. I'd say Macy was a second-rate lawyer who took the case because he needed work. None of the top lawyers in Boston, and there were many, wanted anything to do with this case. Not that lawyers don't like to defend big-name criminals. It's just marquee lawyers saw representing Conti as a losing proposition.

Added to the charges of racketeering and extortion, Conti was also charged with illegal gambling, money-laundering, and murder.

The government's main witnesses were Johnny Greco, Paul Doyle, and Garrett Neeley, all of them willing to testify against Conti. All of them plea-bargained for reduced jail sentences when they learned that Freney and Conti were FBI informants, and Freney was gone, leaving them to take the rap.

Johnny Greco, who was reputed to have killed over twenty-five men, was in prison on charges of murder. He plea-bargained to have his sentence reduced from forty to fifteen years. On the stand, Greco told the court:

"Ya, I whacked a few guys in my time. Umm, let me see if I can remember some of 'em. There was Billy Puddu and Norm Jackson. Those punks was stoolies. Oh, yeah! There was a government informant. His name was Richie Cattaneo. Owned a night club over in Revere. Freney wanted him out of the way. So I whacked 'im, too.

"Freney also ordered me to take out a guy named Phil Newton. He was a Dallas business tycoon. An oil tycoon or sumpthin.' Anyway, Newton found out that Freney and Conti were skimmin' profits off of his company. I think the company was called North American Jai Alai. I goes down to Newton's country club and pop him right in broad daylight as he was teein' off the thirteenth hole.

"Then Freney tells me I gotta whack Ralph Taggert. Taggert, who's runnin' North American in Miami, was the guy who told Newton Freney and Conti was the guys who was robbin' 'im. I told Freney Taggert was a friend of mine. Lent me money when I was on the lam livin' in Florida. But when Jimmy Freney tells ya to do somethin', ya do it. So I goes down to Miami and whack Taggert and stuff his body in the trunk of his Cadillac. Drive his car to the Miami airport and leave it in the parkin' lot there."

Paul Doyle was next on the stand. Doyle was in prison serving five years for extortion and money laundering. Doyle got his sentence reduced to two years for turning state's evidence.

"We laundered tons of money in real estate — buying restaurants, bars, liquor stores, appliance outlets, laundry mats, condos, you name it. My biggest cash cow was buying and selling condos, especially in the Back Bay. The price of condos there was skyrocketing during the Eighties and Nineties. We would buy a condo on Newbury Street for five hundred grand and sell it for a million a year later. A year later, we would buy a condo on Commonwealth Ave and the next year we'd sell it for two million. Parking lots alone with these condos were going as high as one hundred and seventy-seven grand.

"Would you believe? Buying and selling condos is not always a cup of tea. There are guys like this yuppie realtor, Brendan Leland, who you had to deal with. He was negotiating a deal with me to buy two condos. He was asking all kinds of questions, like how much light the unit gets. Whether it needed rehab. Maintenance charges. Electricity. Whatever. A pain in the butt this guy was. And a frigging neurotic.

"Somehow he heard that I had mob ties. One day he calls me up and says the deal's off. He's having nightmares about these condos. Nightmares about finding bodies hidden behind the walls. Waking up with a horse's head in his bed. You know, like what happened in the *Godfather* movie. He says in no way does he want to be owning these condos when the day came one of these guys gets out of jail.

After Paul Doyle, Garrett Neeley took the stand. As Freney's surrogate son and personal body guard, Neeley, more than any of the other gang members, felt betrayed by his boss turning out to be a FBI informant and going on the lam, leaving him to fend for himself. Once the supreme loyalist, who swore eternal allegiance to Freney, Neeley broke down and agreed to testify against his former boss and the boss' partner. Neeley, who was charged with extortion and accessory to murder, plea bargained to get his sentence reduced from fifteen to five years. As part of his plea bargain, Neeley agreed to divulge where Freney and Conti had buried some of the bodies of victims who mysteriously disappeared years ago.

"I don't know where Freney and Conti buried most of da bodies. I can tell ya where Freney dumped some of 'is bodies. Der was Dicky Hudson. Freney had me whack 'im 'cause he was holdin' back money and jewelry he owed us on the Medford bank heist he pulled off Memorial Day weekend back in 1980. Buried ol' Dicky-bird in the Squantum marshes where da marshes grow in Quincy Bay.

"We buried Susan Anderson's body in da marshes, too. Susan was Conti's stepdaughter. Conti and Freney killed her 'cause she was goin' to tell her mother, Marcia Anderson, Conti's wife, she and Conti were havin' an affair.

"I know der were a lot of the bodies buried on Spectacle Island. But you won't find any bodies der now. Der been covered ova with dirt. I personally was neva out der. But Nicky Silanus. He was an enforca. Got bumped off years ago in tryin' to rob a bank. I remomba 'im tellin' me 'bout takin' bodies out to the island and dumpin' 'em der.

"I knowed John MacAllister was dumped der. The guy was workin' for Freney runnin' guns to the IRA. When Freney found out he was rattin' on 'im, Freney whacked 'im and Freney and Silanus dumped the body on Spectacle."

Several weeks after Garett Neeley's testimony, the trial turned from a courtroom drama into a television soap opera. I called the show *All in the Family.*

In his testimony, Neeley said that Freney and Conti had several arms caches hidden in the Boston area. Neeley led state police to one of the caches. What they found in a utility shed in the backyard of the home of Conti's mother in Arlington, Massachusetts, a suburb west of Boston, was an arsenal of weapons. There were thirteen rifles, ten Israeli Uzi submachine guns, nine shotguns, twenty-six pistols, eight silencers, eighty boxes of ammunition, assorted police badges, uniforms, holsters, handcuffs, brass knuckles, knives, face masks, gas masks, and one blue police light and a bullet-proof police vest.

Neeley told the authorities that Conti's brother, Ralph Conti, a retired police officer, had moved the guns to mom's house before the police could find them. Ralph Conti found himself on the stand, defending himself against charges that he helped his brother disperse the gang's huge arsenal.

The government prosecutor, Ronald Bannister, thought that by getting Ralph Conti on the stand, by getting him to tell all about his brother's crime empire, he could deal a final blow to Robert Conti's defense. It turned out that Bannister opened up prima facie evidence about the most dysfunctional American family imaginable.

To testify against Ralph Conti, Bannister called Dustin St. John to the stand. St. John was Ralph Conti's nephew and Robert Conti's son. St. John's real name was Robert Conti, Jr. But under the Witness Protection Program, Conti, Jr. had assumed the name Justin St. John.

St. John knew a lot about James Freney and his father's gang. St. John was a chip off the old man's block. He had an underworld reputation for hiding behind his father's name. He was a con man par excellence. He grossed over two million dollars in ten years by ripping off drug dealers and hapless bookies, who always thought better of retaliating against the son of Robert Conti.

The government figured there would come a time when St. John would turn state's evidence in exchange for dropping charges against him — charges of drug dealing, arson, burglary, and assaulting a meter maid. That time had come.

*Bannister:* Mr. St. John, can you tell the court what you know about your uncle Ralph Conti's involvement in hiding guns at your grandmother's home?

*St. John:* I helped Uncle Ralph move the guns from a warehouse in South Boston to my grandmother's home. If you need evidence of Uncle Ralph's involvement, take a look at who that bullet-proof police vest was registered under — Uncle Ralph.

*Bannister:* Do you know of other activities regarding your father that your uncle was involved in?

*St. John:* Ever since my father went to prison, Uncle Ralph has managed my father's assets. My father has a lot of assets — I'd say millions of dollars — especially in real estate. I know Uncle Ralph talks a lot with Paul Doyle about real estate in the Back Bay. Uncle Ralph approves all the deals Doyle makes for my father. I also know that Uncle Ralph picks up money from bookies that owe my father.

*Bannister:* Could you tell us about your relationship to your father?

*St. John:* Life was pretty good for us growing up in Norwood the children of Robert Conti. We had a swimming pool, a tennis court, and new cars before we were even old enough to drive. Saturday mornings, friends of my father like Garrett Neeley would arrive at our home delivering bags stuffed with cash.

I met Jim Freney once when I was a little boy. He was wearing a Red Sox cap and he talked to me about baseball. He said this was the year the Red Sox were going to win it all. I think it must have been 1986. "What do ya think of my boy Roger Clemens?" I remember him saying. "Clemens' a bull. Told his team –'Just get on my back boys and we'll ride to the World Series.'"

I loved my father very much. We were very close. I visited him in prison regularly for six years. I did whatever he asked. When he asked me to help Uncle Ralph move the arsenal of weapons to my grandmother's house because the police were about to find out where they were stored, I helped my uncle move them.

But one day, when I was visiting my father in Walpole, he told me that he had killed my half-sister Susan. She was only twenty-six at the time. I couldn't believe what I had heard. I was revolted, sick to my stomach. I could have thrown up. His family was expendable. All he cared about was himself.

It was the lies, the murders, especially the murder of my half-sister, committed by my father that drove me to expose my father's legacy of deceit and crime. I wanted to put an end to it. He's menaced everyone he's been in contact with. Not only his family, but his friends.

When I think about what he did to his boyhood friend Lou Farnese.

*St. John began to sob. He took out a handkerchief, wiped away the tears and continued.*

I feel so bad for Lou's kids. It was my father and James Freney who told the FBI that Lou was the one who planted the bomb in that lawyer's car. Remember the government lawyer whose leg got blown off? I know all three of them — Lou, my father, and Freney — were involved. Lou got seventeen years. My father and Freney weren't even charged.

I once wanted to be like my father. Funny thing is now I'm doing something my father told me never to do — trust the government. I'm telling them everything I know about my father because I want all this evil to end.

*Bannister:* Did your uncle ever talk to you about the murder of your half-sister Susan Anderson?

*St. John:* Uncle Ralph knew his brother murdered Susan. He seemed to imply she deserved it. He said my half-sister was having sexual relations with a black man. That she was a stripper and had a drug problem. I asked him "Does that mean she should be dead?"

On the stand Ralph Conti was cross-examined by Conti's defense lawyer Norman Macy.

*Macy:* Mr. Conti. You said that you knew your brother murdered Susan Anderson. Did you know if he killed Richard Hudson, John MacAllister, or any other people?

*Conti:* Look I'm not my brother's keeper and he's not mine. My nephew here, St. John, or whatever he calls himself these days, wants to ruin his father through me. He's afraid of losing his inheritance.

He's trying to get hold of his father's assets. In life, you can pick your friends, but you can't pick your family.

The trial went on for several more weeks, but it reached no climax. It just came to an end. The verdict seemed preordained. The evidence against Robert Conti was overwhelming. Neither Conti nor his lawyer Norman Macy put up much of a defense. Conti on the stand, wearing a rumpled jacket and pants, the glow on his once youthful face gone now replaced with the pallor of jailhouse walls, seemed resigned to his fate.

In May 1999, after three months of trial, Judge David Barton convicted Conti on charges of racketeering, extortion, money laundering, and obstruction of justice and sent him back to prison for another ten years. Conti still faced charges of murder.

Ralph Conti would later be convicted of charges of obstruction of justice, perjury, and possession of weapons. Outside the court building after Robert Conti's trial was over, surrounded by reporters, he shouted "This is nothing but a frame-job by my scumbag nephew St. John. I'm innocent. I'm going to get ten years in prison for doing nothing, just on account of my last name."

Nearby, Conti's lawyer Norman Macy was talking to another group of reporters. "St. John was lying," he said. "He wanted to ruin his uncle because he controlled his father's assets. Look at his motives. By turning state's evidence, in exchange for his testimony, the government is giving St. John a new name, relocation expenses, and twenty-five percent of his father's assets that were forfeited on conviction of these criminal charges."

As Robert Conti was herded away by federal marshals, I heard him yell over the noise of the crowd — "American justice. That's what I was in Korea for?" Then he turned to his lawyer and muttered, "My gang? My gang's all gone and so is Freney. The fuckin' FBI. They're all fucked up."

## THE TRIAL OF WILLIAM O'DONNELL, 1999
Reporter Donald Shay covered the trial of William O'Donnell for *The Boston Chronicle*. This was his account.

The trial began in September 1999. Judge Amos Potter presided over the trial. Ivan Mather was the government's chief prosecutor. He was called Ivan "The Terrible" because of his record of putting behind bars some of the Mafia's top capos. Margaret Mason was the lawyer for the defense. She had the reputation of being a pretty good lawyer, but was not one of the principals of her law firm of Haig & Hennessey, which was representing their client William O'Donnell. The principals were too connected to Boston's power elite to risk the stigma attached to their names if they lost the case.

A jury of six men and six women were selected. The courtroom in the federal court building in South Boston was packed. Boston officials, local celebrities, Justice Department, FBI agents, and other lawmen from all over the country — Washington, New York, Philadelphia, Dallas. Families and friends of witnesses and victims . City, state, and national media, and "the Friends of Bill," a group of crime writers, wannabee law enforcers, and court room junkies that supported O'Donnell.

Prosecutor Ivan Mather delivered his opening statement:

"William O'Donnell is charged with racketeering, obstruction of justice, conspiracy to obstruct justice, and making false statements to the FBI. For more than twenty years, William O'Donnell has helped James Freney and Robert Conti run their rackets with a free hand. He has thwarted efforts of law enforcement to arrest James Freney and Robert Conti by providing confidential information to them and lying to the FBI. In exchange for confidentiality and sensitive law enforcement information, William O'Donnell received tips about the Italian Mafia and accepted gifts from the Freney gang, such as a boat and a diamond ring.

"Not only did he keep investigations of law enforcement away, William O'Donnell also shielded James Freney and Robert Conti from other gangsters who could do them harm. While James Freney and Robert Conti were helping him keep tabs on the Italian Mafia, William O'Donnell was helping them keep tabs on their enemies, including the Italian Mafia. William O'Donnell also passed sensitive law enforcement information to James Freney and Robert Conti that led to the murder of two FBI informants.

"Today's indictment fills out a dark picture of corruption and obstruction of justice by a former FBI agent. The handler of criminals became a criminal himself."

The defense lawyer Margaret Mason delivered her opening statement:

"The defense counsel will show evidence that William O'Donnell is not guilty of charges of racketeering. He is not guilty of associating with the criminal activities of James Freney and Robert Conti. He is not guilty of giving information to James Freney and Robert Conti that led to the murders of two FBI informants. William O'Donnell did not participate in these murders, did not plan these murders, and did not have any advance knowledge about these murders. Nor is William O'Donnell guilty of charges of obstruction of justice — of thwarting efforts to arrest James Freney and Robert Conti, of providing confidential information regarding law enforcement to them, and of lying to the FBI."

After her opening statement, Mason showed an FBI training film of O'Donnell instructing recruits in the art of handling informants. O'Donnell is seen in the film offering the following instruction:

*"Rule Number One of handling informants. Informants are treacherous. They will turn on you when they get a chance to save themselves. Never trust an informant.*

*I find it distasteful to pay informants for information, but I found it's very effective to pay at Christmas time.*

*Agents shouldn't share information about their informants with others in law enforcement. You got crooked cops. Someone then could send that information to the wiseguys.*

*In working with informants, you tell them, 'I don't want to hear about your crimes. Don't tell me something you're doing or I'm going to have to act on it.'"*

"As this tape shows," Mason pointed out, "William O'Donnell had a talent for developing informants. The FBI took advantage of that strength. And it was their choice to use him for that purpose."

After Mason finished, she showed the video tape of the Mafia induction ceremony in Medford, Massachusetts in 1980:

"Acting on a tip from his informant James Freney, William O'Donnell told his bureau about a secret Mafia gathering in Medford," Mason commented as the tape was shown. "This was the first breakthrough in bugging La Cosa Nostra. It led to the government bugging of Mafia headquarters on Prince Street in the North End in 1981. Those incriminating tapes of Mafia underboss Dante Massaroni, and his capos, Guido Massaroni and Samuel Salerno, led to the virtual decapitation of the Mafia's Boston organization. Through the efforts of William O'Donnell, the FBI cut off the heads of the Mafia snakes."

Mason concluded her opening presentation: "William O'Donnell was a scapegoat — a sacrificial lamb for the FBI. Sacrificed so as to preserve the FBI's image of integrity and incorruptibility. He was only following orders from his FBI superiors in Boston and in Washington, D.C. For J. Edgar Hoover, organized crime had an Italian surname. For the FBI, agents like William O'Donnell who handled top echelon informants like James Freney and Robert Conti, were indispensable in bringing La Cosa Nostra down."

Luigi Farnese and Garrett Neeley were witnesses for the prosecution. Farnese took the stand first.

*Mather:* Mr. Farnese, back in 1968, FBI agent William O'Donnell arrested you in New York City. Could you tell the court about this arrest?

*Farnese:* Well, I was on the lam for a few years, after bein' accused of killin' a few people. Ya rememba the gang wars of the sixties? We were all bumpin' each other off. So I got outta Boston and went to New York, thinkin' I would be safe from the cops and G-men down there.

Then one day this G-man O'Donnell arrests me on Third Ave near Gimbels. After that I'm always readin' in the papers what a hero this guy O'Donnell was. Wrestlin' me to the ground, like he caught me single-handedly. That's a laugh. The truth is he comes up to me and asks me to lay down. I did. He had two other agents with 'im. Not to mention a gun at my head.

*Mather:* You were sentenced to sixteen years in prison. What happened when you got out of prison in 1984?

*Farnese:* When I got out of prison, the family wasn't the same as in the old days. In the old days, we did things differently. The admission standards were high. New soldiers were pulled off the streets into a basement where they were inducted into the family. It was all secret. There was no celebration with prosciutto, figs, and vino. Nowadays, everythin' is loose. There's no leadership. Everybody thinks like they're in *The Godfather* movies.

*Mather:* How did you become boss of the Boston La Cosa Nostra?

*Farnese:* I was still in prison when the FBI taped that ceremony in Medford. When I got out of prison, most of the other capos were in jail. Carmen Borgia Junior had taken over the New England operations and he appointed me a "King's Man" — that's top capo, probably 'cause I use to be tight with Junior's father. I reported directly to Junior. In 1987, he got arrested and went to jail. But he still ran the organization from prison, though he pretended he wasn't in charge.

The commission — the five families in New York — decided they had enough of Carmen Junior and gave 'im the boot. They summoned me to New York and I became the boss. My role was to look over the family, the flock, so to speak. I was in charge of all the organization's operations in New England. But I tell ya, it wasn't the same like the old days. The bond of friendship that we had in the past and that kept the dons and their families together was gone. Finito. Many of my associates who I thought were my friends weren't anymore.

*Mather:* How did you end up back in prison?

*Farnese:* I'll tell ya how. 'Cause of that god-damned rat Conti. He was the crud who told O'Donnell I put the bomb in that lawyer Hanratty's car that blew off his leg. It wasn't me alone who did it. Conti and Freney were in it, too. But I'm the fall guy who goes to jail for another thirty years. Bobby Conti — my old boyhood chum. We grew up together. We joined the Winter Hill together, along with Freney. They get off scot-free. And Freney's *still* free.

*Mather:* What made you testify against William O'Donnell?

*Farnese:* My wife, Stella, told me, "Lou, there's no way you're going to stick your neck out and do one more extra day for someone like O'Donnell. Tell them everything." It wasn't an easy decision to testify. I love my wife.

*He gets teary-eyed.*

Ya see, if I cooperated, it would be the end of our marriage. I didn't want her to be in danger, me not bein' able to protect her 'cause I'm away in the Witness Protection Program. No, it wasn't an easy decision to break the code of *Omerta.*

Then Margaret Mason cross-examined Farnese:

*Mason:* Tell me, Mr. Farnese. Isn't it really revenge you want? Wasn't William O'Donnell the person who arrested you in 1968 and sent you to prison for sixteen years? And wasn't William O'Donnell the person who arrested you again and sent you back to prison for thirty more years? Wasn't it payback time behind your decision to testify against William O'Donnell? And in the end, wasn't it really the only way you could reduce your prison time — shave some years off of your life in prison — if you testified?

Garrett Neeley was the next witness to take the stand.

*Mather:* Mr. Neeley, tell us what you know about the relationship between FBI agent William O'Donnell and James Freney.

*Neeley:* Freney was always tellin' me we gotta friend on the pad.

*Mather:* What do you mean 'friend on the pad?'

*Neeley:* Oh, dat means a crooked FBI agent in the bag.

*Mather:* Could you give a specific example of FBI agent O'Donnell being on the pad?

*Neeley:* Ya, I rememba the time Freney was plannin' on takin' out Alec Minihan.

*Mather:* Who was Alec Minihan?

*Neeley:* Minihan was in our gang. But Freney found out he was an informa for the FBI. He'd ratted that Freney had hired Johnny Greco to bump off Phil Newton down in Dallas 'cause Newton had found out Freney and Conti was skimmin' profits off his company North American Jai Alai. Then Greco whacks Ralph Taggert 'cause he was the one who told Newton Freney and Conti were skimmin' profits outta the jai alai company.

179

So like I say, I rememba Freney tellin' me "Don't worry 'bout nothin'. Big Brother is watchin' things."

I don't understand what youse talkin' about, I says to 'im.

A little while later, I figured out what Freney was tellin' me. One day, it was May 11, 1982, I think, O'Donnell is sittin' in his car right near the old Topside Bar. Ya know, the bar on Northern Avenue in Southie. It was about 6:00 o'clock. Happy Hour. O'Donnell's got binoculars and a walkie-talkie so he can talk with Freney. The signal is one click — "Don't move." Two clicks — "All's clear. Move in and whack 'im."

So Minihan comes out of the bar. Freney's wearin' a fake mustache and a wig so's nobody will recognize 'im, gets de two clicks on his walkie-talkie, gets out of his car, and whacks Minihan. *Bam! Bam!* Minihan goes down and rolls off the steps onto the sidewalk.

*Mason:* I object, your honor. My client was nowhere near the Topside Restaurant and Bar on the evening of May 11, 1982. He was doing paperwork at FBI headquarters. He learned about the murder on the evening news.

*Judge Potter:* Objection sustained.

*Mather:* Mr. Neeley. Do you know of other instances where FBI agent O'Donnell was involved in any murders?

*Neeley:* Yeah, der was John MacAllister. He ratted to the FBI that Freney was runnin' guns to the IRA. But O'Donnell tipped 'im off. Told 'im the feds was gonna arrest 'im and Joe Morrow at de warehouse in Southie.

*Mather:* Who was Joe Morrow?

*Neeley:* Joe Morrow was a drug deala from Charlestown. Always tryin' to screw us. Owed us five-hundred grand. He was in on the gun runnin' operation. When the feds get down to the warehouse, Freney is gone. But dey nabbed Morrow and some other guys.

*Mather:* I thought Joe Morrow was murdered? Wasn't it Freney who killed him?

*Neeley:* Nah! 'is wife killed 'im afta he got outta prison. Knifed 'im right in the back when she found out 'e was fornicatin' with another woman.

Mason cross-examined Neeley.

*Mason:* Mr. Neeley. Could you tell us how the Freney gang sized up their victims? How did they find out their weaknesses before moving in?

*Neeley:* As far was we was concerned, everybody was weak. Der wasn't nobody we couldn't intimidate.

*Mason:* You felt there was no one you couldn't intimidate anywhere?

*Neeley:* No. We was only in Boston.

*Mason:* Did James Freney tell you to get a body bag when you were threatening a real estate agent named Raymond Stubbs at the L Street Tavern in South Boston?

*Neeley:* No, Freney told me to get Stubbs a bottle of beer, not a body bag. I don't think bars in Southie have body bags.

*Mather:* I object, your honor. This questioning is irrelevant to this case.

*Judge Potter:* Objection sustained.

*Mather:* Is William O'Donnell guilty of obstructing justice and conspiracy to obstruct justice? I think what we have heard today is that William O'Donnell was associated with, yes, even participated in, at least two murders directed or carried out by James Freney. I think the evidence is overwhelming — William O'Donnell has blood on his hands.

Mason rebutted Mather's remarks:

*Mason:* This indictment is a further example of the outrageous actions of the government, which has been working to conceal its own misconduct and to distract attention from the way they have handled criminal investigations. The government would have us believe the testimonies of Luigi Farnese, a betrayed and beleaguered Mafia boss, and Garrett Neeley, a leg-breaker, grave digger, and protégé of James Freney. Both of them liars, cheats, and killers.

Both of them hated William O'Donnell for turning Freney and Conti against them. For both of them, revenge was their motive for taking the witness stand. Since they cannot physically kill William O'Donnell, they can still kill him just as easily, just as effectively, by raising their right hand, swearing to tell the truth. By lying, they have condemned William O'Donnell to a slow death on the courthouse floor.

Mather then called Paul Doyle to the witness stand to bolster the government's case against O'Donnell.

*Mather:* Mr. Doyle. Could you tell us how James Freney would pay off, let's say bribe, police and other law enforcement agents?

*Doyle:* Freney use to joke that "Christmas was for cops and kids." Every year, around Christmas, I'd deliver envelopes containing from one hundred to five hundred dollars to about twenty cops. The amount depended on how much we felt the cop could do for us, how high up he was in the police command, and how much we liked him.

*Mather:* Could you tell us if James Freney gave William O'Donnell any gifts?

*Doyle:* Oh, sure. I remember as far back as 1975, Freney gave O'Donnell a Claddagh ring. The one he wears on his finger now.

*Mather:* Did you know that Freney was an informer for the FBI? Did you know that O'Donnell was Freney's handler?

*Doyle:* No, I didn't know Freney was an FBI informant. I don't think anybody knew, except maybe Robert Conti. I thought Freney gave the ring to O'Donnell because of their families' friendship. O'Donnell grew up in the same neighborhood of Southie as Freney and his brother Dan. In fact, Dan Freney and O'Donnell were pretty good friends. The Claddagh ring is a ring of friendship, you know.

*Mather:* Were there other gifts Freney gave Mr. O'Donnell?

*Doyle:* Freney told me to transfer title of one of our condominiums to O'Donnell. The transfer took place sometime in the late 1980s. It was one of our best condominiums — a penthouse on Beacon Street in the Back Bay, overlooking the Charles River. Worth at that time almost a million dollars. As soon as papers were passed, O'Donnell took his wife and kids and moved from Southie to the condominium.

*Mather:* Were there any other gifts?

*Doyle:* Freney also gave O'Donnell a twenty-thousand dollar Sea Ray power boat. Freney had painted on the boat's stern "The Handler." It wasn't long, though, before Freney took back the boat.

He decided owning a twenty-thousand dollar power boat on an FBI agent's salary didn't look good.

After Doyle, Karen O'Donnell, William O'Donnell's ex-wife, was called to the stand.

*Mather:* Mrs. O'Donnell. Do you know if your ex-husband, William O'Donnell, ever received any gifts from James Freney, Robert Conti, Paul Doyle, or any other member of the Freney group?

*Karen O'Donnell:* No, I had no knowledge of him ever receiving any gifts from those people.

*Mather:* You didn't know that the condominium where you lived on Beacon Street in Boston was a gift from Freney?

*Karen O'Donnell:* No.

*Mather:* You didn't know the power boat your ex-husband owned was a gift from Freney?

*Karen O'Donnell:* No.

*Mather:* Did you know a ten-thousand dollar, diamond-studded Claddagh wedding ring that your ex-husband gave you was a gift from Freney?

*Karen O'Donnell:* I didn't know Freney gave him that ring. (She responds angrily.) That son-of-a.... I don't even have that ring anymore. He gave it to *that* woman sitting over there (pointing to Charlene O'Donnell, William O'Donnell's attractive, blond second wife, sitting in the first row in the courtroom).

Ray Dewars was another witness who took the stand. Dewars, 60, was a retired Boston police officer, now making a living as a substitute teacher in Florida. For years, Dewars pursued Freney, but resigned in 1995, turning in his Boston police badge after twenty-five years on the job. In his resignation letter, Dewars claimed he was targeted for going after Freney and exposing corruption in the police ranks.

Dewar's story was like Frank Serpico's — the Serpico made famous by Al Pacino in the 1973 movie. Serpico was a NYC police officer who was vilified by his department after exposing police corruption there during the 1960s.

Dewars had a reputation as an outstanding investigator. The problem was that he made allegations against colleagues. But he never substantiated these allegations. All of Dewars' allegations of internal corruption were vigorously pursued, but none ever proven. Every time he pointed his finger at corruption, instead of going after the people he pointed at, they went after him.

At some point in his career, Dewars started to feel he couldn't trust anybody. He became Diogenes, the Greek philosopher who searched for an honest man — the lone Boston police officer walking through the dark with a lantern of truth.

*Mather:* Mr. Dewars. Could you tell us why you suddenly resigned from the Boston police force after twenty-five years of service?

*Dewars:* I was never comfortable working in my department because working in South Boston and working on organized crime just wasn't a popular thing for a cop to be doing in Southie. It was a career-ender for many police officers unless you were on the right side of the Freney gang.

I resigned in 1995 when Freney escaped arrest and became a fugitive from justice. I figured I would never be able to catch him if other law enforcement people protected him. So I gave up. I resigned and retired to Florida.

*Mather:* Which law enforcement people do you believe protected Freney?

*Dewars:* Well, besides a lot of Boston police officers, the FBI protected him — at least William O'Donnell, his handler at the FBI protected him.

*Mather:* How did William O'Donnell protect Freney?

*Dewars:* O'Donnell thwarted any chance I had of catching Freney. O'Donnell worked to sabotage my efforts by portraying me as an unstable, rogue cop. He started a behind-the-scenes whisper campaign to turn my own department against me. He ended up ruining my career.

*Mather:* Could you give us specific examples of how William O'Donnell thwarted your efforts to capture Freney?

*Dewars:* Well, there was the time I had set up with the FBI recording equipment to secretly record a conversation between

Freney and Conti outside Freney's liquor store, Atlantic Wine & Spirits. But all they talked about was the coming Yankee-Red Sox series in Boston. Somebody at the FBI tipped them off that their conversation was going to be recorded. I knew that somebody was O'Donnell.

*Mather:* Were there other instances where William O'Donnell thwarted your efforts to capture Freney?

*Dewars:* I guess Operation Bean Town was the best example of this. Operation Bean Town back in the early 1980s was a combined effort of Boston, state, and federal law enforcement agencies to investigate James Freney's drug operations. I represented the Boston police in this group. Operation Bean Town ended up indicting fifty-seven persons on drug charges. Freney wasn't one of them. O'Donnell told Washington that Freney was an important FBI informant who should be protected and our allegations that Freney and his Irish mob ran a large-scale cocaine and marijuana trafficking organization in Boston were unsubstantiated. He said there was no specific information as to Freney's involvement in these criminal activities.

*Mather:* I suppose this trial is a vindication of all your efforts to tell the truth about William O'Donnell.

*Dewars:* I'm down in Florida enjoying life and O'Donnell's up here worrying about going to jail for life. I knew there were lies and rumors being spread and now the public knows.

Walter Huff, William O'Donnell's supervisor, took the stand as a government witness. Both the prosecution and the defense jockeyed back and forth to establish the role that Huff and others at the bureau played in using James Freney as an FBI informant.

*Mather:* Mr. Huff. Could you tell us about the bureau's handling of James Freney as a FBI informant?

*Huff:* I warned O'Donnell repeatedly about the cozy relationship between him and Freney. I also warned my supervisors that Freney should be terminated as an FBI informant after learning Freney had been involved in killings.

*Mather:* Which killings are you referring to?

*Huff:* The killings of Alec Minihan, John MacAllister, Phillip Newton, and Ralph Taggert.

*Mather:* What did your supervisors at the bureau do when you warned them about James Freney?

*Huff:* They refused to listen to my advice. I'm angry over the fact that people were killed. Murdered. I'm angry over the fact that it went on for so long.

*Mason:* Mr. Huff. Is it true you accepted a bribe of five thousand dollars from James Freney in 1986?

*Huff:* O'Donnell insisted on my taking the five thousand dollars. He told me, "You need to take this. If you don't take it Freney is going to think we don't trust him."

Anyway, that five thousand dollars was a loan. I was going to pay him back in two installments.

*Mason:* Did you ever repay that loan?

*Huff: He begins to sob and takes out his handkerchief to wipe away tears from his eyes.* I admitted I made a mistake and embarrassed the FBI by taking the money. But I've done my penance. I donated the five thousand dollars to my church.

*Mason:* Mr. Huff. Don't you find it an ironic coincidence that you found religion after the government gave you immunity for testifying?

*Huff:* I got serious about religion when Freney became a fugitive from justice in 1995. I prayed every night.

Following Walter Huff, the FBI's Boston bureau chief Martin Compson took the stand.

*Compson:* These allegations of racketeering and obstruction of justice are appalling to me and every other FBI agent. This is a bitter pill for all of us. But don't judge us by a couple of bad apples and rogue agents. Ninety-nine percent of us are decent, hardworking people.

I can attest that there is no FBI policy, official or otherwise, that enables an agent to veer from the law in the development and maintenance of criminal informants. The FBI has no 'wink-and-a nod' policy that condones William O'Donnell's conduct.

Nevertheless, despite some of the things that have occurred at the bureau in the past, rest assured, we will continue to pursue James Freney to the end of the world.

The trial dragged on for some time, as procedural delays and court respites stretched weeks into months. Finally, William O'Donnell took the stand. He was debonair, wore a navy blue pin-stripped suit. His hair was coiffured in a blow-dry style.

*Mason:* Mr. O'Donnell, could you tell us about your role in bringing down the New England Mafia?

*O'Donnell:* I recruited James Freney as my top echelon informer. A TE informer, we called him. The information that James Freney, and through Freney, Robert Conti passed on to me was instrumental, I would say indispensable in taking down La Cosa Nostra in New England.

You have to understand how an agent has to work when handling a TE informer like Freney. You have to out-gangster the gangster. You have to use every trick in the trade that he uses — racketeering, obstruction of justice, extortion, bribery, deception, lying. But in this case, not killing. I knew nothing about those slayings that Freney and Conti have allegedly committed.

Walter Huff and other supervisors at the bureau approved all my actions involving Freney and Conti. They approved them because our orders were to take down the New England Mafia. We were at war with the Mafia and I believed, along with many others at the bureau, that the best way to fight this war was to employ the one person in Boston who could help us bring them down — James Freney.

After O'Donnell finished testifying, everyone in the courtroom expected to hear the prosecution and defense's closing arguments. Instead, Martin O'Hara, a retired FBI agent, who worked in the research section of the Boston bureau, took the stand.

*Mather:* Mr. O'Hara. Can you tell us about the Boston bureau's efforts to bring down the New England Mafia?

*O'Hara:* The Boston bureau believes it was successful in bringing down the New England Mafia. But frankly speaking, the FBI's major concern is no longer the Mafia.

*Mather:* I don't understand what you mean "the FBI's major concern is no longer the Mafia."

*O'Hara:* What I mean is that the Mafia or organized crime is no longer a high priority for the FBI. The Bureau has moved in a new direction. It's assembled its resources and focused its efforts on a different objective. Have you ever heard of the Megiddo Project?

*Mather:* The Megiddo Project? What is the Megiddo Project?

*O'Hara:* The Megiddo Project was a secret document published in 1997 for the FBI's internal use only. The document was released to other law enforcement agencies just last month. The project is the FBI's strategic assessment of the potential for domestic terrorism in the United States undertaken in anticipation of the arrival of the new millennium.

*O'Hara reads from the document.* "The Megiddo Project warns of the potential for extremist criminal activity in the United States by individuals or domestic groups who attach specific significance to the year 2000....The volatile mix of apocalyptic religious and New World Order conspiracy theories may produce violent acts aimed at precipitating the end of the world as prophesied in the Bible."

In short, the FBI is warning that all hell may break loose as we approach the New Year.

The FBI has specifically targeted the activities of individuals and sects who preach apocalyptic violence and who embrace "Christian Identity" — those who believe that the "white Aryan race is God's chosen race."

Christian Identity's interpretation of the Old Testament is that Anglo-Saxons are descendants from the lost tribes of Israel and favored by God. Today, the white supremacist groups like the Aryan Nation sect consider themselves to be these descendants. In their world, Blacks and Hispanics are described as "mud people" and Jews are considered the tools of the devil.

The FBI called it The Megiddo Project because of its Biblical significance. Megiddo is an ancient hill in Israel, which in the Hebrew world was called "Armageddon." The New Testament designated Armageddon as the assembly point in the Apocalyptic setting of God's final and conclusive battle against evil. The name "Megiddo" is an apt title for a project that analyzes those who believe the year 2000 will usher in the end of the world and who are willing to perpetuate acts of violence to bring that end about.

After O'Hara finished testifying, the prosecuting lawyer Ivan Mather delivered his closing statement:

Was William O'Donnell a rogue agent or, as the defense contends, just following standard FBI rules for handling informants with his supervisor's approval?

Clearly, William O'Donnell knew the rules. You, the jury, saw the training video presented by the defense at the beginning of this trial that showed he knew the agency rules. But he didn't follow them because he had switched allegiances to James Freney.

Somewhere along the way, William O'Donnell allowed himself to be corrupted by his prize informant. Somewhere along the way he began doing the criminal activities he was supposed to be investigating. Somewhere along the way, William O'Donnell crossed the line from crime fighter to crime partner.

By working with his criminal informants James Freney and Robert Conti, William O'Donnell betrayed his oath of office, his duty to his fellow agents, and his brothers and sisters in law enforcement.

Gentlemen and women of this jury, the evidence presented at this trial has shown that William O'Donnell is guilty of the charges brought against him — guilty of racketeering, guilty of obstruction of justice, guilty of conspiracy to obstruct justice, and guilty of making false statements to his own agency, the Federal Bureau of Investigation.

The defense lawyer Margaret Mason delivered her closing statement:

An FBI agent faces a constant dilemma. How to gain trust from a criminal informant while still keeping society safe? On one hand, he has to adhere to regulations that require an agent to report those crimes of his informant to the FBI. On the other hand, he doesn't want to dry up his source of intelligence. Did his bureau want to have it both ways?

William O'Donnell was a talented agent under orders to get sources who could help the Boston FBI bring down the New England Mafia. Mr. O'Donnell did not choose to associate with James Freney and his gang. He was told to associate with them to get information and that's what he did.

William O'Donnell's supervisors were eager to nurture top level informants. They agreed to allow James Freney and Robert Conti to continue their gambling and loan sharking operations in exchange for inside information about the Mafia. Mr. O'Donnell's work was approved by his supervisors who decided to use Freney and his Irish gang to bring down the Italian Mafia. That was the FBI's decision, not Mr. O'Donnell's. Mr. O'Donnell had no authority to decide who the FBI should go after.

Mr. O'Donnell's supervisors knew that he grew up in South Boston on the same street corners as James Freney. Who else but a guy from the neighborhood would James Freney have trusted with secrets that could have gotten the informer killed?

Some people say you shouldn't put the hometown boy in charge of the hometown guy. But who else is going to talk to the hometown guy? James Freney wouldn't talk to anybody else.

Is it possible that William O'Donnell's bosses did not understand that his neighborhood connection would be a double-edged sword for the FBI?

Are we to believe that they did not know that angels don't make pacts with the devil? That the goods they wanted from Freney could not be exchanged without compromising those high standards the FBI claims to hold?

How much was the FBI willing to compromise for what it wanted? What ends justified which means? Was William O'Donnell a rogue agent or rather did he represent a rogue agency, a compromised federal law enforcement agency?

William O'Donnell was a devoted agent. He is now a victim of a government cover-up over moral compromises made during the war on La Cosa Nostra. If there were problems, the agency should have stepped up to the plate. Instead, the FBI needed a scapegoat.

Who better than the informant's handler? Somebody at the bottom of the totem pole.

William O'Donnell was a good agent. He did what the FBI wanted him to do.

After days of deliberation, the jury gave its verdict. Standing up in the jury box, the foreman addressed the court:

Your honor. The jury finds the defendant William O'Donnell:

On charges of racketeering, that he associated with the criminal activities of James Freney and Robert Conti...Guilty

On the charge he accepted a condominium, boat, and wedding ring as bribes from James Freney...Guilty

On the charge he delivered a bribe of five thousand dollars to his supervisor Walter Huff...Guilty

On charges of obstruction of justice, that he thwarted efforts to arrest James Freney and Robert Conti...Guilty

On the charge he provided confidential law enforcement information to James Freney and Robert Conti...Guilty

On the charge he made false statements to the FBI...Guilty

On charges of conspiracy to obstruct justice, that he provided information leading to the murder of Alec Minihan, and John MacAllister...Not Guilty.

On Friday, December 31, 1999, the court convened to hear Judge Amos Potter pronounce William O'Donnell's sentence.

"It is always a sober moment when it becomes necessary to sentence a member of law enforcement who has abused his authority and crossed the line from crime fighting to criminal.

"William O'Donnell is convicted of racketeering, obstruction of justice, and making false statements to the FBI. Following the federal guidelines, I sentence William O'Donnell to ten years in the federal penitentiary."

William O'Donnell stood next to his lawyer. The stunned and weary-looking former lawman was dimly aware that he had gone from retired agent to inmate as a federal marshal put handcuffs on him. O'Donnell looked down and pulled the Claddagh ring off his finger and gave it to the marshal.

> *This is the way the world ends*
> *This is the way the world Ends*
> *This is the way the world Ends*
> *Not with a bang, but a whimper*

# CHAPTER XIII    THE GRAVES

Graves Light is a gray, ninety-three-foot high granite structure set on a rocky outcrop known as Graves Ledge. Graves Light marks the main entrance to Boston Harbor and the most northerly point of the Brewsters.

The ledge was named for Thomas Graves, a vice-admiral in the fleet of Seventeenth-century Massachusetts Governor John Winthrop. Over the years, the name has stuck, for it also evoked the shipwrecks that claimed so many lives off the ledges. It has even been said that the rocks surrounding the lighthouse look like headstones, marking the watery graves of the drowned.

While fancy may well have blurred into outright fiction, there is no doubt that countless wrecks occurred off these treacherous shoals. Among a couple of latter-day disasters: in 1938, the *City of Salisbury*, carrying a cargo of wild animals, struck a submerged rock and sank with most of its cargo off the Graves. In 1941 during a winter gale, the fishing vessel *Mary E. O'Hara* hit a ledge west of the light. For hours the crewmen clung to masts swaying above the water until their hands froze and they succumbed to the icy seas.

## EPITAPH FOR ORGANIZED CRIME

With the arrival of the new millennium, organized crime in Boston was history.

The Italian Mafia had become a shadow of its past. The mantel of the Borgia crime family was passed to Sergio Lombardi, an aged, old-world godfather based in Providence, Rhode Island.

He presided over a noxious and unhappy Mafia family with Michael "Sonny" Santoro, who was pushing 80, as Boston underboss. They were nicknamed "the old fellas."

Feuding capos, like Freddy Moretti, Anthony Ricci, and Alex Colombo, vying for power, tore apart the organization, already weakened and demoralized from the stunning 1998 revelation that their allies in crime — Winter Hill gang leaders, James Freney and Robert Conti — were in cahoots with the FBI to bring them down.

Since that time, scores of capos, soldiers, and associates have been put behind bars, many of them for life. Decimated by racketeering indictments, the New England Mafia has been unable to recruit new wiseguys.

As one law enforcement agent put it, "The mob may not be dead yet, but it's dying. Quite frankly, who in is right mind in the twenty-first century would get involved with the Mafia."

***Where They Are Now***

Carmen Borgia, Jr. — Released from prison
Luigi Farnese — Released from prison
Dante Massaroni — Prison
Sammy Salerno — Prison
Gino Moretti — Prison
John Ricci — Prison
Albert Bruno — Prison
Mickey Barbarini — Prison
Frank Colonna — Prison
Vincent Giordano — Prison
Gaetano Villa — Died in prison
Guido Massaroni — Dead
Joseph Brambilla — Dead
Nicolo "Nicky" Gallo — Dead
Vincent Costa — Dead
Biagio Esposito — Dead

By the 21st century, the Irish Mafia was no more. Indictments handed out by law enforcement decimated the higher ranks of the Winter Hill gang. The revelation that James Freney was an informant for the FBI and on the lam, served a crushing blow to the gang, even to the most loyal members like Garrett Neeley.

Leaderless and undisciplined, gang members began to rat on each other, leading to more indictments, more gang members going to prison or into the Witness Protection Program. The Winter Hill gang, James Freney's gang, had collapsed.

### Where They Are Now

Robert Conti — Prison

Garrett Neeley — Prison

John Greco — Prison

Paul Doyle — To be released from prison

Charles McGivers — Released from prison

Patrick Quinn — Released from prison

Howard Summer — Released from prison

Charles Conti — Dead

James Barrow — Dead

Alex Minihan — Dead

Stan Moore — Dead

Craig Reed — Dead

Marty Miller — Dead

James Freney — Fugitive from justice

The Boston bureau of the FBI was hardly in a position to boast about its victory over organized crime in the city. True, the Italian Mafia was now only a faded imitation of its former glory days. And what constituted the power behind the Winter Hill gang, and later the Freney gang, had disappeared.

But the FBI was under siege. A growing number of plaintiffs sought damages totaling nearly $2 billion from the federal government, stemming from William O'Donnell and the FBI's relationship with organized crime bosses. At least ten suites were filed under the civil portion of the Racketeer Influenced and Corrupt Organization (RICO) Act, the same federal law used against the Mafia and organized crime figures.

In 2003, the government released a report entitled: "Everything Secret Degenerates: The FBI's Use of Murderers as Informants." The report, a 40-year history of the FBI's organized-crime informant program, charged that "as a result of the ultra-secret informant, FBI agents became corrupt, encouraged perjury in death penalty cases, let innocent men languish and die in prison, and allowed people to be murdered, all in the name of protecting informants." The report called the FBI's Informant Program "one of the greatest failures in the history of federal law enforcement."

Adding to the FBI's woes was a congressional committee investigating the scandals. The committee decided to probe Dan Freney's relationship to his fugitive brother. In televised hearings watched closely throughout the Boston area, Freney said repeatedly that he did not know where his brother was. He did not know where he had been over the past years. He did not aid his brother in any way while he was a fugitive. And he possessed no information that could lead to his brother's arrest.

Public reaction to Dan Freney's appearance before the congressional committee was one of outrage. Few people believed Freney was telling the truth. Did he really not know anything about his brother's whereabouts over the past eight years? Despite evidence to the contrary, had he really not aided his brother as a fugitive? And for a man who once said that he would never be helpful to anyone against his brother and felt no obligation to help anyone catch him, Dan Freney's testimony that he possessed no information that could lead to his brother's arrest seemed incredulous.

Dan Freney's performance at the committee hearing was the knock out blow his long-time adversaries were looking for. Dan Freney had put loyalty to his brother over the public interest. With public support behind him, the governor demanded that Dan Freney resign his seat from the State Assembly. Dan Freney's seventeen-year reign was over. He sank like a battered ship into his watery political grave.

Not long after Dan Freney's resignation, I spoke to Jack Kirby, and asked him why Dan chose to deny all the charges made of his relationship to his brother. Was it really out of loyalty to his brother, a man, who everyone else in the city knew was a ruthless gangster and crime boss? Would he sacrifice his political career to save his bad brother?

"It was more than brother loyalty," explained Kirby. "You've got to understand. Dan is a fervent Catholic. He's in denial. He can't accept that his brother is a killer because murder is a mortal sin. Moreover, Dan has to deny with all his heart and soul that his brother was an informer for the FBI. Remember what Dan said? 'We loath informers. They are the lowest of humanity. In the *Divine Comedy*, Dante wrote of the ninth circle, the innermost circle of hell, as that place for those who betray.' Dan will not betray his brother."

## THE ODYSSEY

After Freney picked Annie Jones up at the House of Roy in Chinatown, they drove to New York City. This was the first stop of an odyssey that would take them across the country and back — and beyond.

Remember Gordon Smith, the private detective who followed Freney's trail in the Gardner Museum theft? Smith has been on Freney's trail, like a bloodhound, ever since he fled Boston as a fugitive from justice. Here is Smith's story of his pursuit:

Freney and Annie Jones arrived in New York City and stayed at the Gramercy Park Hotel. Today, the hotel is a seventy-year old, seventeen-storied brown brick building located on Lexington Avenue at 21$^{st}$ Street, across from Gramercy Park. Inside, the corridors are dimly lit and in the alcoves are old chairs and musty sofas, where only ghosts now sit. On the dark wood-paneled walls are faded photographs of the Kennedy family, who stayed at the Gramercy in the 1920s; Humphrey Bogart with his first wife, Helen Mencken; and Babe Ruth sitting with his arm in a sling at a piano bar in the hotel's lounge.

I asked the doorman if he remembered anyone who resembled this photo I had of James Freney.

"It was a long time ago," the doorman said, "but I remember this couple arriving here with no bags, nothing, just the clothes on their backs — like refugees.

"The next couple of days I see them come back with brand new suitcases and boxes from Bloomingdale's and Saks Fifth Avenue," the doorman told me. "Every morning at 7:00 a.m. sharp, I'd see this guy jogging around the park. I checked his name out at the registration desk. He had signed it Harry Anderson. He and the woman never said anything while they were here for a few weeks. But after I helped them load up their car with a ton of suitcases and boxes, he gave me a big tip. I think it was a hundred bucks."

Freney was sighted next in South Carolina. I got a call from a guy I often network with, a private investigator named Dave Watson. He asked me if I wanted to come down to Edgefield County, South Carolina. He thinks he knows where Freney is staying. When we meet, Watson tells me this story.

"Have you ever heard of the 'Irish Travelers'"? Watson asks. "There's a village of Irish Travelers here in Edgefield. They've survived for over 150 years by keeping to themselves and keeping outsiders away.

"The travelers are descendants of nomadic Irish traders and tinsmiths, known as Tinkers, who immigrated to the United States in the 1840s, fleeing the potato famine in Ireland. Even today, some of the older folk still speak kind of a Gaelic dialect of their own. Travelers are suspicious people. Their view of the world is shaped by their people's history of persecution in Ireland, where they were seen as an itinerant underclass.

"All marriages are arranged when the girls are seventeen to ensure the outside world is kept out. Cousins marry cousins and always in an arrangement that includes a dowry. That's why there are only about a dozen surnames in the community, like Carroll, Costello, Gorman, O'Hara, and Sherlock.

"The men work at jobs like driveway pavers, barn painters, and roofers. Every spring, they go out from the village in caravans of trucks and trailers to ply their trade. But in recent years the police have been watching them closely because they're getting complaints that some of the Travelers are dishonest. There have been arrests and convictions of a few con artists who have been running home-improvement swindles. A policeman friend of mine calls these operations 'non-traditional organized crime.'

"But because it's such a closed community, the police can find out if there are any strangers coming into the community. My friend told me there is a guy bearing the same description as James

Freney. And he has a woman companion who looks like this Annie Jones. There's a woman named Deirdre Gorman who might talk to you about them."

Deirdre Gorman greets me at the door of her trailer home. "What do you want?" she asks.

"I'm looking for information about a missing person who may be living here," I answer. "Relatives of this person are quite concerned. He's been missing for quite a while and they've hired me to try and find him."

"You must mean Seamus Carroll," Gorman says hesitatingly. "You ain't the first who's been askin' 'bout him. Seems lately, a lot of people have been comin' here lookin' for him. Ordinarily, I don't speak to strangers, but Seamus and his missus are like family and I don't mind puttin' his relatives' worryin' to rest. Yeah, they come down from Boston. He told me they were havin' some trouble with the law and was hopin' kin folk here would offer him protection for a while."

"Where can I find him now?" I ask.

"He lived at that trailer home next to mine," Gorman answers.

"*Lived?*" I ask. "You said *lived*?"

"Oh, he doesn't live here anymore," Gorman responds nonchalantly. "He and the missus left here a couple of days ago."

"Do you know where they were going?" I ask, expecting Gorman to have no idea.

"Come to think of it, I do," she says. "Seamus mentioned this Cherokee Kid person. Talked 'bout givin' him a proper burial. Said he was headed to New Echota, Georgia, where the Cherokees live."

When I arrived at New Echota, I sat down with a tribal chief, Darrell Benge, to discuss where the remains of a person called the Cherokee Kid may be buried and if anyone else had inquired about this person.

"Last week, a Dennis O'Malley visited here and asked me if I knew where I could find the grave of a man named Charlie Hutto, nicknamed the Cherokee Kid," Benge tells me. "O'Malley said he was an old friend of Hutto's and wanted to move him to a proper gravesite.

I told O'Malley we had no records of a Charlie Hutto here, but they might know more about Hutto over in Tahlequah, Oklahoma, where most of the Cherokee Nation lives.

"You see, back in the 1830s, gold was discovered in Georgia. The white settlers began to want the Cherokee land. So in 1838, they rounded up thousands of Cherokee men, women, and children and marched them one thousand miles to Indian territory, known today as the state of Oklahoma. They called the forced march 'The Trail of Tears' because four thousand died from cold, hunger, and disease during the six-month journey."

When I arrived In Tahlequah and sat down with tribal chief Joe Hummingbird, he told me Dennis O'Malley had been there a couple of days ago.

"Charlie Hutto came from Tahlequah," Hummingbird says. "Hutto spent a lot of time in Alcatraz. When he got out and came home, he never could settle down. Drank himself into the grave. Having nobody who cared about him, he was buried in a pauper's grave yard. We found his grave. Mr. O'Malley opened up his wallet and handed me five-thousand dollars to move him to a proper burial site. We moved the remains of Charlie Hutto to the Blackston sacred burial ground in Tahlequah. There, Charlie Hutto will be ensured a happy and peaceful afterlife. There, he will be able to come to terms with the mystery and reality of death."

After Tahlequah, Freney's tracks went cold. Sure, there were more and more Freney sightings as the story of Freney's prolonged disappearance spread over the Internet and on television programs like *Unsolved Mysteries*. People reported seeing Freney and Annie Jones all over the United States: on a ranch near Pinesdale, Wyoming; outside a beauty parlor in Iowa City, Iowa; at the Alamo in San Antonio, Texas; buying Native American jewelry at a Navaho concession in Canyon de Chelly, Arizona; shopping at a Wal-Mart SuperCenter in Galliano, Louisiana; and in the Hotel Richelieu in New Orleans' French Quarter. Most of these sightings turned out to be false, the result of overzealous imaginations. Lured by the

FBI's one million dollar reward for Freney's capture, it seems as if everybody had become a bounty hunter looking for him.

I picked up Freney's trail again in the spring of 1999, when I got a telephone call from a pharmacist in La Jolla, California. He told me a woman had come into his pharmacy looking to buy Atenolol. That's medicine for controlling high blood pressure. The woman fit the description of a photo of Annie Jones that he had seen on the Internet. The woman said she didn't have a prescription. She had been buying it for her husband in Mexico without a prescription, but he had run out of it and it was an emergency. The pharmacist told her he couldn't sell her the medicine without a prescription. She left pretty upset. But the next day, the pharmacist got a call from a Doctor Ramon Hernandez, who said he was writing out a prescription to a Mrs. Anderson for Atenolol. The pharmacist gave me Doctor Hernandez's telephone number to call. He asked me if he would collect some of the reward if the information he gave me led to Freney's capture.

I called and introduced myself to Doctor Hernandez.

"Yes, this is Doctor Hernandez speaking. I treated a Mr. Harry Anderson a few weeks ago. He came into our clinic with his wife. He was experiencing acute angina. He told me the Atenolol he had been taking didn't seem to be working. It was giving him hallucinations and nightmares in his sleep. I told him he might need a heart bypass. I remember that cold, piercing look he gave me as if in no way would I dare operate on him. Here I'm a cardiologist, trying to help him, and I'm trembling in fear before this man. Getting a hold of myself, I told him an angioplasty, a relatively easier procedure, whereby we insert stents into the blocked arteries and the patient goes home the next day, may be a possibility if the arteries in question were not severely blocked. Fortunately, thank God for both of us, the angiogram showed that we could perform the angioplasty.

"Would you believe! The day after the procedure, Mr. Anderson has just dressed. He asks me 'What's the bill, doc?' I hand him the bill and he takes out $25,000 in cash and pays me on the spot. That's the last I ever heard about him until you called. By the way, if they capture this Mr. Anderson, or whatever his name is, would I get a piece of the reward?"

Again, Freney's tracks went cold, until about a year later. I get a call from a Rollie Bateaux. He says he runs fishing charters out of Grand Isle, Louisiana. Grand Isle's a beach resort town on a peninsula jutting out into the Gulf of Mexico, about sixty miles south of New Orleans. Bateaux tells me the photos of Freney and Annie Jones he'd seen on the reward posters in the post office look like the couple who arrived at Grand Isle a year ago. Off I go to Grand Isle.

"When they arrived, the two of them first stayed at the Water Edge Motel off of Highway 1," Bateau told me in his waterfront office. "Then they moved to a beachfront duplex overlooking the Gulf of Mexico.

"I first met him, he went by the name Dennis O'Malley, on my boat dock. He wanted to know if I could take him deep-sea fishing. I said, 'Sure, anytime you want to go.' I took him out several times. He was always asking if there were any shipwrecks in these waters. He wondered if some pirate ships carrying gold might have sunk off Grand Isle. I told him if he was looking for pirate treasure, he'd be better off going to Florida or the Caribbean.

"Two weeks ago, O'Malley asked me to take him by boat over to Bayou Teche. He asked me to drop him off upstream at Irish Bend. That's where the Civil War "Battle of Irish Bend" was fought. When I left him on the dock and pulled away, I saw him talking with a man who I recognized as Captain Smith. I've heard the Captain spends time up your way in Boston. Didn't you say you come from Boston?

"The captain happens to be one of the most notorious drug runners in the Louisiana bayous. Every time the law closes in on him, he disappears into the snake and alligator-infested swamps in the backwaters."

"Where's O'Malley now?" I ask Bateaux.

"I don't know," Bateaux says. "I haven't seen him since I dropped him off at Irish Bend."

I waited a couple of weeks, hoping that Freney would reemerge from the bayous. I checked out the beachfront duplex

Bateaux had told me Freney and Annie were living.   A sign on the house read: 'It's Our Dream.' Inside, the house was empty. Annie was gone. According to neighbors, she had left two weeks ago.

Once again, Freney had eluded me. But a year later, I picked up his trail again. This time, I get a call from Ritchie O'Rourke. He was Freney's drug-running connection in Florida. Hoping to get that million dollar reward, O'Rourke was ratting on his old partner.

"Freney is stayin' in a hotel I own on St. Vincent island in the Caribbean," O'Rourke tells me.   "The hotel is called The Last Resort. He's stayin' in what we call 'the Indictment Suite,'" O'Rourke chortles.

I fly down to St. Vincent and drive over to the Last Resort Hotel. What do you think I find? Freney and Annie Jones had checked out two days before. Destination unknown.

Returning to Boston from St. Vincent, Gordon Smith was pretty dejected. He had spent a good part of his professional career chasing James Freney, always one step behind him, always coming up empty handed.   Freney remained a phantom, an elusive and indefinable being — not only for Gordon Smith, but for others, too.

Although Gordon Smith gave up his pursuit of James Freney, the FBI was still in the hunt. In fact, "We've intensified our efforts. We've assigned a special fugitive task force to pursue Freney," said a FBI special agent in the Boston bureau. "We'll catch him. Whatever it takes to do that, we will do."

In 2002, the manhunt expanded overseas. Scotland Yard reported someone seeing Freney in Piccadilly Circus in London. Investigators scoured the hotels, Internet cafes, and gyms in the city. They found a safe deposit box in London registered under the name Harry Anderson (one of Freney's aliases). No money was found in the box. Only a book called *The World's Top Retirement Havens,* with chapters on a "civilized retirement in Britain and Ireland, as well as "retirement with the Gods" in Greece.

Clearly, Freney had planned to spend his retirement on the run.

Freney's photo — showing him as well-tanned, with balding, close-cropped white hair, and sporting a gray goatee — was posted on the Internet and his fugitive story was featured on BBC's *Crime Watch*. Freney was dubbed "The Ace of Spades" in the deck of cards *The World's Most Wanted Criminals*, produced by a British company.

Freney sightings were reported in London, Manchester, Brighton, Oxford, Hastings, and the Isle of Wight in the United Kingdom, in Dublin, Ireland, and as far away as France, Italy, Spain, and Greece, as Spanish telecommunications carried a series of "virtual wanted posters" of Freney across the continent.

Freney sightings came pouring in. "Most of the leads turn out to be false," said one British crime fighter. "In the hunt for a seventy-four year old, pasty-faced man, Freney is everywhere. Yet he's nowhere. We're ending up chasing old men around the country and around the world. He looks like hundreds of other old guys. We've got people telling us they think their neighbor is James Freney. We'd go around and, yes, he looks like James Freney. But he's not."

After nearly a decade on the run, why hasn't Freney been caught?

Some people say the FBI doesn't want to capture him. If Freney were caught, they think, he could provide embarrassing information about other FBI agents and their relationship with criminal informants. As one law enforcement official put it, "The FBI doesn't want this loose-lipped old gangster turned informant anywhere near a witness box."

Others say that even before 9/11, with the Megiddo Project, the FBI had shifted its priority of fighting organized crime to combating domestic millennium terrorism. Since 9/11, with the FBI galvanizing all its resources to battle global terrorism, it is highly unlikely that capturing an aging gangster ranks as a high priority.

Still others think Freney is dead. There's no Freney to be found.

"He's alive. We'll catch him," said a Boston FBI agent. "We've tracked down 1600 leads since 2002. Our agents have traveled to twenty-five countries, including Greece and the Caribbean pursuing these leads. It's a matter of time and luck. But we'll catch him. The FBI has caught 445 out of the 475 top ten fugitives ever listed."

But so far, all these leads have led to tracks that have vanished.

Where's Freney now?

Frank Doherty, the Seanchie of Southie, thinks he knows. "I'd waga all the gold in Fort Knox, Freney's in Ireland," Doherty says. "He'd been makin' plans to escape long ago. He got a Euro passport through the Four Horsemen in Southie, who got it from the IRA. The passport allows 'im to roam free all ova Europe. Like a magic carpet, it takes 'im any place he wants to go.

"Freney's probably stayin' in an IRA safe house. But I bet yar bottom boots, he's a traveled ova the country, searchin' for 'is great-great granddaddy's grave in Inistioge and for great-great granddaddy's treasure that's said to be buried in Brandon Hill, near Graiguenamanagh."

"Where's Freney? That's not the big question. Freney's an aging gangster. He's no threat. Maybe he'll die in a hail of bullets like John Dillinger or Bonnie and Clyde. Maybe he's going to die quietly in bed. But sooner or later he's going to die," said Hal Shaeffer. "The big question is — *where's Freney's money?*"

Shaeffer took from his brief case two pieces of paper, unfolded them, and placed them on the table in the reading room of the Boston Public Library, where we were meeting.

"I got them from a friend of mine who's with the Quincy police. He cleared out Annie Jones' condo and thought I might be interested in them since I collected things about the Boston Harbor Islands," said Shaeffer.

On the table, Shaeffer had laid two yellowish, dogged-eared maps, crudely drawn, like pirate maps. One was a map of Fort Standish on Lovell's Island. There was an X marking a spot between Battery Morris and Battery Burbeck. The other was a map of the Outer Brewster. On the map was an X placed at the entrance of the concrete bunker that housed Battery Jewell.

Did Freney really bury money on Lovell's and the Outer Brewster? If he did, how much money did he bury there? Is the money still buried there? Has he been back to dig it up?

Or are the maps a hoax — the idle doodlings of a pirate pretender?

I never saw the maps again. Schaeffer died two years ago. The maps disappeared with his passing.

Did Freney bury his money on the islands of Boston Harbor? Only he knows.

# EPILOGUE

In 1996, the U.S. Congress established The Boston Harbor Islands National Park Area. The purpose of creating a national park area was to preserve and protect a drumlin island system within Boston Harbor, along with its natural, cultural, and historic resources; to provide public access to the islands and surrounding waters for the education, enjoyment, and scientific and scholarly research of this and future generations; and to tell the individual stories of islands that comprise one of the last great urban wilderness areas in America.

As of this writing in the Spring of 2004, James Freney is still a fugitive from justice and hope springs eternal in the hearts of the Red Sox Nation, for this could be the year that *The Curse of the Bambino* is lifted and Boston wins its first World Series since 1918.

As the old lady from Logan Way said, "Only ignorant people think a curse lasts forever. That's just a superstition. If you take a scrap of a witch's clothin,' boil it and drink the water, the curse is gone."